AN INTRODUCTION TO
MODERN
WESTERN
CIVILIZATION

AN INTRODUCTION TO MODERN WESTERN CIVILIZATION

Edmund Clingan

iUniverse, Inc.
Bloomington

An Introduction to Modern Western Civilization

iUniverse books may be ordered through booksellers or by contacting:

iUniverse
1663 Liberty Drive
Bloomington, IN 47403
www.iuniverse.com
1-800-Authors (1-800-288-4677)

ISBN: 978-1-4620-5438-1 (sc)
ISBN: 978-1-4620-5439-8 (e)

Printed in the United States of America

iUniverse rev. date: 10/13/2011

CONTENTS

PREFACE

After more than twenty years of teaching courses in western civilization since 1789, I experienced growing difficulties assigning a textbook to my classes. Many were very expensive and had sacrificed text for color pictures. Many contained mistakes of fact or interpretation. My students wanted an affordable text that would be closer to my lectures. This text is designed for the course at Queensborough Community College, but I hope that other students or any with a desire to understand the modern world will find this text useful. There are no pictures or maps. I provide my students with supplementary material, and other readers are urged to consult relevant maps and illustrations on the Internet. Each chapter consists of the text, key terms to review, a time line to help keep things in order, and primary source references that will enrich the reader's understanding of the period. This book also ends with the dissolution of the Soviet Union in 1991. It is not because history ended here, but after this date, the hoard of secret documents is so great that there can be no honest attempt to depict contemporary events as history. In the 1920s, Europeans were astonished when the secret documents that led to World War I came out. These shattered their views of their countries and world. This is a short introduction that I hope will encourage more reading in history. I have only scratched the surface of the historical record, have omitted much, and have simplified for the sake of clarity.

Over my career, I have deplored professors who assigned their own textbooks, yet here I am. I pledge that all profit made from this book will go the Queensborough Community College Fund.

Chapter 1

THE GLOBAL ECONOMY OF THE EIGHTEENTH CENTURY

The modern history of western civilization begins around 1770. The modern world rests upon hundreds of years of earlier developments, and these first two chapters will provide the necessary background. They will introduce you to some terms that will recur throughout the course.

INTRODUCTION

There are four basic things to understand about the world of 1770:

1) It was united

The world of 1770 was going through a transition. The world of 1500 had existed in three separate areas at varied levels of development: a) the Old World, which includes all of Europe, Asia, and Africa; b) the New World, which includes North America, Central America, and South America; and c) Australia, which was still a Stone Age economy. These three areas had their own plants, animals, and diseases. By 1770, all the major areas had been united. There were still significant areas of the inland of the Americas, Africa, Asia, and Australia that were outside the world system because of disease and/or difficult transportation, but those areas were shrinking each year. By 1870, the "unknown" areas of the world were just a few pockets. By 1770, there had been a full exchange of plants, animals, and diseases with extraordinary results. Disease, especially smallpox and measles, had killed most of the population of the Americas. This made

1

European settlement much easier. The Europeans in turn imported African slaves to build a labor pool to exploit the natural resources of the Americas.

2) It was agricultural

For the previous 3,500 years, virtually every area of the world that could support agriculture did support agriculture. The non-agricultural areas of the world were too hot or too dry. Most economies relied on farming, and most people farmed for a living.

3) It was rural

Most people still lived outside cities, even in the states of Western Europe. The rural setting produced most of the economy, even manufacturing. Wage-paying jobs were scarce in the cities. The unemployment rate in cities was very high in the best of times. Many who tried to move from the countryside hoping to find a job would end up dead of hunger, cold, or violence.

4) It was dominated by absolutist empires

Rural, low-density populations made effective communication and transportation, and therefore control of the population, very difficult. Monarchies controlled most of the civilized world. **Monarchy** comes from a Greek word meaning "one man rules." We may use the term **absolutist** to describe these monarchies: **a political system where a great degree of power is concentrated in a pre-industrial centralized monarchy or administration**. "Politics" refers to the exercise of power. "A great degree of power" is not total power. Kings had to share power, most commonly with **noble** families who inherited their wealth and power rather than earning it. They often were the richest people and usually owned land. They kept order in local areas for the king, and the king gave them privileges in return. Because most kings and nobles gained wealth and power through a lucky accident of birth, they were often stupid, lazy, and incompetent. The ordinary people had to pay for this (sometimes with their lives) in the wars started to satisfy a king's vanity. Sometimes a king was so incompetent (or just a boy) that advisers and officials of government would run his nation. You did not need a strong or skilled or smart king to have an absolutist government.

Absolutist governments also controlled their nation's official churches, which were Roman Catholic in France, Spain, and Austria, Orthodox in Russia, Protestant in Prussia, and the Church of England. The governments would accept or appoint the leaders of these churches, and dissent by a priest or minister could merit harsh punishment. This was known as **the alliance of throne and altar**. There was no separation of church and state. Governments did not tolerate people who were not members of the official church or at most granted them limited rights. Many absolutist kings believed (or said they believed) that God himself had made them king. Therefore they were only answerable to God, and an attack or insult on the monarch was an attack on God. This was called the **divine right of kings**. Priests and ministers promoted this to Christian worshipers, further bolstering the power of the king.

The fifteenth and sixteenth centuries saw the establishment of powerful regimes in England, France, Spain, Turkey, Russia, China, Northern India, and Japan. In the seventeenth century, however, all these regimes saw popular uprisings that taught the kings that they had to move slowly. The people would only surrender a certain portion of their blood and treasure for the absolutist rulers.

RICH AND POOR

We understand instinctively who is rich and who is poor, but historians understand that there are degrees of wealth and different ways of measuring wealth. There are also different levels at which we consider wealth: the individual (or family), the corporate (people organized as a group, most familiarly a business or corporation), and the nation.

	Family	Corporate	Nation
Revenue	Paycheck or Annual Income	Sales	Gross Domestic Product
Assets	Assets	Assets	Total National Assets
Change in wealth	Savings/Loss	Profit/Loss	National Account

Rich and poor are more complicated than we thought. If all three measurements are moving in a positive direction, then obviously a family, corporate body, or nation is becoming richer. But what about a family that cleans out its savings and borrows money to buy a house (an asset)? The family may feel richer even if the numbers tell a different story. Assets are probably the most important measurement, but many can change value and are hard to keep track of. Attempts to list the total assets of the U.S.A., for example, are very approximate.

The three levels (family, corporate, nation) can also move in different directions in the same period. We will see times such as the Industrial Revolution in Britain where no doubt the British nation and many corporate bodies were getting richer, but most families were getting poorer. This happens when there is growing **inequality** and just a few people gain the most profit. Thus, the **distribution** is important to consider.

When looked at most simply, economics is simply the study of the relationship between anything one may put value on (capital) and human labor. Different economic systems have organized this relationship in different ways.

THE RISE OF EUROPEAN CAPITALISM

The **capitalist** economic system dominates the economic world today. Like everything, capitalism started and grew at a particular time. It began in Western Europe during the historical period called **the middle ages** (roughly 500–1500).

Definitions of Capitalism

Unfortunately, many people have different definitions of capitalism. Some identify it with market structures or social structures or even political systems. Marxists identified capitalism with an industrial economy. Some identify it with free trade though capitalism has often existed and prospered under restricted trade. I will offer three related definitions:

1. An economic system where the person who puts the money into an enterprise receives a share of the profit, rather than people directly involved in enterprise.

2. An economic system where individuals or groups of individuals place capital at risk with an expectation of receiving back a profit equal to the risk. A clear relationship between risk and return is at the heart of capitalism. When the relationship becomes unclear, there is a crisis of capitalism.

3. An economic system where production is primarily for profit rather than consumption.

The Pre-Conditions for Capitalism

Western Europe after the fall of Rome was a unique society for several reasons. Never before had a society with a heritage of civilization and a high level of social organization been based in the countryside. Also, there was a relative shortage of labor and a surplus of resources. Labor had always been the cheapest commodity in every previous world society, so that there was no incentive to increase labor efficiency and productivity because it would lead to mass unemployment. Slaves were common in these civilizations. The Europeans lost one-third of their population in the 125 years after the fall of the Western Roman Empire. Now labor was very valuable and these societies needed a capital-intensive system. The West had no way to take advantage of this as long as fear and uncertainty kept trade routes effectively closed and it lacked enough **hard money** (gold and silver). After 1000, the Western Europeans had subdued the Vikings and driven the Muslims from Sardinia, Corsica, and Sicily. Early pioneers in building regular trade routes included Jews, who were not bound by Christian restrictions and as second-class citizens in both Christian and Muslim societies engaged in trade rather than farming. Flanders in the north and northern Italy in the Mediterranean began to flourish as trade centers. To this day, if you draw lines from Flanders to northern Italy, the resulting area of land is the core of Europe and the major institutions of the European Union are located in the "power corridor": Brussels, Strasbourg, and Frankfurt.

Growth of Trade

Merchants in twelfth-century Italy set up a new kind of shipping business, the ***Commenda***. A private investor or a group of investors would lend money to a traveling party expected to invest in a commercial operation for the duration of a round-trip voyage. The lenders assumed risks and would get three-quarters of the profits. These contracts made long-distance trade much more efficient and many early ones specified what goods would be sold, to whom, and at what price. By one estimate, trade with Italian city of Genoa increased fourfold from 1274 to 1293. Families of merchants diversified among a home office, carriers, and branches. They pressed for and gained better and more secure roads, bridges, and passes through the Alps Mountains. The growth of trade enabled the Europeans of the Middle Ages to transform farm surpluses into usable money in a way the ancients never had. This is a form of **monetizing national assets**. It soon led to a new form of business as port cities of Italy dominated marine insurance that had developed by 1318.

Banking

The banking system also grew in the thirteenth century: pawnbrokers who would lend money in exchange for holding collateral; deposit bankers would protect money and keep accounts; and merchant bankers fostered investment in commercial ventures. Deposit and merchant bankers had grown out of money changers who transferred credits and changed currencies in accounts of clients. The word "bank" comes from the French for "bench" where the moneychangers sat at the fair. Problems came in relations with the state because kings would often borrow money for wars and then repudiate the debt, bankrupting the bank. In 1342, Edward III of England defaulted on his loans and bankrupted the Italian Bardi and Peruzzi companies. In the sixteenth century, the Fugger family of bankers had lent 55 percent of their assets to the Habsburg emperor Charles V and went broke when he defaulted. To get something out of the government, the bankers charged high rates of interest, even above 40 percent a year. They hoped that the government would pay interest for a year or two before repudiating the debt (refusing to pay). You could not sue an absolutist king. These high interest rates meant that affordable credit was scarce for everyone.

Accounting

Arabic numerals (actually originating in South Asia) replaced Roman numerals after the Italian mathematician Fibonacci popularized them in 1202. It is far easier to do both simple and complex operations with Arabic numerals, and Roman numerals have pretty much disappeared except for the Super Bowl. The fourteenth century saw the invention of **double-entry bookkeeping**. An accountant kept credits and debits in separate columns and the profits made or lost from a transaction. Single-entry bookkeeping had only recorded the debts owed and the proprietor would not know until the end of the year whether there was a profit or a loss. Single-entry bookkeeping cost less but did not distinguish between capital and revenue and made the concealment of fraud easy. Accountants had noticed that receipt of cash involved two entries: a discharge in the account of the debtor and a charge in the record of the cashier. This was a rational way of dealing with money and keeping accounts.

Joint-Stock Companies

The harnessing of waterpower in water mills was a crucial part of medieval development. By the mid-twelfth century, there were dozens of new mills. Local nobles controlled and financed some of these. The eleventh century also saw the first primitive joint-stock ventures. Several partners would buy shares in a project, usually a wheat mill, employ laborers to construct the mill, and share in the profits according to the percentage owned. The Societé du Bazacle of Toulouse financed the mills of the Garonne River in southwest France. The problem was that the partnerships were short-lived and the partners tried to squeeze as much money as quickly as possible. The *commenda* was a form of joint-stock agreement but only existed for individual trips and not continuing businesses.

An Ideology for Capitalism

The Usury Problem

By 1250, capitalism was running into the prohibition on usury and the prevailing Christian ethic that condemned wealth. Jesus had thrown the moneychangers out of the temple and had said it was as easy for a rich man to get into heaven as for a camel to pass through the eye of a needle. In the early middle ages, the rich had lent money to free peasants at interest rates up to 50 percent a year. When the peasants could not pay, the rich took away their land. By 1139, the Church had officially banned **usury**, which it defined as lending money at any interest rate. Only Jews, not bound by the Christian rules, could make these loans. It is a measure of religious intensity in the Middle Ages that there were few unscrupulous Christians who defied the ban and risked hell. But this prohibition threatened development by cutting off all credit. The interest rates of Jewish moneylenders could be as high as 33 percent. An unscrupulous Christian offered a loan at 20 percent in 1161.

A prominent Christian scholar named **Thomas Aquinas** solved the crisis. He identified the difference between usury and investment: the element of risk. In Aquinas' view, it is usury only if you know you are going to get your money back. If you get a peasant in your debt and can take his land, that is usury; if you invest in shipping and commerce, you run the risk of the ship being lost to a storm or pirates. You would then lose your entire investment. In the mid-fourteenth century, the Catholic Church formally modified its prohibition on usury to accept Aquinas' changes. By the sixteenth century, deposit bankers regularly paid 5 to 12 percent interest annually.

Aquinas provided an ideological basis for investment and capitalism by making money respectable. After Aquinas, there was a great surge of civic pride. People were proud of their wealth and showed it off by giving lavishly to the church. The age from 1250 to 1350 is the high point for the construction of Gothic cathedrals that still stand today.

THE AGE OF EXPLORATION

The European Age of Exploration marked the culmination of trends in nationalism and capitalism. Only capitalistic means, long-term planning, and investment could finance it. Nationalistic competition spurred nations to invest this money, sustain the effort, and occupy new areas. European societies had tried before 1300 to expand into new areas and mostly failed. After 1300, they succeeded.

The Portuguese in the East

The Motives

Mansa Musa, the king of Mali in West Africa, staged a magnificent pilgrimage to Mecca in 1324 and 1325. He brought his entourage and a caravan of camels carrying hundreds of pounds of gold with him. This deeply impressed the Europeans and gave them a sense of how much wealth was in West Africa. It directly inspired the kingdom of Portugal to establish contact with the gold sources of western Africa. There was further need because Europe was suffering from a shortage of silver starting in the 1340s. In 1346, a Spanish sailor was shipwrecked looking for the sea route to Mali. Portugal had scanty natural resources and a population of one million at most. They begged, borrowed, and stole money to finance these voyages. The Europeans were freed from hugging the coast in the 1400s by better shipbuilding, sail manipulation, and the introduction of the compass from China. With methodical research and development, they studied Arab vessels on the Indian Ocean and learned of the lateen sail that was small and triangular. They put together the lateen sail with multiple masts and sternpost rudders from the Chinese to make the **caravel** ship. They started with a fifty-ton caravel in the 1440s. (That meant that the ship could carry fifty tons of cargo). By 1500, the Portuguese were building 200-ton caravels with a third mast and a combination of triangular and square sails that could move in almost any wind. These heavy ships could carry cannons and were highly maneuverable. Sometime after 1180, European sailors equipped themselves with the **magnetic compass** from China, which told them direction, and the **astrolabe** from the Arab world, which told them how far north or south they were.

Atlantic Exploration

The Portuguese discovered and seized the Azores and the Canary Islands. They carefully made ever-better maps, sea charts, and logs with descriptions.

8

They kept them very secret. The Portuguese settled the Madeiras in the 1420s and then dedicated the islands to raising sugar cane. The Portuguese enslaved the first four men they met on the Senegal River in 1441 and began a new phase of the slave trade. The Canary Islands became a major source of slaves until the Europeans exterminated the natives entirely. From 1450 to 1500, the Europeans enslaved 150,000 Africans. Sugar production from slave plantations expanded rapidly with the Portuguese conquest of the Cape Verde islands in the 1460s. Sugar plantations began in the Canary Islands themselves in 1484. By 1490, the price of sugar had fallen by two-thirds. Madeira was a big producer at a thousand tons a year and Antwerp in the Netherlands had emerged as a major sugar refining center. The European demand for sugar kept growing and growing, especially as new delights such as coffee, chocolate, and tea could be used with sugar.

In the 1450s, the Portuguese pushed up the Gambia River and found that the Songhai Empire had shattered Mali. They finally reached the "Gold Coast" of Africa (present-day Ghana) and set up a gold-trading post at Elmina in 1482. They could not venture into the interior because of disease. In 1483, they reached the mouth of the Congo River. The king of Portugal sent a group of eight into Africa; only one survived. On the coast, the Portuguese set up colonies and sugar plantations worked by slaves. After 1530, they had gained most of the gold they could and slave trading became more lucrative. The initial goal of direct trade with the gold kingdoms had failed, but the Portuguese had set a greater goal.

On to the Indies

By the late fifteenth century, reaching India had become the main goal of the Portuguese. They wanted to outflank the Muslims who controlled the rich spice trade with southern and southeast Asia. It had taken the Portuguese over a hundred years to get to the mouth of the Congo River, but only four years later they reached the Cape of Good Hope, the southern tip of Africa. The Portuguese slowly raised money for the next trip that would bring them into the Indian Ocean, and they sent spies to Persia and India to scout ahead. In 1498 **Vasco da Gama** reached India on behalf of Portugal. His large vessels and cannon made him master of the Indian Ocean. The Indians realized that he was disrupting trade and drove him out, but he returned in 1502 with troops. Da Gama's fleet devastated cities and his sailors mutilated people. The Portuguese sacked many cities and set up a chain of forts. Da Gama's 1502 trip made a profit of 3,000 percent. The Portuguese soon discovered the law of supply and demand: Da Gama's pepper flooded the market and caused the price to fall 90 percent. At the 1509 **Battle of Diu** off the Indian coast the Portuguese defeated a Muslim fleet. They soon reached the Strait of Malacca near Singapore and made contact with the Spice Islands. They opened trade with Japan in 1542.

Columbus, Spain, and the Americas

The announcement that Portugal had reached the southern tip of Africa in 1487 pushed its neighbor Spain into action. It financed the unlikely voyage of Christopher Columbus in the hope that he could reach eastern Asia ahead of the Portuguese. Columbus was wrong: he stated that Portugal is 2,760 miles east of Japan, but it is actually 12,000 miles. Instead of dying at sea, he got lucky and found an unexpected continent. Spain and Portugal began to conquer the Americas, soon joined by the Dutch, French, and English. In 1564/5, the Spanish found a fast route from the Philippines to North America via Japan. Through a series of marriages, the Spanish rulers gained control of Portugal and the "Low Countries" (present day Belgium and the Netherlands). They brought in even more money for the crown of Spain than the silver and gold mines of the Americas, but Spain mismanaged them and faced revolts. The Netherlands gained control of much of the Spice Islands and many trading bases. European expansion led to contact with very different cultures and civilizations. They found new medicines, diseases, foods, and manufactures. So many different systems made people wonder if their system was right. Other religions seemed acceptable.

THE ESTABLISHMENT OF NATIONAL FINANCE

Financial Changes and the Need for Cash

After breaking free from Spain, the Dutch discovered a fast route to the Spice Islands by sailing far south of Africa and using the winds of the "roaring forties." To handle their new trade empire, the Dutch set up the **East India Company** in 1602. It was the first immortal corporation. Each partner had a number of shares, but when the partner (shareholder) died, the partnership would not dissolve. Instead the shares would be sold or inherited or reassigned. After 1612, the shares became negotiable and the company encouraged their sale. It soon became common practice for shareholders to buy and sell and swap shares even while alive and a **Stock Exchange** began to grow. This fostered an interest in long-term development and future profits, rather than quick riches.

Coinage and banking remained problems. The Dutch had fourteen mints with all sorts of coins and there were thousands of different European coins floating around. The Dutch government chartered the **Bank of Amsterdam** in 1609. It fixed exchange rates for thousands of European coins and minted gold florins which were universally accepted (and all those trading with the Dutch had to accept them for large trades). Investment capital flooded into Amsterdam. Merchants could borrow money from the Bank of Amsterdam at half the interest rate charged in Britain or France. It allowed the government of the Netherlands to borrow considerable amounts at reasonable interest rates. By 1700, the Dutch owed 250 million florins while their annual income was only 13 million. In the seventeenth century, Britain and France founded colonies in North America and India. These nations were larger than the Netherlands and gradually they drove the Dutch out. Then they fought wars against each other. By the late 1600s, Britain and France were fighting a costly war around the world.

Establishment of the Bank of England (1694)

Because England had a smaller economy and population than France, the costs of war were more difficult to bear. England had run deeply into debt and its creditors were worried. The first step in paying this debt was to raise taxes on land and many consumer goods in 1692. The government announced an official national debt in 1693. It had issued **bonds**, which means "promise," but governments around Europe had often broken these promises. In 1694, instead of repaying some of its leading creditors, the government gave them a charter to operate the Bank of England. The creditors raised over £1 million from the public and lent it to the government at 8 percent interest.

This bank would issue banknotes and hold government accounts. The profit was considerable, so the creditors gained much more than if the government had simply repaid its bonds. As England continued to fight and win wars, it kept borrowing more money. England (which absorbed Scotland and Ireland and became Great Britain) finally reached a period of peace in 1713. The terms of the peace treaty gave Britain the right to administer the slave trade to the Spanish American colonies and the government chartered the **South Sea Company** to run this. Naturally, leading creditors jumped at the chance to exchange their bonds for shares of Company stock. For a while, the price of shares rocketed up, far beyond the value of the company. This formed a **Bubble** (that is, mostly made of air), and in 1719 the bubble burst. The Company went bankrupt, and its shares were worthless. Those who had held bonds and traded them for shares asked the British government for relief, and (amazingly) the government paid them for the value of their bonds. This created tremendous investor confidence in the British government. Creditors to the government were assured of payment. The government would not have to worry so much about debt. This gave tremendous fiscal backing to Britain that France did not have. Britain would have very deep pockets to draw on in times of war. By 1740, Britain could borrow four times as much as it had in the 1690s. Low risk meant a steady fall in interest rates, which encouraged business expansion. This also had effect of monetizing production from the economy.

France

France tried to follow Britain in modern finance. It chartered the Bank Royale in 1716 in imitation of the Bank of England. Like Britain, it swapped government bonds from the war for shares of a new **Mississippi Company** that would draw on the imagined profits of that river. A Bubble also grew as the value of shares grew thirty times in value. The Mississippi Bubble burst in 1719, but the French government refused to compensate the shareholders. In fury, they attacked the Bank Royale physically and financially and caused its collapse. French investors now tended to put their money into land instead of paper securities. Investors influenced and at times controlled England, but not France. Unlike Britain, France's tax system remained confused and decentralized. British and Dutch borrowers enjoyed interest rates half that of France in the eighteenth century.

MERCANTILISM AT ITS PEAK

Mercantilism was an early form of national economic planning. Leaders of European nations believed that the wealth of a nation depended on how much gold or silver it had. The way to increase this was to run a **trade surplus** (selling to other nations more than it buys from them.) If a country buys more from other nations than it sells, it is running a **trade deficit**. Since measuring economic activity was very difficult, governments had trouble judging the effects of their policies. Governments fostered or subsidized industries they deemed important, imposed high tariffs, rigidly regulated prices and qualities of manufactured goods, sponsored royal monopolies, and encouraged colonial expansion as a way of getting more raw materials without having to import them from another country and to create a market for manufactured goods. **Import substitution** means a government creates and pays for factories to make things that its people have usually bought from abroad. Productivity is usually lower and thus the product is generally more expensive and of worse quality than if tax money was not lowering the cost. There is no incentive for these companies to become more productive so import substitution rarely helps real growth. Home countries tried to ban manufacturing in colonies to force them to buy goods made in the home country. This caused tremendous resentment in the colonies, and smuggling was common.

THE "TRIANGLE TRADE"

Most foreign European trade was linked with the Americas and Africa. The key was sugar, grown in the Madeiras and Canary Islands then planted abundantly in the West Indies of the Caribbean. From 1713 to 1792, Britain imported £162 million in goods from Americas and £104 million from India and China. The sugar economy was based on plantations owned by absentee British or French landlords, managed indirectly, and worked by slaves. The richest single sugar colony was Haiti, owned by France. After 1650, the slave trade to the Americas was very substantial: the British brought 610,000 to Jamaica from 1700 to 1786. The slave trade kept growing because sugar-growing was hot, backbreaking, and often deadly work. The average life expectancy for a slave out in the fields was seven years but many others died or were maimed from the sugar-processing machinery and the boiling pots used to make sugar syrup. By 1790, slave-produced goods (tobacco, cotton, sugar) accounted for one-fourth of the British imports. Sugar would be manufactured into rum. The Europeans brought it and other spirits to Africa along with gunpowder, flints, and textiles to trade for slaves, thus the name "Triangle Trade."

From 1600 to 1800, the Europeans brought some 9.5 million slaves from Africa to the Americas; it is estimated that an additional million died during the brutal passage across the Atlantic where slaves were chained together in tight quarters. If disease broke out, it could kill nearly everyone aboard. Records were not carefully kept and some estimates range to 13 million captured or killed. About three million slaves went from Angola to the sugar plantations of Brazil. Other slaves went from West Africa to the sugar islands of Indies, where death rates were very high, or to the tobacco plantations in the south of what would become the United States. Europeans would either establish factory-forts or invite African dealers out to ships. Slavery spread in African societies as rulers were eager to make money. Some non-Europeans did well in the global economy: the tribal chiefs in Africa who sold slaves, Chinese and Indian merchants who sold porcelain, textiles, tea, silk, and spices. The lion's share of the profits went to the Europeans who supplied capital and technical and organizing abilities.

While Vasco da Gama had gone around Africa in 1498, no Chinese ship came back the other way until 1851. Profits piled up especially in Britain, France, and the Netherlands. The wealthiest did quite well. The middle class became more comfortable, larger, and more literate. The lower classes tended to be worse off in Europe.

TIMELINE

1268	Aquinas redefines usury
1324	Mansa Musa's pilgrimage to Mecca
1420s	Portuguese begin to settle Madeiras
1487	Portuguese captain rounds Africa
1492	Columbus reaches America on behalf of Spain
1498	Vasco da Gama reaches India on behalf of Portugal
1567	The Netherlands begin revolt against Spain
1588	Portuguese pepper fleet destroyed as part of Spanish Armada
1602	Dutch East India Company founded
1609	Bank of Amsterdam founded
1694	Bank of England founded
1713–1740	Peace between Britain and France
1719	South Sea and Mississippi Bubbles

KEY TERMS

Absolutist
Noble
The Alliance of Throne and Altar
Hard Money
Commenda
Vasco Da Gama
Dutch East India Company
Bank of Amsterdam
Bank of England
South Sea and Mississippi Bubbles
Mercantilism
"Triangle Trade"

PRIMARY SOURCE DOCUMENTS

Thomas Aquinas on usury, http://www.fordham.edu/halsall/sources/aquinas-usury.html

Chapter 2

THE ENLIGHTENMENT

THE SCIENTIFIC REVOLUTION

The Scientific Roots

To paraphrase R.R. Palmer and Joel Colton, science is important first of all because it affects practical life including health, wealth, and happiness. The population of Europe increased after 1650 largely because of the introduction of new crops and scientific farming. Scientific discoveries led to breakthroughs in manufacturing and transportation that would lift many out of poverty. Medical science brought life to billions and allowed them to live fuller lives. Misuse of science could also lead to mass destruction and death. Secondly, science affects modern thought. In this book, we shall see how the scientific writing of Newton, Freud, and Darwin affected humanity's vision of itself. Seventeenth-century changes upheld the view of an orderly universe, the ability of human reason, and led to the intellectual movement known as the Enlightenment. Like European technology, European science borrowed from many traditions and civilizations. In the **early modern period** (1500–1789), it combined the rigor of ancient Greek logic with pragmatism and experimentation from the Middle Ages.

Scientific Method

It was necessary first to establish a regular scientific method. There had been a big gap between "natural philosophers," who ran experiments to discover basic principles, and practical inventors and tinkerers, who invented or improved existing devices and practices. The philosophers paid little attention to the inventors (who were generally trying to get rich), and the inventors did not consult with the philosophers for help. Communication is vital for scientific advance so that everyone knows about the experiments that succeed and fail. This prevents a waste of time and effort duplicating what has already been done.

Two writers led the way in creating scientific method: the Englishman **Francis Bacon** (1561–1626) and the Frenchman **René Descartes** (1596–1650). Starting in the 1620s, they outlined a program that started from scratch to prove basic principles. They understood that investigation led to physical laws. Using scientific method, you do not start with a belief and then try to find some examples to back this up. You start with all the examples you can find and see if you can derive general principles. Bacon criticized the ancient Greeks for their insufficient experimentation. Bacon strongly believed that the only science worth exploring was that which affected everyday life. He therefore helped unite science and technology. Descartes was a great mathematician and ensured that most science would be expressed in numbers and equations. Descartes completely separated matter from spirit, so matter could be studied in its completely mechanical form. Both agreed that once people understood nature, they could manipulate it to build a perfect society.

Scientific method, which can be applied in a wide variety of fields from biology to baseball, works as follows. You start with a particular problem. You gather as large a group as possible to investigate the problem because there are always random variations and the smaller the group the larger the possibility that something can happen by pure chance. After carefully noting and measuring all conceivable aspects of the group relating to the problem, the scholar should notice some patterns. He may then form a **Hypothesis**: a possible explanation. He will then test the hypothesis: does it hold up in all or at least most cases? Most hypotheses have had to be discarded or modified, no matter how much this disappointed the scholar. If some conclusion remains, it may be presented as a **Theory**. Others will then test the theories to see if they hold up or must be further modified. A scientific theory such as evolution of species or climate change is not just "some guy's opinion." It has been tested thousands of times and has held up with modifications. The scholar should publish results of the investigation, no matter the outcome, so others may learn. **Laws** of science mean things happen the same way all the time under the same circumstances.

Governments founded institutions to foster research such as the Royal Society of London in 1662 and the French Royal Academy of Sciences in 1666. These societies and others held conferences, published journals on all subjects, and sent the journals to scholars across Europe. A scientific community could grow and build on members' work.

Isaac Newton (1642–1727)

Astronomy and physics led the way in the seventeenth century because they could apply a wave of math advances including the use of decimal fractions, the standardization of algebra, the invention of logarithms, the development of coordinate geometry (by Descartes), and finally calculus by Newton and Gottfried Leibniz. **Johannes Kepler** had developed the theory that planets go around the sun in elliptical orbits in 1609, but no one knew why the orbits worked. Why did the planets not fly off into space? To measure the movement more precisely, Newton invented the reflecting telescope in 1671; this could see further. He also developed calculus to describe movement along an arc at any moment. Newton came up with three basic laws of physics: **The Inertial Law** (a body at rest or in motion at a constant velocity along a straight line remains in that state of rest or motion unless acted upon by a net outside force), **The Force Law** (the change in a body's velocity due to an applied new force is in the same direction as the force and proportional to it but is inversely proportional to the body's mass), and **The Reaction Law** (for every applied force, a force of equal size and opposite direction arises). With these laws, Newton derived the **Law of Gravitation**: every body in the universe attracts every other body; this force (gravity) depends on the distance between the bodies and their mass. Newton published these findings in his 1687 book *Mathematical Principles of Natural Philosophy*. In 1704, Newton followed this up with his book *Opticks* which explored the properties of light and colors. Both books contained many equations, and the books were hard reads even for other scientists. While many grasped that Newton had proved important and even revolutionary ideas, the details were hard to absorb.

Consequences

Sailors had always understood that the gravitational pulls of the earth, moon, and sun affected the tides. Now gravity allowed a precise mathematical measurement and could be predicted far in advance, aiding sailing and trade. Calculus curves and trajectories led to more accurate use of artillery. Better guns made it easier to subdue rebels and the eighteenth century saw fewer revolts in the countryside. Modern revolutions would occur in the narrow twisting streets of cities where gun trajectories were useless. Scientific achievements thrilled many. The Europeans had answered many questions that had existed for thousands of years. Scientific method might solve the world's problems and lead to a perfect society, as Bacon hoped. But science frightened others. Newton proved that the sky's color in an optical illusion. Even Newton's improved telescope found no sign of God in the heavens.

HOBBES, LOCKE, AND ENGLISH POLITICAL THEORY

The rise of scientific method and political turbulence in seventeenth-century England made that area fertile ground for new ideas of politics that either supported absolutism without the divine right of kings or challenged absolute kings. The rulers of England had growing financial problems after 1600. Tax rates were low, and the absolutist kings had to share power with the landowners who controlled the English Parliament. These landowners refused to grant the large permanent taxes that the king of France enjoyed because that king had then ruled without calling the French Estates-General (the equivalent of the Parliament). In 1629, King **Charles I** (ruled 1625–1649) tried to rule without Parliament. Eleven years later, he was out of money and had to recall the angry Parliament. Relations worsened and the **English Civil War** (1642–1649) broke out with the king's army losing to a new army raised by Parliament. The winners then cut the king's head off.

Thomas Hobbes, *Leviathan* (1651)

Thomas Hobbes (1588–1679) was materialistic and atheistic. He had opposed Parliament in the civil war and fled to France to tutor Charles II, the son of the dead king. Parliament's victory did not last long. The general of its army, **Oliver Cromwell** (1599–1658), sent Parliament home in 1653 and ruled as a military dictator. Hobbes was friendly with scientists such as Bacon, Descartes, and the Italian Galileo Galilei. He wanted to apply scientific principles to human society and politics, just as Galileo and Descartes had worked on astronomy and math. In his book *Leviathan*, he wanted to separate absolutism from God and religion. He began with a low opinion of humans. People are nearly equal in mind or body so that whatever one holds, another can hope to acquire. The weak can kill the strongest if they use some brains. Without power to overawe them, "notions of right and wrong, justice and injustice have no place." In the state of nature, life is "nasty, brutish, and short." To escape the chaos, people surrendered their freedom of action and natural rights to an absolute ruler who maintained order. The ruler is the source of morality, property and perquisites. Hobbes emphasized that all absolutist actions should be for the public good; the state cannot kill. People have no right to revolt against the state unless they are threatened by death, or the ruler has failed to protect them. Absolute power can belong to a king or a parliament. Hobbes advocated using the church to pound the idea of the state's supremacy into people's heads. The state should ensure peace and the contentment of the people. This is why Hobbes was so upset about the Parliament's rebellion. It threatened to bring back the state of nature, which was worse than the most bloody despot. The publication of *Leviathan* angered the exiled royalists because it denied that God made kings.

Levellers and Diggers

The confusion of the English Civil War allowed many political groups to grow. Levellers were some parliamentary soldiers who put forward a written social contract, "Agreement of the People," to give people control over the government. There should be elections to the Parliament every year in districts with equal populations. The state should pay salaries to members of Parliament so all could participate. This immediately led to a discussion of property since some people inevitably had more influence. Levellers grudgingly accepted that propertyowning men represented the country not just their selfish interests. Lower classes would not have the vote. Some talked of limiting landed wealth. The state would pay administrators but would move them around so that permanent parties did not form. Gerrard Winstanley of the **Diggers** had a different answer: confiscate property and put the common treasury under "overseers" with sweeping powers of punishment. Some Diggers mutinied against Cromwell's dictatorship, and he jailed them.

John Locke (1632–1704)

Oliver Cromwell died in 1658. His government had become much hated as it had waged more wars while imposing a rigid moral code on the English people. He banned public dancing and card playing, among other things. Charles I did not look so bad. Parliament returned and offered the crown to **Charles II** (ruled 1660–1685) if he would behave himself. Once he was king, Charles II did not talk about divine right of kings but did rebuild much of the absolutist system. He was much more clever than his father, and the opposition remained small and divided.

John Locke opposed the return to absolutism and fled to the Netherlands in 1683 because he feared arrest. Charles II died in 1685 and was succeeded by his younger brother **James II** (ruled 1685–1688). James was more like his father: he promoted divine right, reduced the Parliament, and abused the law. Although England was a Protestant nation, James had converted to Roman Catholicism, which alarmed strong religious elements. In 1688, some in Parliament combined with the Dutch ruler **William III** (ruled 1688–1702) to throw James out of England. Parliament became the main political force in England, sharing power with the monarch. This was not democracy since most people were not allowed to vote. It was called the **Glorious Revolution** because not as many people died as in the civil war of the 1640s.

Locke returned to England and published the book he had written earlier. This was the *Two Treatises of Government*. He saw Nature as benign and rational and people as basically good. The natural state is peace. There is no need for a massive "Leviathan state," but since there will always be disputes, society needs judges. The government makes laws and protects the natural rights of life, liberty and property. People have not consented to being enslaved (although Locke justified the enslavement of Africans), having their property seized, or handing over power to others. The executive (king) defends and carries out law. The legislative branch (parliament) is supreme and makes law. The Parliament has two houses: the House of Commons and the House of Lords (those who inherited a title or were appointed by the King). Locke believed that the Commons was the people's house although rich landowners controlled it just like the House of Lords. Hobbes had said that people only have a right to rebel if the government directly threatens their lives. Locke said people have the right to revolt if government breaks the contract with them. People would have the good sense to use this right very rarely.

Locke published a second book on a very different topic. This was an attempt to apply science to learning. In *An Essay Concerning the Human Understanding* (1690), Locke wrote that everyone was born with a blank slate (*tabula rasa*) for a mind. Knowledge grew from experience; in this, he followed Bacon and rejected Descartes who believed that people were born with certain ideas. Education and mental discipline could improve people. One needs all three aspects to learn: experience, education, and mental discipline. Locke made an important breakthrough by stating that almost everyone can learn. If you believed that people were born smart or stupid, then trying to teach the stupid was a waste of time.

Out of Locke would spring the Enlightenment and the ideas of liberalism. His radical ideas that governments are responsible to their people and that everyone could learn would soon lead to democracy and the proposal that everyone should learn at government expense. The German-speaking state of Prussia would take the lead by making elementary education mandatory in 1717.

THE WORLD OF THE PHILOSOPHES

"Enlightenment" refers to a common program of intellectuals in France, the Netherlands, Germany, Italy, Scotland, and elsewhere that lasted from about 1713, the end of a round of European and colonial wars, until 1789, the beginning of the French Revolution. There were many different currents and disagreements, but most Enlightenment writers shared the following ideas:

1) universal principles exist governing humanity, nature, and society

2) human reason, given enough time, will discover all these principles

3) a belief in the perfectibility and progress of humanity

4) a hostility to supernatural revelation as they attacked all based on revelation. This often brought conflict with religious leaders.

Before 1713, rich patrons commonly supported writers. These patrons could be members of the king's family, nobles, church leaders, or rich merchants. The emergence of a global economy had changed things. The middle classes had grown richer and larger in France and England and were the main consumers of Enlightenment literature and new novels. French colonial trade grew from 25 million livres in 1716 to 263 million (952%) in 1789, while British colonial trade grew from £10 million to £40 million (300%) in the same period. Catholic parish schools educated enough people for the French literacy rates to double in the eighteenth century. Perhaps half the men and one-quarter of the women in France could sign their names. In England, around 60 percent of the men and 40 percent of the women were literate. In 1713, there were 2.5 million newspapers sold in England; this rose to 16 million by 1801. The Enlightenment saw the beginning of modern publishing businesses, newspapers, the bestselling book, libraries, and all things that go with a reading public. Half the books published in 1700 had a religious theme; in 1780, only 10 percent had a religious theme. *Philosophes* were free-lance writers. The reading public had grown, and the middle and upper classes wanted to keep up with progress. Britain had ended censorship in the 1740s, but the rest of Europe censored books in various ways or banned them entirely. The *philosophes* had to use the abstract or face punishment. However, readers prized banned books. The authorities would imprison writers but breaking into the houses of nobles and other wealthy families was not a good idea since the taxes and loans from these families paid for the government.

Philosophes from 1713 to 1748 popularized the complex ideas of the Scientific Revolution. One early popular writer took the name **Voltaire** (1694–1778) to write more freely. He had been born Francis Arouet but began to call himself a nobleman (Francis d'Arouet) falsely. The real noble families beat him viciously. Voltaire hated the nobles and the Church for the rest of his life. His early works explained the meaning of Newton, Bacon, and Locke in simple language.

The Enlightenment reached the height of its power from 1748 to 1776. Most of the important works of the Enlightenment were published in this era. We cannot go into all of them in a survey such as this, but we will discuss a few influential ones in this chapter and in later chapters two others from 1776: Adam Smith's *Wealth of Nations* and Thomas Jefferson's "Declaration of American Independence."

Cesare Beccaria

The Italian Beccaria applied the scientific method to the criminal justice system. In his *Essay on Crimes and Punishments* (1764), he called for abolishing torture and all cruel punishments, along with capital punishment; the punishment should fit the crime. At time, hundreds of laws could result in death or long sentences. For example, in 1744 England hanged a man named John Burton for stealing two wool caps. Governments should emphasize prevention, not punishment. Punishment should be severe enough so that a rational person learns that crime does not pay, but the state should treat prisoners humanely. Crime was an injury to society.

Montesquieu

Baron Charles de Montesquieu (1689–1755) was a noble and sat in one of the French regional courts as a judge. In *The Spirit of the Laws* (1748), he asserted that the climate, size, population, religion, and social customs determined the type of government. He opposed centralization and royal absolutism. He called for a **separation and balance of powers** among the king, legislature, and judiciary, and national, provincial, and local levels. There would be **checks and balances** among groups, so no one would be very powerful. Montesquieu tried to develop what we would call today comparative political science. He said there were three basic types of government:

DESPOTISM—One man rules by whim with no fixed law
    Courtiers or eunuchs have considerable influence
MONARCHY—One man rules
    There is a known and regular system of laws
    Knowledgeable counselors advise the Monarch
    Judicial tribunals register laws
    A good system for large territorial states
REPUBLIC—People govern themselves and make the laws
    1) Aristocratic
       Less than half of the population makes or carries out the laws
    2) Democratic
       More than half participate
       Exists only in small states
       Requires no great discrepancy in wealth and power

Britain did not fit the three models. Montesquieu called it a "moderate government" between a monarchy and a republic. It consists of three units of government: the executive enforces the law, the legislative makes the law, the judiciary oversees the law. *Montesquieu was wrong in this description.* The judicial branch has never been an equal, and no British judge would ever dare to strike down an act of Parliament. Montesquieu wanted to limit the power of absolutist kings and increase the power of nobles like himself. It has lasting influence because it helped inspire the frame of the United States Constitution.

Jean-Jacques Rousseau (1712–1778)

Rousseau lived during the Enlightenment and is always included among the great Enlightenment thinkers, but he did not fit in very well. Most *philosophes* came from noble or middle-class background, but Rousseau's father was a watchmaker who abandoned him at the age of ten. He ran away from Geneva at the age of sixteen and arrived virtually penniless in Paris. He had doubts about whether humanity had made any progress at all and found pure reason untrustworthy. Feelings and emotions were at least as important, and impulsive judgments were often the best. Had he written forty years later, he would have fit comfortably into the Romantic movement that we will describe later.

After laboring for years in obscurity, Rousseau suddenly gained attention by winning a prize for his *Discourse on the Origin of Inequality among Men* in 1755. He agreed with Locke that the state of nature was good. Like earlier writers he praised the "noble savage" that he imagined lived in the Americas and Asia. People became too sophisticated and lost touch with their basic nature. As population grew, the idea of communal property faded; men competed for resources, especially land. The real problems began with private property; this was a sharp break with Locke, who thought property was a fundamental right. Property caused people to move closer to Hobbes' view of the state of nature. In the present day, even if society were destroyed, there could be no return to the state of nature.

The *Social Contract* of 1762 tried to describe the ideal state since people could never return to the state of nature. People should give up their power to the "**General Will**": the common interest of all. Men must be educated to learn their common interests. He moved beyond Locke and urged that the government pay for public schools for all so people would learn their self-interest. Everyone must be equal under the law without special privileges for nobles or discrimination against religious minorities. Rousseau wanted direct democracy, not representative democracy or intermediaries such as nobles. This vision was in direct opposition to Montesquieu's. The people would never turn the "General Will" over to an agent. It is not quite "majority rule" but rather the "true will" of each citizen if they were truly informed of proper interests; we might call it a consensus. How would this start? There should be a supremely wise legislator to write the laws and then step aside. Citizens would approve further laws in referenda. This would be the best state because it would give everyone a stake and they would contribute more blood (as soldiers) and treasure (as taxpayers) than people in an absolutist state who had no say in government. Given the state of transportation and communication in his time, Rousseau believed that this kind of system could only exist in small states, with no great wealth or power divergences, just as Montesquieu had said for democratic republics. The government of France ordered the burning of *Social Contract*.

When he was asked to write a model constitution for the dying nation of Poland, Rousseau wrote quite a conservative document. It maintained serfdom and denied most people political rights. Rousseau recognized that you could not go from the old way to a democratic republic, especially when most people could not even read or write. Though he had strong romantic tendencies, Rousseau could be realistic when needed. Many inspired by Rousseau could not say the same.

TIMELINE

1605	Bacon, *The Advancement of Learning*
1609	Kepler, *The New Astronomy*
1627	Bacon, *The New Atlantis*
1637	Descartes, *Discourse on Method*
1642–49	English Civil War; ends with execution of King
1651	Hobbes, *Leviathan*
1660	Charles II returns to England as King
1687	Newton, *Mathematical Principles of Natural Philosophy*
1688–89	Glorious Revolution ousts King James II of England
1690	Locke, *Two Treatises of Government*
	Locke, *An Essay concerning Human Understanding*
1704	Newton, *Opticks*
1713	Peace treaty between England and France
	Enlightenment begins
1733	Voltaire, *Elements of the Philosophy of Newton*
1748	Montesquieu, *The Spirit of the Laws*
1755	Rousseau, *Discourse on Origin of Inequality among Men*
1762	Rousseau, *Social Contract*
1764	Beccaria, *Essay on Crimes and Punishments*
1776	Smith, *Wealth of Nations*
	Jefferson, "Declaration of American Independence"
1787	United States Constitution
1789	Enlightenment ends

KEY TERMS

Francis Bacon
René Descartes
Isaac Newton
Law of Gravitation
Thomas Hobbes
Levellers and Diggers
John Locke
Voltaire
Baron Charles de Montesquieu
Jean-Jacques Rousseau

PRIMARY SOURCE DOCUMENTS

Francis Bacon, http://www.bartleby.com/39/20.html

Isaac Newton, http://www.fordham.edu/halsall/mod/newton-princ.html

John Wallis, http://www.fordham.edu/halsall/mod/1662royalsociety.html

John Locke, http://libertyonline.hypermall.com/Locke/second/second-8.html

Thomas Hobbes, http://www.fordham.edu/halsall/mod/hobbes-lev13.html

Voltaire, http://www.fordham.edu/halsall/mod/1778voltaire-lettres.html

Beccaria, http://www.fordham.edu/halsall/mod/18beccaria.html

Montesquieu, http://www.fordham.edu/halsall/mod/montesquieu-spirit.html

Jean-Jacques Rousseau, http://www.fordham.edu/halsall/mod/Rousseau-inequality2.html

Chapter 3

THE AGRICULTURAL AND INDUSTRIAL REVOLUTIONS

THE AGRICULTURAL REVOLUTION

As stated before, most people in Europe (and the world) in the eighteenth century were farmers and lived in the countryside. A fundamental change in farming would shake a nation. European farming before the modern period varied according to laws, customs, family traditions, soil quality, climate, and many other factors. Generally, we may say that there was a rotation of crops usually involving a grain such as wheat, barley, or rye, and protein-rich crops such as broad beans. Animals and their manure were relatively scarce, which meant both fertilizer and meat were far more limited than today. For most farmers in Western Europe, the only choice was to let part of the soil rest and recover its nutrients. The land would lie **fallow**: farmers would plow and remove any weeds that appeared, but they would not plant crops. They left roughly one-third of the farmland fallow, and this has led historians to create a general model called the **three-field system**. The population grew very slowly and village life remained much the same from generation to generation. There were a few very fertile, densely-populated areas such as the Netherlands and the Po river valley in Italy that used more intensive techniques, but they were not suitable for Europe as a whole. **Thomas Malthus** (1766–1834) had described the early modern situation well: population increased more rapidly than the food supply, thus insuring constant poverty and periodic cycles of famine.

New Foods and Demographic Revolution

1650 marked the low point of European population in the early modern period. It had just suffered terrible wars, bad weather, and crop failures. After that year, population would grow at an accelerating rate for the next three hundred years. The biggest contributor to the growth from 1650 to 1800 was new food. Explorations had brought the Europeans in contact with many unfamiliar foods, but the most significant were **corn** (which the Europeans call maize) and the **potato**. Corn was developed in central Mexico and had spread through most of the Americas by 1492. Even more important was the potato, one of the hardiest plants in the world. It is native to the Andes Mountains of South America and almost single-handedly supported the complex society of the Incan Empire of Peru. It is an excellent source of carbohydrates, can be prepared in a variety of ways, and has many uses for human and animal consumption. An acre of potatoes could feed up to five times as many people as an acre of wheat. A farmer could harvest a crop of potatoes in three or four months whereas many grains took ten months to ripen. Better food and a decline in the virulence of the plague brought down the death rate and boosted the population. Entire areas of Europe such as Ireland and the southwest German states became dependent on the potato. That proved to be dangerous. From 1650 to 1800 the population increased in England from 5 million to 9.25 million, France from 21 million to 29 million, the German areas from 17 million to 29 million, and Russia from 17 million to 36 million.

Improvements in agriculture led to a change in many facets of everyday life. Men and women often lived with their parents until they married. For men, the average age at first marriage was about twenty-five to twenty-seven, for women it was around twenty-one. Then they would move out, having saved up enough money to buy enough land for themselves. During early adulthood, children often worked for several years away from home. Social pressures had worked to keep levels of children born to unmarried women very low. The spread of the potato allowed farmers to set up a household more easily because they did not need as much land if they planted potatoes. After 1750, the age of marriage began to drop. Earlier marriage meant more children and a larger population.

Other new foods included increased planting of the turnip, which people could eat in an emergency but was mostly for animals. There was also scientific cultivation of the sugar beet with the aim of increasing its sugar content. In the nineteenth century, sugar from beets increasingly replaced sugar from cane, which could only be grown in the tropics and was largely the product of slave labor.

New Tools

The time around 1700 also saw the invention of some simple but ingenious new tools that increased farm productivity. The Englishman **Jethro Tull** (1674–1741) introduced a deeper mold board on the plow. The plow was lighter, and horses or oxen could pull it. Plowing would be faster even as it dug more deeply. When one stirs up more soil, it brings more oxygen. This means that the microbes that help fertilize soil will increase and work faster making the soil more productive. Tull introduced a new seed planting method of "seed drilling" in 1701 rather than broadcasting. This meant a family did not have to save as much seed from the previous year's crops and this increased its food supply. It had a modest impact in more advanced Western Europe, but Central and Eastern Europe increased their yield per seed by 24 percent.

Big agricultural machines such as reapers and chemical fertilizer would come only in the nineteenth century. The U.S. wheat yield in 1866 was eleven bushels per acre, about three times medieval Europe's yield. The yield increased to sixteen in 1914, twenty-four in 1960, thirty-six in 1983, and forty in 1998; the growth since 1960 has mainly been because of chemical fertilizer derived from natural gas. The price of wheat in 1919 hit a high of $2.16 per bushel (which equals $43.20 in 2007 dollars) as opposed to the current prices of four to seven dollars. What would your life be like if all the prices in the grocery store cost six to ten times as much? What would you buy and not buy? How much would be left after you paid for food and rent?

New Means of Cultivation

During the political turmoil in seventeenth-century England, outlined in the previous chapter, a number of English spent time in the Netherlands and observed the more intensive methods. The scientific revolution inspired some to apply the scientific method to farming. Tull proposed a process of mowing fields while the root plants grew. **Charles Townshend** (1674–1738) proposed a scientific model of cultivation based on his experiments on soil fertility. This became known as the **four-crop rotation.** The farmer would plant wheat in the late Fall. It would grow in the winter (thus known as "winter wheat") protected by snow from the cold and then the farmer would harvest it in the early spring. Then the farmer would plant root crops such as potatoes and turnips. The farmer could mow to remove weeds while these grew underground. The farmer would grow a summer grain such as barley and oats that were mainly for animal consumption; autumn would see him plant so-called artificial grasses such as alfalfa and clover or legumes (peas, beans) to fertilize the soil and replenish nutrition. Thus two cycles (wheat and root crops) would take nutrition out while the summer grain and the autumn cycle would replenish nutrition and make the soils ready for winter wheat. Scientific farmers found that on many soils, there would no longer be a need to leave a part fallow, so you could plant the entire area year after year.

Farmers also applied science to animal breeding to create larger animals for meat or milk or (as with the new sport of thoroughbred horse racing) speed. The ability to feed and keep more horses meant that the average English farmer had about 67 percent more horsepower to help them than the French farmer in 1800. **Robert Bakewell** (1725–1795) was a leading breeder. During his lifetime, the average weight of cattle doubled and sheep tripled from twenty-eight to eighty pounds.

Enclosure Acts

There was strong resistance among farmers to the new techniques. For many they seemed physically impossible, and farmers complained that the scientists must have used special soils in special conditions. They would not risk their family's lives on something so uncertain.

The big landlords, however, were eager to increase their profits and turned nasty. They controlled Parliament. Only 250,000 men (3 percent of the total population) had the right to vote for the House of Commons. But there was no equal distribution, and by one estimate of the time just 5,723 men (.07% of the population) controlled the House of Commons. After 1700, the Parliament passed many **Enclosure Acts**. On the one hand, they cut off farm lands owned or traditionally rented by peasants from common land and waste land. The commons and the wastes were areas of lesser fertility that the village would use communally for less-demanding plants or pastures for animals or foraging areas. The commons and wastes could make the difference between life and death even though a local noble or big landlord often owned the lands. Because the productivity of these lands was low, peasants had used them by custom. Now there were fences or hedges and penalties for "poaching." The Enclosure Acts also imposed fees for surveying land that many peasants could not afford. The result of enclosure was that many sold or gave up their lands or cooperated with their landlords in converting the land to the new system. From 1761 to 1792, the Parliament enclosed seven times as much land as in the previous thirty years, and the pace accelerated after 1792. By 1800, the nobles or gentry held 80 percent of the land in Britain.

Results of the Agricultural Revolution

From 1700 to 1870, the number of farm workers in England grew by 14 percent, while production of crops grew 181 percent. Labor productivity therefore grew 146 percent. Measured another way, the land productivity of wheat, oats, and legumes doubled. Farmers not only eliminated most fallow land but reclaimed swampy and hilly and infertile land so the total amount of land planted grew 72 percent. Production of potatoes went from 1.31 million bushels to 50.14 million bushels. The general population of England and Wales rose from 5.75 million to 25 million (335 percent) in this time. England had been a food exporter from 1660 to 1770; now it had to import food. Sixty percent of the English workers had been mainly food producers in 1700; that fell to 22 percent by 1850. The increase in population would tend to lead to a rise in food prices, but the increase in productivity offset this and brought prices down. Sara Horrell found that 48 percent of the budget went to food in the 1787 to 1796 period in Britain, but only 40 percent on average went to food in the 1830 to 1954 period. By another estimate, in 1688 58.5 percent of the British G.D.P. was spent on food, drink, and textiles; that would fall to 16 percent by the 1990s.

The agricultural revolution spread to northern France by 1770. One hundred years later the process was largely complete in that country. From 1780 to 1810, the amount of French land planted with potatoes increased by more than one hundred times. From there it spread across the rest of western and central Europe. The process was faster than Britain's and there were few enclosures. Farmers would often split their land among many sons. After several generations, the family was left with "microplots": farms too small to support a household. At that point, families would plant potatoes or introduce the four-crop rotation.

INDUSTRIAL REVOLUTION

Basic Shifts

The Industrial Revolution involved three basic shifts: machines replaced and amplified human labor. Wood burning gave way to coal burning as world coal production grew from 10 million tons in 1800 to one billion tons in 1900, a one hundredfold increase. Thirdly, animal or water or wind power gave way to the steam engine. Instead of many separate activities carried out by families across the countryside, unified factories would carry out production with many different machines and either would be centered in cities or new cities would grow up around the factories.

Why England?

England had several advantages for industrialization:

Financial: the Bank of England provided a strong anchor for a credit system to provide financing for projects. Interest rates were lower than in most other European nations. The number of banks outside the capital of London grew from twelve in 1750 to 400 in 1793 and 900 in 1815.

Geographic: England, being a long and narrow island, had many navigable waterways, making transport cheaper.

Economic: the Agricultural Revolution, pioneered in England, made for lower food prices and thus more disposable income for manufactured goods. Landowners used their agricultural profits to develop many coal fields.

Natural resources: coal and iron were abundant. Because the gentry ran the country, there were few regulations on agriculture or industry and landless workers could move where they pleased.

These four factors were necessary to start an industrial revolution. Nearby Ireland had similar geographic advantages and also went through the agricultural revolution. However, Ireland did not industrialize. It did not have much coal or iron. Also, its banking and credit system was underdeveloped. Ireland also suffered as a British colony. Cromwell had brutally completed the colonization process in the 1650s by taking land away from most Catholics. Although 90 percent of the Irish were Roman Catholics, Protestants owned 86 percent of the land and were often absentee landlords. What wealth Ireland produced was frequently transferred to Britain. Those who rented the land had no incentive to improve their land because that would only raise the rent. Ireland's textile industries suffered from British competition, and Ireland actually deindustrialized during the late 1700s: 48% of the Irish had been employed in farming in 1775, it was 75% in 1845. The Agricultural Revolution brought rapid population growth in Ireland as it did in Britain, but it also brought a dangerous over-reliance on the potato. Not only was this the main food for many, but raising potatoes was also the main job of many. If anything should happen to the potato crop, the Irish would have nothing to eat and no job to provide money to buy other food. 1,750,000 Irish left for England and America before the Great Hunger of the 1840s.

New Textile Inventions and Innovations

After agriculture, textile production was the second biggest occupation. Most clothes were made of wool, which comes from sheep. Silk and cotton were very expensive and had to be imported, often from China and India. In the putting-out system, merchants gave wool to peasants to spin into thread, then weave into cloth, and then sew together as clothes. In 1717, Thomas Lombe set up the first true factory, which would be carry out these functions in one central place. In 1733, **John Kay** invented the **flying shuttle**, which sped up the weaving process. This created pressure to speed up the spinning of the thread to meet the weavers' demand. **James Hargreaves** solved the problem of thread by inventing the **spinning jenny** in 1765. The **water frame** of **Richard Arkwright** could turn out coarser yarn even faster than the spinning jenny after 1775. Finally, **Samuel Crompton's "Mule"** combined the speed of the water frame with the fine thread of the jenny. The Mule could spin two to three hundred times faster than a hand spinner. However, the Mule required water power, so businessmen built factories near water and cottage spinning declined. The number of hand-weavers kept growing to weave the enormous amounts of spun thread, which grew tenfold from 1770 to 1790. In the 1820s, **Edmund Cartwright's power loom** (invented 1785) became dominant in weaving. These inventions all occurred in England. It was not because Englishmen were smarter than men of other nations. These inventors had incentive because credit was cheap, and many of these inventors became very wealthy men. They could borrow money at low interest rates to set up a new business or expand existing business. Often they borrowed from friends, relatives or members of their church. Life was harder for businessmen in France and Spain because interest rates were much higher and it was harder to make a profit. They found it easier to put money into land.

The next key problem was the supply of cotton. The North American colonies and India were the main sources of cotton. Cotton production was very slow because cotton seeds had to be picked out by hand. In 1793 the American **Eli Whitney** invented the **cotton gin** to pick out seeds automatically. This caused an upsurge in the cotton industry. Britain imported 2.5 million pounds of cotton in 1760, 22 million in 1787, and 366 million in 1837. It also caused the expansion of cotton plantations across the southern U.S. and with it slavery.

The Transportation Revolution

As textile production grew after 1760, it became more important to ensure cheap and reliable transportation. Roads were mostly unsuited to wheeled vehicles:

a rainstorm turned them into quagmires. Only a few special coaches on the British roads of the 1760s could travel sixty miles a day. Water transport was cheaper and more efficient. A horse could pull 100,000 pounds loaded onto a water barge, but only 250 pounds on land. After 1760, Britain and France launched many projects to build canals to link rivers and to deepen many waterways. In 1815, engineers led by **John McAdam** built new roads made with crushed stones over a solid foundation to accommodate wagons.

The "rail road" had long existed in the mines, usually made of joined wooden rails. Miners would push carts on grooved wheels loaded with tons of rock. The heavy weights were constantly breaking and splintering the wooden rails, which necessitated replacement. Innovations in iron and steel made better rails possible; mines installed the first iron rail track in 1767. In 1801, the first general railroad was established, pulled by horses to link the canals. The barge would be unloaded on to special carts that sat on iron rails.

Transport improvements caused the price of commodities to fall as goods became cheaper. The first steam-powered railroad line opened in 1830. The railroad expanded horizons of travel and movement, made cheap overland transport possible, and shrank distance for the first time in European history.

Growth in Iron and Steel

The European iron industry had grown steadily from the fifteenth century, when the water-powered blast furnace operated in Italy to increase the production speed of cast iron. Blast furnaces are used to extract the metal from the raw ore. Heating was done with **charcoal**, the result of wood burned in the absence of air to make a smokeless fuel. Europeans had cut down many forests to make charcoal or to build ships or warm people in their homes. From 1540 to 1640, coal and iron production in Britain increased 800 percent, but limits on mining from water and the nature of coal prevented further expansion.

With the price of wood climbing, especially in Britain, people began to turn to coal for heating. Although very efficient, coal was very smoky and could not be used in houses that did not have chimneys. Iron makers could not mix coal with iron because coal had many impurities that made the iron brittle. Another problem was that coal would turn soft and clog the furnaces. **Abraham Darby** borrowed the process of charring coal to remove impurities in coal from the brewing industry. This created **coke**. He used it to smelt iron in 1708.

The Application of Steam Power

The problem of pumping water from mines still limited coal use. Before 1700, the only sources for the continuous driving of machinery were wind, water, and living muscle. Scientific experiments of the late 1600s on vacuum and atmospheric pressure had shown the power of steam, pistons, and vacuums. Thomas Savery (c.1650–1715) built an early steam engine in 1698, but it was **Thomas Newcomen** (1663–1729) who built the first continuous engine in 1712. It pumped 120 gallons of water a minute from the mine. He used steam to create a vacuum that worked a pump at a cycle of twelve strokes a minute. The Newcomen engine produced five horsepower, about the same as an average water mill. By the time of his death, 100 of his engines were in use, mostly in the coal belt in the British Midlands.

In 1763, a small working model of the Newcomen engine was brought to a professor at Glasgow University for repair. **James Watt** recognized the great waste of energy in the engine and worked to improve its efficiency. A problem arose with the Watt engine that the main cylinder had to be snugly contained or steam would escape. Ironmaster **John Wilkinson** had devised in 1774 a new way of boring holes into cannon and the same thing could be done to cylinders and other automatically guided precision tools to within a thousandth of an inch. In 1797, Richard Trevithick developed the **high-pressure steam engine**, which was more efficient than Watt's engine and could produce twenty horsepower, four times the power of the Newcomen engine. Trevithick invented a locomotive that could haul ten tons at five miles an hour.

Steam power sped up production in industrial areas. Blast furnaces pumped air to speed iron manufacturing. Henry Cort simplified the entire iron production process in the 1780s and produced high-quality iron. Later, steam powered the entire textile process. Factories could be located away from water sources. Canals linked coal fields to the centers of industry. Britain began to export iron in 1797. British iron production was 260,000 tons in 1806. It reached three million in 1844. By 1852, Britain accounted for half of the world's iron production and was exporting over a million tons a year. In 1777 Abraham Darby III built the Iron Bridge, the first large work of civil engineering in iron. In 1829, **George Stephenson**'s locomotive *The Rocket* operated from Liverpool to Manchester at twenty-seven miles per hour.

Adam Smith: Economic Theory for the Revolutionary Age

With the tremendous growth in farm and manufactured goods, the emergence of a national work force and more cohesive national states united by railroads, an international market was emerging more clearly. The old principles of mercantilism were clearly outdated as were old regulations dating from the Middle Ages.

Adam Smith (1723–90) of Great Britain published the *Wealth of Nations* in 1776. Smith had met with Voltaire and applied Scottish Enlightenment theories to economics: by serving their own self interests and applying reason, people will actually serve a greater good by bringing into effect the "invisible hand" as long as they are properly informed (as with Rousseau). Another important step is the division of labor: each person doing one small repetitive task can increase productivity. Production lines were already common in Enlightened Europe. The larger the market, the larger the division of labor could be, and thus the government should lift all restraints on trade. Smith was the founder of the classical liberal economic school.

Many heads of big corporations who cite Smith with approval want to "get the government off their backs," but Smith also attacked big corporations venomously: those that had begun to separate boards of directors from management and from the stockholders. This leads to management cheating the true owners of the company. If companies get too big, they invariably manipulate and distort the free market so the invisible hand cannot operate properly. Smith advocated government interference of a sort that only Communist governments have ever implemented.

With attacks against restraints on trade, Smith founded an economic liberal philosophy that would combine with political liberalism to create one of the most powerful political movements of the nineteenth century.

TIMELINE

1698	First Engine (Savery)
1708	Use of Coke in Smelting Iron (Darby)
1712	First Continuous Engine (Newcomen)
1730s	Townshend promotes four-crop rotation
1733	Flying Shuttle (Kay)
1733	Jethro Tull, *The Horse Hoeing Husbandry*
1765	Spinning Jenny (Hargreaves)
1765	Improved Steam Engine (Watt)
1775	Water Frame (Arkwright)
1776	Adam Smith, *Wealth of Nations*
1779	Crompton's "Mule"
1781	Rotary-action steam engine (Watt)
1783	Steamship (d'Abbans)
1785	Power Loom (Cartwright)
1793	Cotton Gin (Whitney)
1797	High-Pressure Steam Engine (Trevithick)
1803–4	Steam Engine Locomotive (Trevithick)
1807	The *Clermont* (Fulton)
1815	Macadamized road (McAdam)
1829	The *Rocket* (Stephenson)

KEY TERMS

Three-Field System
Thomas Malthus
Jethro Tull
Four-Crop Rotation
Enclosure Acts
Flying Shuttle
Spinning Jenny
Water Frame
Crompton's "Mule"
Power Loom
Cotton Gin
McAdam
Abraham Darby
Thomas Newcomen
The Rocket
Adam Smith

PRIMARY SOURCE DOCUMENTS

Accounts of the "Potato Revolution," http://www.fordham.edu/halsall/mod/1695potato.html

Letter from the Leeds Cloth Merchant, http://www.fordham.edu/halsall/mod/1791machines

Adam Smith, http://www.wsu.edu:8080/~dee/ENLIGHT/WEALTH1.HTM

Adam Smith, http://odur.let.rug.nl/~usa/D/1776-1800/adamsmith/wealth02.htm

Edwin Chadwick, Report on Sanitary Conditions, http://www.victorianweb.org/history/chadwick2.html

Chapter 4

THE REVOLUTION IN POLITICS

What does "Revolution" mean?

A revolution is not simply toppling a ruler (time immemorial) or even shifting the political system (Aristotelian cycles). It is not peasant revolt (time immemorial). It is remaking society in a progressive manner to bring it closer to God's kingdom or some ideal equivalent. It requires the Christian idea of progress in a linear fashion. Revolutionaries are self-aware. While it involves religious and ideological underpinnings, it must also avoid the trap of the pure being "above politics." A key moment came with Aquinas' *Summa* (1268) that politics is natural to man, not a result of the fall of Adam and Eve. Revolutionary movements are preceded by the spread of Christianity because it stresses the linear nature of time. When this idea comes to non-Christian cultures, revolutions become possible. Many things are retrospectively called "revolutions" in ancient and medieval times, but those leaders were not planning a full overhaul of society and politics. These movements were grabs for power or a return to the past (such as the Gracchi or Caesar in Rome) or slave/peasant revolts (Spartacus). Although the execution of King Charles was a revolutionary act, the installation of a military dictator, Oliver Cromwell, soon put an end to any revolution. The "Glorious Revolution" of 1688 was more of a Dutch invasion and substitution of kings than any real revolution.

THE ANGLO-AMERICAN REVOLUTION

George III's Enlightened Ambitions

King George III (ruled 1760–1820) of Britain dreamed of being an **Enlightened Despot**. These were rulers on the European mainland who combined absolutist rule with a belief in the Enlightenment. George's father and grandfather had spoken little English and had been content to let Parliament run things. Under the settlement of 1688, the king still had sweeping power, especially handing out jobs and monetary honors, and George was determined to use it. In the middle of the Seven Years' War against France, George dismissed the Prime Minister (head of the day-to-day government) and replaced him with his personal tutor. George III maintained his own group in the House of Commons with payments and government honors. This group was called "the **King's Friends**." They let France have an easy peace in 1763. The king tried to increase his control over the thirty-one governments in the British Empire (the North American colonies all had separate governments). The only exception to this centralization was that the king gave more power to Protestant landowners in the Irish Parliament. Eventually, however, Ireland rebelled with the help of French troops and its Parliament was abolished in 1801. To run an empire required taking account of the needs of West Indian sugar planters, American Indians, French Canadians, and British taxpayers, not just North American colonists.

Calls for Political Reform

Calls were also growing for political reform on two fronts: the way of election and corruption. Most members of Commons were elected from **boroughs** (towns); many of these boroughs had few electors ("rotten boroughs") or were under the control of the local notable ("pocket boroughs"). There had been no **reapportionment** (division to match how many people lived there) since 1688. There were only eight members of the House of Commons to represent the eight million living around London, while forty-two members represented 100,000 in Cornwall. Fifty-one English and Welsh boroughs with fewer than 1500 votes chose 100 members, about one-fifth of the House of Commons. The opponents of reform said that it was unnecessary and unwise. The British system, unlike today's American system, rests on the idea of **virtual representation**. Members of the House of Commons do not represent the district that elected them but all British possessions and people. There was no need for British workers or peasants or women to vote because the wise rich landowners of Britain already provided them with a fair representative.

The Wilkes Affair

John Wilkes (1725–1797) was a reformist member of Parliament who had written articles critical of the king and the Peace with France. The government charged Wilkes with libel. The "King's Friends" expelled him from the House of Commons in 1764, although Wilkes had won his court case. Wilkes reprinted the article, was outlawed, and fled to France. When he returned in 1768, he was arrested. Demonstrators filled the streets chanting "no justice, no peace." Troops fired on the unarmed crowd, driving it into a frenzy. Wilkes was released from prison and elected to the Commons. The Commons refused to accept the result or let Wilkes take his seat. This happened three times. Then the Commons proclaimed the election loser as winner. Nevertheless, slow change began. In 1771, there was full press publicity of debates so the Parliament could no longer operate in secret. In 1774, Wilkes once again won election to the House of Commons. This time, with uneasiness about the king growing, he was allowed to take his seat. He immediately introduced a reform bill.

North American Problems

George III's biggest headache came with North America. Since the 1680s, Britain had allowed these colonies to govern themselves and had not taxed them. It governed through colonial assemblies, some of which were quite democratic; 95 percent of adult men got to vote in Massachusetts, for example. During the Seven Years' War, London struck down laws in Virginia and South Carolina and tightened royal control of colonial courts. The British taxpayer had borne the entire cost of the war, and the British army had done most of the fighting. The population of the British colonies had grown from 250,000 in 1710 to 2.5 million by the 1770s. Many of these were young people from England who had not found work, and oppressed people from Highland Scotland and Ireland who bore grievances against the Crown.

Pontiac's Rebellion and the Tax Acts

The fight was not over. After the war, the British settlers began to squeeze the Indians' territory. **Pontiac's Rebellion** erupted in 1763. The government decided to maintain 6,000 troops as a border force and forbade colonists from settling west of the Appalachian Mountains, lest it cause more Indian wars. That angered the colonists. Britain was determined to get its money back through a series of increased taxes. At one time, the Land Tax of 1692 had paid 20 percent of revenue, but there had no reassessment as the landowners controlled

Commons, and other taxes from sales and trade filled the gap. Britain had to pay £2 million a year interest on the money borrowed for the Seven Years' War plus another £3.5 million to defend the empire. The Revenue Act of 1764 (called the **Stamp Act**) effectively doubled taxes from one to two shillings per American while British residents paid twenty-six shillings per person. It would only raise £150,000 per year.

The largest colonies of Virginia and Massachusetts protested against the Stamp Act. Virginia delegate Patrick Henry proclaimed that there could be "no taxation without representation." This was a direct challenge to Virtual Representation. If King George yielded and gave the North American colonists a few representatives, it would encourage Wilkes and the reformers to demand their proper representation. Thus the king was in a difficult position. Mob violence began to spread in Boston, the capital of Massachusetts. Nine colonies met in a Stamp Act Congress (New Hampshire, Georgia, North Carolina, Virginia, and the Canadian colonies were not present). Parliament repealed the Act in 1766. The British tax situation grew worse as Parliament, against King George's wishes, reduced Land Tax enforcement.

This led to the **Townshend Acts** (1767) on imported paint, glass, lead and tea. The American colonies ran a trade deficit of £2 million and had to balance it with illegal trade. New England had outgrown its food supply and felt the burden of mercantilism most keenly. Britain's Sugar Act of 1764 cracked down on smugglers. Boston tried to refuse imports and violence culminated in the **Boston Massacre** (March 1770) where British troops who had been redeployed from the frontier killed five Americans. **Lord North** had just become Prime Minister of Britain. North was young at thirty-eight (the same age as George Washington and only two years older than King George) and had been a leader of the King's Friends. He had been a major force in expelling John Wilkes from the House of Commons and keeping him out. North now repealed all the Townshend Acts except for a symbolic tea tax. Parliament kept this just to show that it had the right to tax the American colonies.

The Boston Tea Party

The tea issue became critical when the British East India Company, which had borne most of the costs for the Indian theater of the Seven Years' War, pleaded for help and was given a monopoly over the American tea trade; this would force a payment of tax. In December 1773, Bostonians destroyed the tea by throwing it into the harbor. North now put through **Coercive Acts** to close the port of Boston and revise the Massachusetts colonial charter.

The Continental Congress

Massachusetts leaders called for a meeting of colonies to discuss a common response; all but Georgia and the Canadian colonies sent delegates to Philadelphia. It condemned all the acts since 1763. While **John Jay** claimed they were asserting rights as Englishmen, the radical Patrick Henry said that the contract of government in a Lockean sense had been dissolved and it was now a state of nature. Using the Enlightenment language of Montesquieu and Beccaria, the Congress sent letters to the Canadian colonies and to the colonies of East and West Florida asking for help, but got little. The Parliament dominated by the King's Friends declared the New England colonies in rebellion in February 1775. Radicals and others called for reconciliation but lost in the Parliament by a vote of 270 to 78. The revolution began in 1775 as local militia in Massachusetts fired on British troops. The Continental Congress called for the formation of an army and put it under the command of **George Washington** (1732–99), an American officer from the Seven Years' War. This army expelled the British from Boston in 1776.

Declaration of Independence

Authority became an issue as royal assemblies were overthrown and chaos swept government and tax collection. Public enthusiasm was whipped up by the recently-arrived English radical **Thomas Paine** and his pamphlet *Common Sense* (1775), which sold 150,000 copies from January to July 1776. About 6 percent of the whole populace bought the book over a seven month period. **Thomas Jefferson** (1743–1826) of Virginia took the lead in drafting a Declaration of Independence (July 4, 1776) that used the terms of Locke and the Enlightenment to bring a bill of charges against the king and state the reasons for a separation of the thirteen colonies from Britain. This included a condemnation of the slave trade, but Congress removed it from the final document. Nine state assemblies followed up the Declaration by drafting new state charters. Six states solicited authority from the voters in advance; two submitted drafts for popular ratification. These charters varied widely: North Carolina reserved voting rights for the wealthy, while Pennsylvania extended voting rights for all male taxpayers over age twenty-one with annual elections. In Massachusetts about one-quarter of the free adult men participated in voting.

Defeat of the British

France shipped massive quantities of arms to rebels but did not intervene until it thought the rebels had a chance to win after 1777. Spain entered the war in 1779, the Netherlands in 1780. War again erupted in India. France sent troops and ships. French money and the French navy helped the rebels gain local superiority. As was typical in colonies, home troops ran into trouble beyond cannon range of ships when faced with a hostile population. The British had paid for 37 percent of the cost of the Seven Years' War with loans. They had to borrow 40 percent of the cost of the American War of Independence. The Dutch held more than 40 percent of the British debt and when they cut off further loans, it threatened the entire British debt structure. The main British force surrendered in 1781 at **Yorktown**. The Commons overturned the resolution fixing the election against Wilkes. In 1782, the reformers in the House of Commons invented a new device: they asked the members to state that they had confidence in Lord North and his government. Although North survived this **vote of no-confidence**, it was so close that he had to resign. The British debt in 1783 was nearly double what it had been in 1763, and the British government was paying an unsustainable 66 percent of its annual revenue just to pay interest on the debt.

The **Peace of Paris** (1783) won U.S. independence, and Spain gained Florida and Minorca in the Mediterranean. The United States would be the area between the Atlantic Ocean and the Mississippi River. Many Americans who had supported the British lost their land. 3 to 5 percent of the total population left the United States forever. In both land confiscation and emigration, the American Revolution was far more radical than the later French Revolution.

After the War

The Congress continued to run affairs, but unlike Parliament, it had no taxing authority. The states contributed $6 million, and Congress borrowed more than $7 million. Congress also issued paper money. Some northern state constitutions provided for the gradual freeing of slaves: Pennsylvania began the process in 1780, New Jersey in 1804. New York put in a gradual process from 1799 to 1827. As late as 1830, there were still 3500 slaves in the North. The northern states plus Maryland, Delaware, and Virginia all banned the African slave trade.

In March 1781 the **Articles of Confederation** were ratified. The Union was a "league of friendship," and each state had one vote. Problems soon rose over debt payment by states, paper money, and the general postwar recession. The Articles could only be amended unanimously. Washington and a New York lawyer, **Alexander Hamilton** (1755–1804), called for a meeting in Philadelphia to correct the defects in the Articles.

The U.S. Constitution

The Constitutional Convention of 1787 wrote a constitution and carefully separated powers among executive (the President), legislative (the Congress), and judicial branches. It was heavily influenced by the radical reformers in Britain, the Enlightenment (especially Montesquieu), and the ideas of ancient republics. In a radical departure, there would be no king or possibility of absolutism. As Locke would have wanted, the legislature would be supreme. The Constitutional Convention modeled the two houses of Congress on those of the British Parliament but since there were no nobles in the U.S., and the Constitution forbade the creation of a nobility, state legislatures would choose U.S. Senators. The House of Representatives would be elected under voting rights that differed from state to state. Equal districts for the House meant no rotten boroughs or pocket boroughs. There would be no property or religious qualification for any office, unlike Britain where only members of the Church of England could serve in Parliament. Many of the leaders of the revolution such as Washington and Jefferson were not Christians but **Deists**: they believed that God had created the universe but then left it alone and did not intervene in human affairs. When Hamilton was asked why Jesus' name was nowhere in the Constitution, he joked "We forgot!" In 1788, half of the states provided for popular election of presidential electors; not until 1828 did this become the general rule. The federal government gained the power to levy taxes and regulate interstate and foreign commerce while the Constitution forbade states from diplomacy or taxing imports and exports.

As state conventions considered the Constitution, several demanded a **Bill of Rights**. The first ten amendments guaranteed various rights to all people under American authority (not just U.S. citizens), including freedom of the press, freedom of religion, the right to a jury trial, and no imprisonment without charge. Inspired by Beccaria, the Bill of Rights banned cruel and unusual punishments. The old ideas of federalism, limited government, and constitutionalism had been associated with reactionaries and nobles trying to fight the power of the king. Now these ideas became progressive.

IMPACT OF THE AMERICAN REVOLUTION

The American Revolution and the Constitution showed the *philosophes* that their ideas could be put into practice. In 1778, American revolutionary leader Benjamin Franklin embraced the aged Voltaire to symbolize how the United

States was inspired by the Enlightenment. Jefferson followed Franklin as Ambassador to France while John Adams was in the Netherlands.

Impact on the British Isles

An Anglican elite had long governed Ireland. Just 10 percent of the population owned 83 percent of the land. Absentee landlords were common. George III had put in some reforms such as elections every eight years, not just at the king's death. Ireland got a resident viceroy. The American Revolution caused a trade disaster in Ireland. The British feared a French invasion and armed "volunteers," but after Yorktown these volunteers pressed demands. North granted more independence for the Irish Parliament and allowed Ireland to export more items, relaxing the mercantilist stranglehold that was destroying the Irish textile industry. The Irish Parliament allowed Catholics to buy land starting in 1782 and a few to vote starting in 1793. A reformist attempt to abolish rotten boroughs in Ireland failed.

The American catastrophe caused fall of the King's Friends and the rise of a new generation led by **Charles James Fox**, who had supported the American rebels and the Irish volunteers, and **William Pitt the Younger**. Pitt introduced an electoral reform bill that was defeated by a vote of 161 to 141. In 1785, as Prime Minister, Pitt tried to abolish the thirty-two most depopulated boroughs. After this failed, Pitt's interest in reform waned and he became North's successor as King George's trusted minister. Fox was his great opponent. Parliament voted down attempts to allow non-Anglican Protestants to hold civil, military, or town office.

The Netherlands

The population was small (under 2 million) but it held 40 percent of British debt and in 1796 all of the U.S. debt. The regents, hereditary aristocrats who controlled town councils, clashed with the Stadholder (a hereditary Dutch noble who controlled the army) over American relations. In 1786, "Patriot" regents got control of Holland, the largest state in the Netherlands, and two other states. This broke into civil war in 1787 with Britain and France arming the two sides. The German state of Prussia intervened with British backing to drive out the Patriots.

To the south were the Austrian Netherlands. Their leaders rebelled against Emperor Joseph II in 1789 when he tied to tighten his control as King George had tried in North America. They passed a Declaration of Independence and then an Act of Union based on the American Articles of Confederation. The Church and the nobles rallied the peasants against the rebels, and Austria regained control in 1790.

Impact on Latin America

Of the 14 million persons living on the mainland of Iberoamerica, about 1 million were slaves, 9.5 million were Indians or of mixed race, and the remaining 3.5 million were Spaniards either born in Spain (*peninsulares*) or America (Creoles). Since the establishment of Spanish colonialism, the *peninsulares* had been dominant, much to the annoyance of the Creoles.

Enlightenment reforms in Spain allowed Creoles into local governments. The Creoles formed a militia in Mexico. Discontented Creoles sought to thread a needle: they wanted to increase their opportunities against the ruling class while preserving their property rights against the lower classes. They looked to the radicals of the United States and Britain, not to the Spanish liberals who opened trade and imposed taxes. Spain raised liquor, tobacco, and sales taxes to pay for its colonies' defense while tax collecting became more efficient because of enlightened reforms. The Creole elite had read the Enlightenment works and was familiar with events in British North America. With more efficient tax collection, town councils had revenue and they became the bastions of the Creoles.

Revolts among different ethnic groups in different regions grew more frequent after 1750: there were only five in the 1740s, eleven in the 1750s, twenty in the 1760s, and twenty more in the 1770s. The Creoles began to realize that only the state protected them from the lower classes. The most violent was the **Tupac Amaru** rebellion in Peru that lasted from 1780 until 1783. He was a descendant of the sixteenth century Incan emperor who was trying to abolish draft labor of Indians in his province while seeking recognition by Spain as a noble and heir to the Incas. The Creoles at first sympathized. Then came his social policy to abolish slavery and a call to wage total war against the Europeans and reconsider property laws. With 40,000 to 60,000 supporters, Tupac Amaru besieged Cuzco in 1781. He was defeated, captured, and then torn apart by horses. 100,000 died in the punishment that followed. Spain reformed the government of Peru as seven intendants replaced a multitude of local governors, but the draft labor system persisted. The tax laws of Spain touched off the **Communero Revolution** of 1781. There were riots in Socorro and other towns of New Grenada (the northern coast of South America) after the government published the tax edicts. An Indian peasant army led by Creole captains marched on Bogota, was delayed, and then betrayed.

THE FRENCH REVOLUTION

Attempts at Reform

The Seven Years' War compelled King Louis XV of France (ruled 1715–1774) to take strong measures. He imposed a 5 percent tax on net landed revenue in 1749, which he raised to 10 percent in 1756, and 15 percent in 1760. He tried to take offices from corrupt officeholders. The nobles were getting completely out of hand. They imprisoned royal governors and military commanders who tried to carry out the king's commands. In 1771, he stripped much of the power from the noble court of Paris and exiled the judges.

The Aristocratic Reaction

Failure of Reform

King Louis contracted smallpox and died. His grandson, **Louis XVI** (ruled 1774–1793) wanted to be loved by all at the beginning of his reign and repealed the previous decrees. Nobles whipped up the mob of Paris to ensure there would be no reversal. Like George III, Louis XVI fancied himself an Enlightened Despot. He would not address the issue of taxing the nobles. Before the government could deal with education or poor relief, the nobles forced even mild reforms to cease. There were some limited rights given to Protestants. France abolished its tax on Jews. The call for reform grew.

Fiscal Crisis

French aid to American colonies during their revolution had put a heavy strain on the French Treasury. Instead of raising taxes, the Treasury under **Jacques Necker** (1732–1804) borrowed a billion livres at interest rates as high as 10 percent from 1777 to 1781. By 1787, the monarchy was up against the wall: heavy debts, no way to raise taxes, no way to borrow more money. Finance Minister **Charles de Calonne** (1734–1802) called for a new property tax and the abolition of internal grain tariffs to create free trade. When the nobles resisted, the government called an **Assembly of Notables**. 144 men met to discuss the problems of France. This upper-class group rejected the Calonne proposal and said that only the **Estates-General** could raise taxes. The was the French equivalent of the British Parliament and had not met in 175 years. The notables demanded that control be given to provincial assemblies, which they expected to control, in return for taxes.

The Debt

The government debt was 4 billion livres. The French budget of 1787 would have 475 million livres' in taxes and borrow 145 million. It spent 50 percent to service the debt, 27 percent on the military, and 6 percent to maintain the king and his palaces. This left only 17 percent for useful spending. France had only half of the equivalent debt of Britain and less than a fifth the per capita debt of the British. Since France had a much larger economy than Britain, there should not have been a problem, but unlike Britain, France did not have a solid banking and credit system.

The Revolution of 1789

Calling of the Estates General

The king tried to decree taxes, but the court of Paris refused to register them. The king banished the court but had to recall it after a month due to popular outcry. The court sensed blood and in January 1788, it presented a list of grievances. The king abolished it and called for the Estates-General. The nobles insisted that the Estates-General should meet as it had in 1614: three separate estates of clergy (First Estate), nobles (Second Estate), and everyone else (Third Estate). This would control the middle class. The public had seen the nobles as its only defense against the tax-hungry state but now grew angry at the naked power grab which would certainly raise the ordinary person's taxes. The middle class began to find its voice in the work of **Abbé Emmanuel Sieyès'** work *What is the Third Estate?* (1789) which said that the Third Estate is everyone. As such, the Third Estate should have 600 representatives as opposed to 300 each for the nobles and clergy. Sieyès claimed that he was a "patriot" (like the Dutch revolutionaries) and reformers took this label, identifying themselves with the nation. The royal council agreed and doubled the Third Estate. The nobles and clergy raised no objection because they believed that voting would be by chamber and they would always control two of the three chambers.

The Nobility

To raise money, the government had opened more offices for sale in the eighteenth century. Men would pay for these offices because they conferred nobility. From 1715 to 1789 there were 6,500 new noble families; this made up between 25 and 33 percent of all noble families, so the nobility was relatively new. Many rich town dwellers bought land, many nobles served as investors. Noble families comprised 400,000 persons (about 2 percent of the population) and owned about 25 percent of the land. The French nobles had largely avoided taxation and had other privileges: only they could carry a sword in public, sit in the first pew in Church, or be buried in a cathedral or its grounds. They walked in the front line of processions. Nobles could appoint judges in their area, could punish civil and minor criminal offenses, and could sell crops first to local merchants when the price was highest. They received payments made by peasants in the form of money, goods, and services. About one-third of the nobles in the Estates-General were "patriots."

The Church

In France, there were about 240,000 clergy (1 percent of population) during the Enlightenment. It held about 10 percent of the revenue-producing land. Most money in the church went to bishops, who were nobles. There were many non-noble priests who were unhappy with the rule of the nobles in the church. Parish priests were key figures in the villages: they were often the only literate men in the village and would announce new laws and had outside contacts. They were often the spokesmen for the village. A little under one half of the clergy in the Estates-General were "patriots."

The Commoners

The upper part of the Third Estate became influential as trade increased 500 percent from 1713 to 1789. The **bourgeoisie** (the upper class of the cities that was not a part of the nobility or the clergy) grew to about 8 percent of the total population of France. It resented noble privileges and felt shut out from government. Outside of the upper part, commoners were not well off compared with nobles. Price inflation rose 65 percent from 1730 to 1780, while wages rose only 22 percent. About half of the peasants owned land. About one-sixth of the commoners elected to the Estates-General were conservatives; the rest were "patriots."

The Election Process

There were several stages: primary assemblies chose regional assemblies of electors. The electors then chose deputies to the Estates-General. The assemblies also drew up grievance petitions at each level. The king decreed that all men over the age of twenty-five who had paid taxes equal to three days' wages could meet in the primary assembly. Most of the grass roots petitions complained about the high burden of taxes and the obligations to nobles. The regional and national petitions were more radical: an unequal tax system, a middle class excluded from politics (particularly from local politics), an inefficient government, and finally, the fiscal crisis. Paris had 30,000 voters eligible; 12,000 (40 percent) showed up at sixty primary assemblies. Most of the 407 Paris electors chosen in this process were lawyers and government officials. The 1789 elections for the Third Estate were much more democratic than the British elections of the time. Only some American states were more generous in voting rights. Not a single peasant or artisan was part of the Estates-General at the king's palace of Versailles outside Paris.

The Tennis Court Oath and the National Assembly

The Estates-General opened on May 5, 1789. The king had recalled Necker as finance minister to try to win some reformist support. The "patriots" were not as radical as the Americans and wanted to keep a king as long as he was subject to a Constitution and the Estates-General. They also wanted a guarantee of liberties and liberal economic reforms such as eliminating internal trade barriers.

The Estates-General met in its three estates: clergy, nobility, and commoners. The commoners demanded a single assembly where all three would vote together. Otherwise, the commons would be overruled by the other two estates. The swing group was the clergy, divided between wealthy bishops and poorer parish priests. On June 13, a few clergymen went over to sit with Third Estate. The clergy's first vote on sitting together failed by a vote of 133 to 114. King Louis' own family was divided: his brothers sat in the Estates-General as conservative nobles, but his cousin Philippe, the Duke of Orléans, was aligned with the patriot nobles.

On June 17, 1789, the Third Estate declared itself a **National Assembly** and invited the other two estates to join it. The clergy now agreed to join, giving it legal authority. King Louis, never a strong personality, was distracted because his infant son had died a week before. The king closed the meeting hall to the National Assembly on June 20, so it met on a nearby tennis court, where it took the **Tennis Court Oath** not to disband until it had written a constitution for France. King Louis went back and forth: first he was conciliatory, then harsh. 18,000 soldiers began to mass around Versailles at the end of June.

The Great Fear

The winter of 1788/89 had been the coldest of the century. The bread price had doubled and was at its highest since 1715. Families had spent 50 percent of their budgets on bread in 1788, 80 percent in 1789. With food so expensive, many workers had lost their jobs and wandered the roads as beggars and robbers. The harvest was poor. When the king dismissed Necker on July 11, the 407 electors of Paris met to form their own provisional government committee and arm themselves. Necker was popular in Paris because he had imported grain to feed the people. The mob raided prisons. On July 14, it grabbed cannon and 32,000 muskets from the Invalides, and then a mob of 8,000 **stormed the fortress of the Bastille** to gain arms. Ninety-eight Parisians were killed. The mob killed the governor and put his head up on a pike and displayed it, just as the government had done to so many criminals.

Louis immediately backed down as he believed the troops were unreliable. He recognized the citizens' committee as the city government of Paris. The **Marquis de Lafayette** (1757–1834), who had fought in the American Revolution, took over command of the guard. They displayed a new **tricolor** flag: the red and blue colors of Paris with Bourbon (the king's family) white. Rumors swept the countryside that conservatives were gathering an army of beggars to reassert their privileges and ancient taxes. Revolts broke out in the countryside as peasants burned tax records and refused to honor feudal dues usually done in the summer. Mobs robbed or murdered grain dealers. 20,000 conservative nobles left France. Provisional governments now took power in twenty-six of the largest thirty cities.

The End of Privilege

On August 4, the nobles agreed to give up privileges (including their tax privileges) in exchange for an amount of money that was never paid. The peasants had won. On August 27, the National Assembly issued the **Declaration of the Rights of Man and Citizen**, a combination of British and American demands for rights: freedom of thought, freedom of religion, all equal under the law. Only citizens or their representatives could enact laws and taxes. The natural rights were "liberty, property, security, and resistance to oppression." The State could take property but only with fair compensation. The Assembly elected a patriot noble named **Honoré de Mirabeau** (1748–1791) as its president and began to compose a constitution.

The Lower Classes in Action

The Move to Paris

Rumors swept Paris that the king would not accept the reforms and that he would use troops. King Louis' brother-in-law was the ruler of Austria and a member of the Habsburg family. Perhaps the Austrians, already sour on the revolution in the Austrian Netherlands, would aid the king. False stories spread of members of the King's Bodyguard wearing Habsburg colors. On October 5, about 6,000 women walked the thirteen miles from Paris to Versailles to ask what was going on and demand relief from the high food prices. The men of the National Guard joined them the next day. The king was conciliatory, but a scuffle broke out in which one Parisian and two bodyguards were killed. The mob dragged the king back to Paris, along with his wife Marie Antoinette, their son, and wagons full of flour. The National Assembly followed. From this point on, the Paris mob was the dominant force; shouts from galleries would drown out speakers not liked by the mob. More conservatives began to go back to their estates or form a second wave of emigration.

The Jacobin Clubs

During the debates over constitution in the fall of 1789, many men formed societies to debate constitutional issues. The most important was the Society of Friends of the Constitution, known as the Club of St. James or **Jacobins** because they met in a former monastery. Dues were fairly expensive so only people from the middle class and upper middle class could join the Jacobin club as they tried to coordinate strategy among their few members.

Constitutional Monarchy

The Assembly wrote a constitution allowing the king a veto for four years, and limited suffrage that gave 4.3 million Frenchmen full voting rights (about 16 percent of the total population and close to two-thirds of the adult male population). Men over age twenty-five who paid a small tax would vote for electors from a pool of 50,000 men who paid taxes equivalent to fifty-four days of labor. The electors would then vote for a legislative assembly. The constitution favored country districts over the towns and cities. The Assembly abolished internal tariffs, erased old provincial boundaries, and replaced them with eighty-three Departments of roughly equal size. These consisted of smaller districts and cantons. Municipal government became uniform. All local officials would be elected locally. It seemed that the revolution was over.

The Quarrel with the Church

The upheaval did not solve the financial crisis which had started the process. The call for "patriotic" loans fell upon deaf ears. Necker announced a budget deficit of 294 million livres, worse than ever. The Assembly took the radical step of confiscating all lands of Catholic Church and the monasteries in November 1789. This land was to be collateral for 400 million livres' worth of ***assignats***, a 3 percent bond; by September 1790, another 800 million livres were being printed up in smaller denominations (fifty livres). 1,200 million livres was less than the value of the land, but people were hoarding hard money or taking it out of the country. Bad harvests had led to a trade deficit as France tried to buy wheat. When they gained power after August 1792, the Jacobins printed small-money notes, which they would exchange for *assignats*. The government then issued 100 million livres in five-livre *assignats*. This led to a spiral of inflation as the government printed more and more in smaller denominations. At the end of 1791, they were being accepted at 75 percent of face value; four months later, at 60 percent, as counterfeiters had a field day.

The government then sold church land in large, undivided blocks, so most peasants could not afford to buy it. Without its land, the Church had to be supported by the government as employees of the state. Under the **Civil Constitution of the Clergy** passed by the Assembly, priests and bishops would be chosen by the same electors who voted for the Assembly, including Protestants and Jews. In April 1791 Pope Pius VI condemned this arrangement and the entire Revolution. Half of all the priests in France resigned, and the new priests were not liked by the people. Only seven of 130 bishops were willing to swear the oath of loyalty to the constitution. An underground church with the old priests sprang up.

Polarization of the King and the Assembly

Mirabeau's death in April 1791 weakened the moderates. Another wave of strikes by disgruntled workers swept through the cities. On June 20, 1791, the king and his family made a desperate attempt to flee, leaving a note behind repudiating the revolution. They were caught and dragged back. The "patriots" who dominated the Assembly were now stuck. They did not want an American-style republic and were saddled with an unpopular king. A growing number of people wanted a republic and they took over the Jacobin clubs. In September 1791, the Assembly declared the constitution in effect and held the first elections under the new system. No one from the first National Assembly was allowed to run for another term so there would be no candidates with the advantage of incumbency. Participation in the election was disappointing: only 25 percent of active citizens (or about 4 percent of the total population) bothered to vote. Even Paris, the center of the revolution, had a turnout of only 10 percent of voters. When the new National Assembly met October 1, 1791, the conservatives had vanished. The political groups were the old "patriots," trying to preserve a constitutional monarchy, squaring off against the Jacobins who favored a republic. Of 745 votes in the Assembly, neither side had 200 votes. The center, called the **Marsh** (because it was soft and squishy), voted with whatever minority it feared more.

International tensions grew. The Revolution inspired the lower classes in the German-speaking lands, the Austrian Netherlands, England and Hungary. Businessmen wished they could dominate their governments as the French had. The Jacobins pushed the idea of seizing the papal land of Avignon, a small independent area surrounded by French territory. Absolutist rulers grew more oppressive. French émigrés centered in the Austrian capital of Vienna lobbied Marie Antoinette's Habsburg brothers for an attack on France. The leaders of Prussia and Austria issued the Pillnitz Declaration on August 27, 1791, and declared they would protect Louis as a brother monarch and go to war if all joined them. This was nonsense because they knew that financially-burdened Britain was completely opposed to another war with France.

Rights of Women

The *philosophes*, even Rousseau, had generally been silent or negative about the place of women in their progressive society. The language of the Anglo-American radicals began to change that. American women sewed uniforms, made gunpowder, ran farmsteads, fought and died promoting the idea of American freedom. In New Jersey, for a brief time, women even gained voting rights. The French Revolution featured women playing a key role with the transfer of the king to Paris. The Declaration of the Rights of Man overthrew privilege. **Olympe de Gouges** (d.1793) wrote a "Declaration of the Rights of Women and Female Citizen" in 1791. In December 1790, the Dutch baroness Etta Palm d'Aelders called for civil rights for women. The *philosophe* Marquis de Condorcet considered the "Admission of Women to Rights of Citizenship."

The French Revolution was bitterly condemned by the Briton Edmund Burke in his *Reflections on the Revolution in France* (1790). Britons Tom Paine (*The Rights of Man*) and **Mary Wollstonecraft** (1759–1797) (*A Vindication of the Rights of Man*) defended the Revolution. Wollstonecraft, who had founded a girls' school, then made the next step, *A Vindication of the Rights of Women* (1792). Anger in Britain forced both Paine and Wollstonecraft to flee to France. However, Jacobin leaders had no interest in women's rights; they soon dissolved the Society of Revolutionary Women and when the Terror was at its height, women were seen as the leading defenders of old religion. The Jacobins executed Gouges as a royalist.

WAR WITH EUROPE AND THE "SECOND REVOLUTION"

The Fall of the Monarchy

The Move to War

A left-of-center group, the **Girondists**, controlled the Jacobin clubs and called for war. They believed that it would discredit King Louis and be the final step that would cause his fall and allow the Jacobins to establish an American-style republic. They urged France to spread the revolution, and on April 20, 1792, the French National Assembly declared war on Austria, supposedly because of the Pillnitz declaration. Only seven deputies opposed the war. Patriot leaders such as Lafayette believed that appearing as a war leader would improve Louis XVI's damaged image. The king could then enforce the constitution and crush the radicals. Émigrés who had grown in number were happy, wanting to see revolution strangled. Prussia joined Austria as its general swore that he would restore Louis to his full absolutist power and punish Paris. Inflation was in high gear by the spring of 1792 as counterfeit *assignats* circulated and the market was breaking down. From 1790 to 1793, the price of bread rose by 27 percent, beef by 136 percent, and potatoes by 700 percent.

War Hysteria Rules

To understand why France went berserk, one must always recall that there was war hysteria. Victory by the Austrians and émigré nobles would mean terrible retribution not only against the leaders of the revolution, but also the many peasants who had risen in the countryside. Some French nobles, including two brothers of the king, were helping the enemy. This spread the fear of a "hidden enemy" inside France. Winning was worth any price, and there was a terrible logic. Those who opposed the increasing pace of trials and executions might be secret enemies themselves. The government applied torture which only brought a flood of false accusations and more witch hunts. The war was at the root of the Terror.

The war went very badly. Only nobles had led the army before the revolution. Two-thirds of the army officers had fled. The army was disorganized, and many officers were inexperienced. The government could not afford mercenaries. The radical Jacobins claimed that King Louis was supporting the enemy. In June, Lafayette tried to raise the National Guard to crush the Jacobins. On August 1, 1792, the Assembly ordered the arming of all able-bodied men. Any man who volunteered for the army would gain voting rights.

The Convention Takes Over

On August 10, 1792, the mob, swelled by provincial recruits, stormed the Tuileries Palace, killed 600 Swiss Guards, and arrested the king. The radical Jacobins, led by the lawyer **Georges Danton** (1759–1794), allied uneasily with the moderate Jacobins. Danton took command of a provisional government and suspended the constitution. Even though the constitution had only been in effect for a year, the Jacobins said a whole new one must be written in a Constitutional **Convention**. All men would be allowed to vote for the Convention, about 28 percent of the population. Turnout varied wildly depending on the area: between 10 and 50 percent of those eligible turned out for the election. Despite the wider electorate, there were only two workers in the Convention.

The old Patriots such as Lafayette had fled or retired from politics. All the leaders of the Convention belonged to Jacobin clubs, whose membership swelled as more and more joined. Tom Paine was one member of the Convention. The Girondists controlled about one-quarter of the seats as the right wing, representing mostly great provincial cities. They were opposed by **the Mountain**, drawn from Paris and controlling about 40 percent of the seats. Danton was the main figure, backed by the bloodthirsty failed doctor **Jean Paul Marat** (1743–1793) and the lawyer **Maximilien Robespierre** (1758–1794). This group had opposed the war earlier but now were determined to spread revolutionary republicanism across Europe. The Mountain's supporters in Paris were known as *sans-culottes*, because they wore long trousers rather than the knee-length breeches common to the upper and middle classes. Fear led to summary executions of prisoners in the **September Massacres** in major cities, including between 1,100 to 1,400 persons in Paris. Good war news finally came in September when the French army beat the Prussians at the Battle of Valmy. The French moved into the Austrian Netherlands, Savoy, Mainz, and the left bank of the Rhine river.

The quasi-religious fervor that accompanies many revolutions was evident after the Jacobin takeover. They proclaimed the Year 1 with a new revolutionary calendar named after weather events. They expanded and highly regimented education almost in a parody of Rousseau. Dechristianization began: the government fostered cults of reason and the Supreme Being, although Robespierre tried to preach tolerance. Their equivalent of God's kingdom on earth was the "Republic of Virtue." The Convention found the king guilty of treason. On January 21, 1793, Louis XVI was executed. His head was cut off by a new "humane" device called the **guillotine**. Dr. Guillotin had complained that ax men were too likely to miss their targets and need several chops to take the head off. His device fit the head securely into a bracket. A heavy, sharp blade would do the job every time with little awareness by the victim. It would become known as the "revolutionary razor."

The Convention ordered a military draft to raise 300,000 new soldiers as it expanded the war and declared war on Britain, Holland and Spain. A royalist revolt in western France protested the draft and demanded the return of the Old Regime and the old priests. More men, including a general and the son of the Duke of Orléans, went over to the Austrian side. There was a vast tax shortfall because of the chaos in the provinces; the government issued more *assignats* and sold the lands of the Church that were supposed to be collateral for the *assignats*. The Austrians and Prussians pushed into France. Mobs demanded that hoarders of food be killed and called for price controls. This led to charges of treason being thrown about. Marat was tried but acquitted. The government authorized trials without jury or appeal. It set up Revolutionary Committees in each section or town to look for traitors.

The Jacobins were in a difficult position. The French armies were again collapsing, and the entire power structure was lined up against them. Reactionary nobles controlled much of western France; Prussia and Austria were pressing on the eastern border. The underground church told its followers that the Jacobins were devils. If the reactionaries won, it would mean the restoration of the king and absolutism and certain death or exile for the revolutionary leaders. They were fighting for their vision of a better world but also fighting for their lives. There was no possibility for compromise once the king was under arrest. The Jacobins now "doubled down" on the Revolution, hoping that a much larger and inspired army could defeat the reactionaries internally and externally. They had no money for trained soldiers so they would have to draft young Frenchmen. Since they would be paid little, these young men would have to be given a cause, the cause of revolution and the future. The government would have to print money and deal with the debts after it gained peace. Printing money caused price inflation and the Jacobin government's only choice was to freeze prices and wages. To prevent the spread of rebellion or undermining of the war effort, only the harshest of penalties would suffice: death. Step by step, there was an awful logic to the Terror.

The Convention set up a **Committee of Public Safety** in April 1793. The name came from the English Civil War; it had the power to oversee the Executive Council and suspend its decrees. The Duke of Orléans was suspected of trying to follow his cousin as king; the Committee arrested and executed him. The Convention wrote a new constitution establishing a liberal democratic republic, then suspended it immediately. Danton set up a Commission of Twelve to investigate treason. The sans-culottes accused the moderate Girondists of treason, and the first arrests came on May 31, 1793. The radical Mountain group led by Danton and Robespierre now took complete control.

The **Reign of Terror** (1793–1794) began. The arrest of the Girondists triggered waves of revolts, the crippling of the army, and the advance of the enemy. Robespierre was put on the Committee of Public Safety on July 27 and became its guiding force. The Committee temporarily stopped inflation by freezing prices and warned that it would regard any merchant breaking the price law as a traitor. The government replaced locally-elected officials with centrally-appointed administrators. On August 23, 1793, the desperate government ordered the *Levée en masse*: all unmarried Frenchmen aged eighteen to twenty-five had to join the army. Older and married men would engage in war work, women would work in hospitals and make tents and clothing; old men should engage in propaganda. The government confiscated gold and silver and foreign currency. The Committee imposed strict wage and price controls, punishable by death. Resistance and black markets sprang up. Peasants stored or destroyed goods. The government outlawed pastries and white bread, confiscated supplies and ordered production of items needed for the war. Orders made the army more mobile and filled it with revolutionary fervor. By the end of 1793, France's army topped 700,000 men. Nine months later, it was well over a million.

By end of 1793, Danton and others began to call for end to the Terror. Robespierre in 1794, after military success, began to relax the economic controls. The most radical sect, led by Jacques Hébert, a writer and publisher, formed a conspiracy to redistribute all property and plotted to overthrow Robespierre. Instead Hébert was executed. Danton's allies criticized the Committee of Public Safety for abuses of civil rights and challenged the Convention. The Committee arrested Danton and executed him April 5, 1794.

The Terror officially executed 17,000 and imprisoned 500,000 persons. 20,000 died in prison or were killed without a trial. Convention attendance was often below 100, for it had no power and no one would cross Robespierre. France was mobilizing its full strength and power for the war, and the world would tremble.

The Thermidorian Reaction

The executions of Hébert and Danton led to the question: who's next? New laws sped up executions tenfold and deprived the accused of their right to a defense attorney. On July 26 (8 Thermidor under the Revolutionary calendar), Robespierre spoke to the Convention and asked it to investigate a possible conspiracy, but the Convention referred it to a committee. The next day, he returned with specific accusations but found that his enemies controlled the mob in the galleries and shouted him down. The Convention moved before the Paris Commune or Jacobin clubs could organize themselves. On July 28, Robespierre was arrested and guillotined, ending the Terror.

The Convention stripped the committees of power, disbanded most revolutionary committees, and restored legal rights. There were fewer executions, and suspects were released. Price controls ended in December 1794. Inflation returned: the *assignats* had fallen to 34 percent of face value by Thermidor, then 20 percent by winter 1794. They would fall to 8 percent by the spring of 1795, and 4 percent by the summer 1795. Bread prices rose 1300 percent from March to May 1795. Beef prices rose 500 percent, pork and eggs more than 100 percent. In general, the cost of living rose 900 percent from 1790 to 1795, while wages did not keep pace. The government closed the Jacobin clubs in November 1794. The Convention recalled the Girondists in March 1795. Economic suffering was great but the most radical Paris leaders had died in the Terror, and the new government suppressed the mob of Paris when it imprisoned 1200 after a demonstration on May 22, 1795. The Jacobins who had ousted Robespierre were themselves removed in the "White Terror." The government ordered the execution of the members of the revolutionary committee as the émigrés began to return. It granted toleration of the Church in February 1795; the underground priests began to resurface.

The Terror sputtered to an end, but its impact was felt for two centuries. For the next two hundred years, the rich and members of the power elite knew that if they went too far in oppressing the lower classes, there could be an upsurge of violence and they could all wind up hanging from lampposts or shaved by the revolutionary razor.

The Directory

The Convention wrote yet another constitution. It limited voting rights to about 8 percent of the population and reduced the pool of electors to 30,000 from 50,000 in 1791. There would be two chambers, as in the United States. The

Council of 500 initiated bills and passed them after three readings. One-third of the 500 had to retire each year. The Council of Ancients (all members were over age forty) could not initiate or amend but passed bills from the Council of 500. The Council of 500 chose five Directors and one had to retire each year by random lot. The Convention automatically put two-thirds of its surviving members into these councils.

This constitution caused much discontent. Royalism began to grow. The son of Louis XVI and Marie Antoinette had died in prison in June 1795. His uncle proclaimed himself Louis XVIII and called for full reaction and to turn the clock back to 1789. In October 1795 a royalist mob outnumbered troops by four to one, but the troops had cannon and were led by a young general named Napoleon Bonaparte. The Government was becoming dependent upon the army. Bandits multiplied on the roads. There were also conspiracies on the radical left. Gracchus Babeuf organized the "Conspiracy of Equals" in 1796 to abolish private property. The Directory smashed this conspiracy and executed Babeuf.

The Directory tried to repair the damaged economy. It oversaw the rationing of scarce resources, foreign exchange, and the stock market. Metal coinage began to return. It imposed high tariffs to protect industry and reduced spending. Most people were tired of the revolution. They were no longer seeking God's kingdom on earth or a Republic of Virtue. Many wanted the peace of the old days, including a king. The Directors were also tired of revolution but knew that if Louis XVI's brother returned, he would have their heads.

The Revolution Expands outside of France

In December 1794, the French army moved into the Netherlands and proclaimed the **Batavian Republic** on the French model. France made peace with Prussia and Spain at the **Peace of Basel** in 1795. France gained much land west of the Rhine River and annexed the Austrian Netherlands (Belgium). The Belgians, Dutch, and Rhineland Germans had been dissatisfied with their rulers and did not rise against the French. In many areas, people welcomed the French as liberators. In Paris, revolutionaries from across Europe had gathered to work on revolutions in Ireland, Poland, Switzerland, the German lands, and the Italian lands.

The Netherlands

The Republic continued the Patriot movement of 1780s that had been stopped by Britain and Prussia. Many leaders turned radical and revolutionary only under the circumstances. 4 to 12 percent of adult males had belonged to Dutch Jacobin clubs before the French invasion. The French reassured the moderates: all they wanted was the ouster of the English and the stadholder. There was no Reign of Terror. Once they were victorious, the French demanded some Dutch territory, the maintenance of a French army of occupation, a payment of indemnity, and for the Dutch to declare war on Britain. In exile, the stadholder authorized the British occupation of all Dutch colonies. The British also captured Dutch ships and suspended payment on their debt to the Dutch.

In February 1796 a Dutch Constitutional Convention was elected by all men except paupers. Too many compromises led to a popular rejection of the proposed constitution in August 1797. In January 1798, a coup drove the conservatives from the convention. This led to a new constitution creating a unitary government. It gave more power to direct elections rather than electoral colleges, and gave citizens the ability to initiate amendments. The voters approved this constitution overwhelmingly, and it would survive the fall of the government.

Italy

In 1796, a French army poured through northern Italy to attack the Austrian-held lands there. The governments were afraid to arm their own people lest they lead a revolution. After breaking up the Paris demonstration in 1795, Napoleon had received a commission. With just 30,000 troops and outnumbered two to one, on May 10, 1796, Napoleon personally stormed across the bridge at **Lodi** in a hail of gunfire and led his troops in a rout of the Austrians. His army was intensely loyal. What had begun as a diversion from the center and north became the breakthrough area. Napoleon lived on local requisitions in Italy and established his own foreign policy. The cities rebelled against the old rulers and Austrians and aided the French. Napoleon established the **Cisalpine Republic** with Milan as its capital. Napoleon extorted funds from fearful cities and stole art treasures. The liberation of Italy echoed across Atlantic: in 1798 the American Senator Andrew Jackson praised it and hoped that England would be next. Napoleon concluded the **Treaty of Campo Formio** in October 1797 with Austria: France kept Belgium and the left bank of Rhine, and Austria recognized the Cisalpine Republic. Austria annexed Venice. Revolutionary activity, aided by Napoleon, swept through Italy in 1798 and 1799. Genoa changed into the **Ligurian Republic**. In Rome, the Pope lost his temporal power and a republic was set up. Most of Italy was now divided into French-dominated republics. Only Britain was left at war. The British blockaded most of the French fleets and their Dutch and Spanish allies making a Channel invasion impossible.

Ireland

The British government feared that Napoleon would next be sent to Ireland, but he was actually dispatched to Egypt, with major consequences that will be discussed. In 1791, **Wolfe Tone**, an Anglican lawyer, founded the Society of United Irishmen. It first called for parliamentary reform. In 1793, the British allowed a small number of wealthy Catholics to vote (but not serve) in the Irish Parliament. In 1794, the Society entered into secret correspondence with the French and desired independence. In 1796 the French landed in Bantry Bay, but the Irish were not ready and the fleet withdrew. The Dutch planned in 1797 to invade Scotland and Ulster after naval mutinies racked Britain, but the plan failed because of bad winds. In 1798 the United Irish rose in a bid for independence. 140,000 British soldiers under Cornwallis crushed the rebellion and killed 30,000 men, women, and children. A French force of several hundred landed too late on west coast. The 1801 **Act of Union** abolished the Irish Parliament, and until 1922 Irish voters would have to send representatives to London. The enemies of France were confused and divided: Prussia was out, Austria had been defeated, and Britain was torn by the anti-war, political reform group at home and the Irish revolt.

The French Imperial Possessions

The eighteenth century had been depressing to *philosophes* who believed in progress, for slavery had accelerated in the Caribbean. The French West Indies in 1770 had 379,000 slaves in a population of 430,000 (88%). This increased after 1770 with 30,000 new slaves arriving each year from 1785 to 1790; even if half died, this still meant 75,000 young slaves. Most people in San Domingue (Haiti) were African and in their twenties.

When news came of the storming of the Bastille, lower-class whites in San Domingue broke out their revolutionary clothes. The colony split between the pro-independence south and the colonial north. Free coloreds, who had generally supported slavery, now found their race was most important. Vincent Ogé led a revolt of 300 free coloreds in the north in 1790. Another colored rebellion killed the governor after he refused to promulgate an Assembly decree allowing free coloreds to vote. This disunity gave an opening to a massive slave uprising of 12,000 in August 1791 in San Domingue. By the end of 1791, whites and coloreds were each arming slaves to use against the other. Some slaves actually brandished royalist symbols.

In spring 1792 France recognized all free persons as citizens and sent 6,000 troops to unite the groups and put down the slaves. When the king was overthrown, the commissioners deported the governor and replaced white colonial officials with free coloreds. War with Spain now gave slave rebels a place to hide on the island. The Convention sent a new governor who clashed with the Commissioner in a new war. The Commissioner then appealed to the slaves. In August 1793 the Convention announced the abolition of slavery. Former slave **Toussaint Brèda**, who took the name **L'ouverture** (the opening), had been a commander with the Spanish/slave forces and emerged as a leader.

These events convulsed the Caribbean basin. The British, with 300,000 slaves in Jamaica, were deeply upset, as were the southern states of the U.S. The events in Haiti inspired slave revolts in the U.S., culminating in **Gabriel's Rebellion** of 1800 where at least two thousand slaves in Virginia organized an uprising. In Guadaloupe, a radical French commissioner liberated the slaves. Martinique put down its slaves by asking for British protection. Britain and Spain invaded San Domingue in 1793/94 and restored slavery. This was complicated by disease . To bolster their ranks the British organized black units by offering freedom to some. In May 1794, Toussaint turned against the Spanish and offered his services to the beleaguered republic. The war had ruined the economy. The Peace of 1795 temporarily drove out the Spanish from the island. Five forces contended in the western third of the island. The British increased their force to 30,000, but disease struck down many. Toussaint's strategy was to be loyal to whatever government ruled Paris.

TIMELINE

1763	End of Seven Years' War between France and Britain leave both deeply in debt
1763–64	Pontiac's Rebellion in North America
1764	House of Commons expels John Wilkes
	Stamp Act
1767	Townshend Acts
1770	Boston Massacre
1773	Boston Tea Party
1775	American Revolution begins
1776	Declaration of Independence
1780–83	Tupac Amaru rebellion in Peru
1781	Communero Revolution in New Granada
1781	French and Americans defeat British at Yorktown
1782	First vote of no-confidence in British House of Commons
1783	Peace of Paris
1787	United States Constitution
	Civil War in the Netherlands
1789	U.S. Bill of Rights
May 5, 1789	Estates-General convenes at Versailles
June 17, 1789	Third Estate declares itself the National Assembly
June 20, 1789	Oath of the Tennis Court
July 14, 1789	Storming of the Bastille
July–Aug. 1789	The Great Fear in the countryside
Aug. 4, 1789	National Assembly abolishes feudal privileges
Aug. 27, 1789	National Assembly issues Declaration of the Rights of Man
Oct. 5, 1789	Parisian women force royal family to return to Paris
Nov. 1789	National Assembly confiscates church lands
July 1790	Civil Constitution of the Clergy establishes national church
	Louis XVI reluctantly accepts a constitutional monarchy
June 25, 1791	Arrest of the royal family while attempting to flee France
Aug. 27, 1791	Declaration of Pillnitz by Prussia and Austria
April 20, 1792	French Assembly declares war on Austria
Aug. 10, 1792	Parisian mob takes Louis XVI and family prisoner
Sept. 1792	September Massacres
	Convention declares France a republic
Jan. 21, 1793	Execution of Louis XVI
February 1793	France declares war on Britain, Holland, and Spain
	Assembly asks levy of 300,000 soldiers; revolts break out
April 6, 1793	Robespierre and the Mountain organize the Committee of Public Safety
May–June 1793	Girondist leaders arrested
Aug. 23, 1793	*Levée en Masse*—all unmarried Frenchmen 18–25 called to the army

Sept. 1793	Price controls to aid the *sans-culottes*
1793–1794	Reign of Terror in Paris and the provinces
Spring 1794	French armies victorious on all fronts
March 24, 1794	Hébert executed
April 5, 1794	Danton executed
July 27, 1794	Execution of Robespierre; Thermidorian Reaction begins
Nov. 12, 1794	Jacobin Club in Paris ordered closed by the Convention
1795–1799	The Directory
April 14, 1795	Ratification of Peace of Basel with Prussia: France gains west bank of the Rhine
May 1795	Radical rising in Paris by *sans-culottes* ends
Oct. 3–5, 1795	Royalist rising in Paris broken up by Barras and Bonaparte
Oct. 17, 1797	Treaty of Campo Formio with Austria: Napoleon triumphant
1798	Austria, Great Britain, and Russia form the Second Coalition Napoleon's expedition to Egypt ends in disaster
1799	French force under Humbert lands in Ireland but is repelled

KEY TERMS

John Wilkes
U.S. Declaration of Independence
The U.S. Constitution
Estates-General
Storming of the Bastille
Declaration of the Rights of Man and Citizen
assignats
Georges Danton
Maximilien Robespierre
Committee of Public Safety
Reign of Terror
The Thermidorian Reaction
Toussaint L'Ouverture

PRIMARY SOURCE DOCUMENTS

Patrick Henry, http://www.law.ou.edu/ushistory/henry.shtml

Thomas Jefferson, Declaration of Independence, http://avalon.law.yale.edu/18th_century/declare.asp

U.S. Constitution and Bill of Rights, http://avalon.law.yale.edu/18th_century/usconst.asp

Arthur Young, http://history.hanover.edu/texts/young.html

French notebooks of complaints, http://www.historyguide.org/intellect/cahiers.html

Abbé Sieyès, http://www.fordham.edu/halsall/mod/sieyes.html

Tennis Court Oath, http://www.historyguide.org/intellect/tennis_oath.html

Declaration of the Rights of Man and Citizen, http://avalon.law.yale.edu/18th_century/rightsof.asp

Levée en Masse, http://www.fordham.edu/halsall/mod/1793levee.html

Mary Wollstonecraft, http://www.fordham.edu/halsall/mod/mw-vind.html

Olympe de Gouges, http://www.fordham.edu/halsall/mod/1791degouge1.html

Chapter 5

THE AGE OF NAPOLEON

Napoleon's Background

Napoleon Bonaparte was born in 1769 to Corsican nobility. France had taken over the island the year before, so he was a French citizen. He went to military school where he mastered calculus and trajectories and joined the artillery corps. Even in school he had a reputation for brilliance, but because he was Corsican he had no chance of commanding a French army while the Old Regime lasted. He became a general during the Terror. Napoleon was brilliant, full of energy, and a master at being able to manipulate people and events. He could work eighteen hours at a stretch and sleep at will. He was also a superb organizer.

The 1797 elections saw the royalists do well. The Directory asked Bonaparte to help it in annulling elections. On September 4, 1797, the Directory and Chamber removed their royalist and Jacobin elements, including two of the five Directors. In 1798, Napoleon invaded Egypt, alarming the British. The goal was to assure the French a share of the decaying Ottoman Empire. The adventure became a disaster when the British navy destroyed the French fleet, trapping Napoleon's forces. He escaped to Paris where he told a more favorable version of the story and preserved his reputation. The British held his soldiers as prisoners for years.

Napoleon's Coup of 1799

The 1798 elections would be difficult because with the purge of 1797, the Chamber would have to elect three of the five Directors. The Directory fixed the elections of 1798 to elect centrists, and the Chamber refused to seat 127 newly-elected deputies. The Directory tackled the financial problem in 1799. It repudiated two-thirds of the national debt, including the *assignats*. It established new indirect taxes. This settled the issue of French debt that had hung over the country for so long, but it had come at a heavy cost. Corruption filled the Directory as many members sold their votes and influence. To make matters worse, war resumed with Austria. France occupied Piedmont and built a friendly government called the **Parthenopean Republic** in Naples and southern Italy.

Emmanuel Sieyès had joined the Directory in 1799 and sought to strengthen the executive. Then the war turned bad. An Austro-Russian force pushed through Switzerland and northern Italy and rolled up the republics allied with France. The Councils ousted three Directors and chose three Jacobins to join Sieyès and Barras. Sieyès gave up on constitutional government and was willing to try a military coup. On November 9, 1799, Napoleon, Sieyès and another director staged a coup and set up **the Consulate**. Napoleon had a following among soldiers and the intellectual élite: in Egypt, he had talked of Suez Canal building and antiquities. He was only thirty years old.

Government under the Consulate

There would be three consuls with Napoleon as First Consul. An overwhelming vote approved the new system. Napoleon wanted to combine the best of Old Regime and Revolution. He ended all feudalism and centralized administration and justice. Citizens would rise based on their merit. There would be no tax exemptions based on birth. The vote had shown that Rousseau's "General Will" was embodied in Napoleon. The people called for order and Napoleon answered. Napoleon used the secret police and administration to keep peace and put down marauders. He gave a general amnesty, and most of the émigrés from 1789 returned, except for the royal family and about 1,000 monarchists.

The Russians withdrew from the war, leaving the Austrians to fend for themselves. At the **Battle of Marengo** (June 14, 1800) Napoleon beat Austria. France occupied Northern Italy and Southern Germany. The **Treaty of Lunéville** (February 8, 1801) confirmed Campo Formio. Spain ceded Louisiana to France. Pitt the Younger's government fell over the issue of removing the civil disabilities of Irish Catholics. The new government was friendlier to Napoleon and signed the **Peace of Amiens** on March 25, 1802. The British gained the Cape Colony at the southern tip of Africa from the Dutch.

The Haitian Revolution

Fox and the British opposition had embarrassed Pitt by denouncing the loss of perhaps 100,000 lives and £10 million in fighting the San Domingue war. By March 1798, the British had made a truce. Now San Domingue fell into another civil war between Toussaint and his remaining rival who commanded mulatto forces. By January 1801, Toussaint controlled the entire island. A new constitution declared Toussaint governor-general for life. Perhaps one-third of the population had died. Toussaint invited the white planters to return and did not yet declare independence from France. Haiti was now a military regime with compulsory labor.

Napoleon sent 20,000 troops; the mission became more urgent with Lunéville and the gaining of Louisiana because he needed Saint Domingue to anchor a planned American empire. At first, the French were able to capture the ports in savage fighting, but then yellow fever took its toll and killed half the French force. The French trapped Toussaint and sent him to France where he died in April 1803. When word came that Napoleon would restore slavery, the guerrillas gathered strength. **Jean Jacques Dessalines** broke with the French and fought the most atrocious war yet. But France's resumption of war with Britain in 1803 led to a blockade, and France could not supply its force. On January 1, 1804, Haiti became independent. It was the first nation freed by a slave rebellion. When he could not regain Haiti, Napoleon sold the French territory of Louisiana to the U.S.

The Reforms of Bonaparte

The government concentrated its authority in paid agents. No one was above the law. The Minister of the Interior (Napoleon's brother Lucien) appointed prefects to control the regions. The government finally pacified regions such as Brittany and Vendée that had been in revolt for years. This meant they would pay taxes. Napoleon drew military officers and administrators from the élite of the nobles and the middle class. The professional tax collectors were much more honest than their royal predecessors, which greatly enhanced tax collection. Napoleon made France's first simple budget. He introduced a sound currency in 1803 by regulating the silver content in the **French franc** and fixed the value of silver to gold. Thanks to the Directory wiping out the *assignats*, the debt was secure. Taxes on consumption, such as salt and tobacco, contributed more and more to the revenue. The Bank of France was established in 1800. It would discount promissory notes, make loans to the treasury, and receive and manage some government assets. It issued 30,000 shares of 1,000 francs each. The biggest 200 shareholders could elect regents to govern the Bank.

Lawyers had toiled for years to overhaul the French legal system. Before the Revolution, it had been divided by province and marked by inequality based on the social class of the accused and the victim. The committees working on the law codes finished their work while Napoleon was in charge, so naturally he named it after himself. The **Napoleonic Code** included a civil code (1804), commercial code (1807), penal code (1808), and civil and criminal procedure (1806). The law was the same throughout France and privileged private enterprise by banning unions. It gave men rights over women. It favored the prosecution over the defense as the local prefect selected the jury, a majority was sufficient to convict, and the accused was presumed guilty until proved innocent.

Napoleon ended the fight with the Church in the **Concordat** (1801) which put all French bishops under the Pope's authority for the first time in four hundred years. It permitted seminaries. The Vatican in return dropped its demands on the confiscated land and Avignon. The treaty put all clergy, Catholic and Protestant, on the state payroll. France became the first European country to recognize Jews as full and equal citizens.

The Revolution was mostly over with the settlement. The Third Estate had gained most of its demands. France was at peace, and its borders reached to the Rhine. Many émigrés quietly regained their land. In May 1802 Napoleon created the Legion of Honor as a first step towards the establishment of a new nobility.

Landowners enjoyed prosperity as rents rose, but they did not reinvest money into making the land more productive. Economic conflict and technology caused the price of textiles to fall by 30 percent. The silk price fell 97 percent as cotton became more popular. The population rose from 27.9 million in 1789 to 30.2 million in 1814. The marriage age dropped, especially as men tried to avoid the draft. Birth control spread from Normandy, Languedoc and the Ile-de-France. Peasants and townsmen increased their share of land from the nobles and church. An 1803 survey of the 1,000 biggest landowners found that 339 were former nobles, 144 were investors who rented land out, 370 were in the liberal professions (lawyers, doctors), and 130 were manufacturers.

In 1802, a popular vote made Napoleon Consul for Life. It was not a secret ballot but taxes were lower than in 1791, and the draft had taken one-tenth the number of soldiers claimed at the height of Directory. In December 1804,

Napoleon crowned himself Emperor of the French, supported by a vote of 3,572,329 to 2,569. Napoleon could name his successor. It seemed the Bourbon dynasty had given way to the Bonaparte dynasty.

Napoleonic Warfare

The first consideration was that the French often controlled larger numbers of troops than their opposition. Secondly, the army trained soldiers to be more mobile. Thirdly, they had higher nationalistic morale. Early modern armies had consisted of soldiers from all language backgrounds of Europe, many of them simply there for pay or plunder. The French had not been able to afford mercenaries and had compensated by filling the soldiers with patriotic and revolutionary enthusiasm. Promotion was on the basis of ability. Of Napoleon's twenty-six marshals, none were nobles. Three had been sergeants in 1789, and three had been privates.

Large numbers meant new strategies. Columns would charge with fixed bayonets. Napoleon scored his greatest strategic triumphs at the battles of Marengo and Austerlitz when he was outnumbered. Napoleon had a basic strategy: maneuver the enemy to an unfavorable terrain, then force the main battle and a full commitment of troops. At the key moment, he would use his reserve troops on the enemy's flank or rear.

France had the largest population in Europe and 40 percent of its men were in their fighting prime. A strong economy supported the war effort. Army desertion and draft evasion remained problems. Communes were responsible for draft-dodgers and had to find substitutes for them. France asked more from what had been the eastern frontier of France and less from the unstable west and Rhine provinces. Napoleon called fewer men to the colors, but a greater percentage complied. The draft term was usually five years. From 1800 to 1814 France conscripted 2 million (7 percent of the total population). The wealthy could pay for substitutes and 5 to 10 percent of the draftees were actually substitutes. In World War I from 1914 to 1918, France would conscript close to 20 percent. In the early years, Napoleon only drafted 60,000 a year, but that gradually grew to 120,000 in 1810. There was no massive levy until after the Russian disaster. France drafted a million young men in 1813 and 1814. Supplies were spotty, contrary to Napoleon's philosophy of "an army travels on its stomach." It lived off the country in some areas but not in north Germany, Poland, or Russia, where careful staff work and supply trains kept the army provisioned for a while. Napoleon reorganized the army in 1800 and 1804 into seven separate corps with their own artillery, cavalry, and infantry. Napoleon had the ability to improvise and shift regiments among the corps and redefine the corps' roles. The battles killed more officers than the military academies could produce, so after 1808 20 to 25 percent of the officers came from the ranks.

Napoleon and the Spread of Revolution

In 1805, war broke out with the **Third Coalition**: Austria and Russia joined Britain. Napoleon planned to invade Britain, but the British smashed his combined French and Spanish fleet at the **Battle of Trafalgar** in October 1805. This battle assured British of naval supremacy. Napoleon marched with 200,000 men from the Channel to the Danube and routed Russia and Austria at the **Battle of Austerlitz** (December 2, 1805). Napoleon forced the **Treaty of Pressburg** (1806) on the Austrians: Bavaria and Württemberg became kingdoms, Baden a Grand Duchy in Germany with a puppet **Confederation of the Rhine** including the smaller German states. The Treaty took Venetia from Austria and gave it to the Republic of Italy.

Napoleon's German policy pushed Prussia into war. At the **Battle of Jena** in October 1806, the French smashed the Prussian army. Napoleon then beat the Russians at the **Battle of Friedland** (June 1807). Czar **Alexander I** (ruled 1801–1825) did not want to retreat into Russia because he feared that the lower classes might rise in revolution if the French soldiers crossed the border. At the **Treaty of Tilsit** (July 1807) Napoleon took much land from Prussia and Hanover (a German kingdom under Britain's control) and gave it to the new kingdom of Westphalia ruled by Napoleon's brother Jerome. In the battles of 1805 to 1807, Napoleon had lost 65,000 men of original 210,000, but made it up with early draft call-ups and help from Switzerland, Holland, Spain, Poland, and Italy. He used loot and contributions to fund the army.

The Continental System (1806)

Britain refused to negotiate peace even though its allies were beaten. Since Trafalgar, it was safe from invasion. The French emperor gathered all his allies and recently-defeated enemies and forced them to sign a treaty that built the Continental System. This was a tariff fortress to harm British trade and force them to make peace. The British made up the lost trade by turning to Latin America. It actually hurt Europe more and the middle-class outside of France became disillusioned with Napoleon. In the Dutch port of Amsterdam, 1,350 ships had entered in 1806, but only 310 in 1809. Land transportation was too expensive. Other countries felt that France was benefiting at their expense. Dependent states paid heavily for "French defense."

Napoleon at the Height of His Power

Austria declared war in April 1809 but was turned back at the **Battle of Wagram** (July 6, 1809). Napoleon called up the draft classes of 1809 and 1810 early and mobilized troops from the Confederation of the Rhine, Italy, Holland, and Warsaw. Many of these soldiers eagerly joined the French not only because they hoped for victory and plunder but also because they supported the French Revolution. The Poles had seen Prussia, Austria, and Russia destroy their country and remove it from the map of Europe. Napoleon had restored part of Poland as the **Grand Duchy of Warsaw**. The Austrian empire, amazingly, sustained four defeats without a revolution or internal collapse. At the **Treaty of Schönbrunn** (1809) Napoleon increased the size of the Grand Duchy of Warsaw. Bavaria and Russia, now allies of Napoleon, benefited. The Treaty took Dalmatia, Slovenia, and Croatia from Austria and merged them into the French-run Illyrian Provinces. Napoleon divorced his wife Josephine, who had borne no children, and married Marie Louise, the daughter of the Austrian emperor.

By 1810, Napoleon's empire consisted of France, Belgium and the Netherlands, the German coast to the West Baltic Sea, the left bank of the Rhine River, and the Italian coast down to Rome. The Swiss Confederation was republican. Napoleon's relatives sat on the thrones of Westphalia, Spain, and Naples. His stepson was viceroy for him in northern Italy. Prussia, Austria, Denmark, Russia, and Sweden had signed alliances binding them to Napoleon.

French domination went through three steps: conquest by the army, establishment of a satellite government, and the drafting of treaties and a constitution on the French model. Italy and Germany and Spain underwent the third stage and had a massive internal reorganization. Napoleon believed in one European civilization and one law for all and tried to promote this as an ideology to bring all together. All people were equal. He abolished noble privileges, but gave them compensation. He tried to free Polish serfs. Liberals welcomed Napoleon at first and saw him as great hero. The German Goethe said: "Napoleon was the expression of all that was reasonable, legitimate and European in the revolutionary movement." There would be religious toleration for all. Most Catholic states followed the terms of Napoleon's Concordat: the church tax ended, the churches lost their land, and most monasteries closed.

France introduced the decimal and metric systems and modernized taxes and finance. However, Napoleon refused to introduce a representative assembly. His model for European civilization was French civilization, his model for European law the Napoleonic Code. This would cause trouble down the road.

NATIONALISM AND THE FALL OF NAPOLEON

Nationalism in Germany and Italy

The German-speaking middle states were reasonably happy but Prussia and Austria smarted. German nationalism found its roots in J.G. Herder's book *Ideas on the Philosophy of the History of Mankind* (1784). Herder called for the separate development of cultures, based on the *volksgeist* (national spirit) of the common people, not the upper classes. Against the internationalism of Enlightenment, Herder emphasized differences among peoples. In 1808, J.G. Fichte, originally a supporter of the French Revolution and even the Terror, delivered *Addresses to the German Nation*, calling for a unified German state. This attracted many German patriots.

Italy did not revolt against Napoleon. The continental system did not hurt the Italian middle class. It welcomed religious toleration and the reduction of papal influence and the expulsion of Austrian domination. Italy had been rationalized and hopes grew for a possible Italian unification. The middle class enjoyed French manners and culture. In Italy, Poland, and France, Napoleon remained a hero long after his death.

Reform in Prussia

The defeat at Jena severely shook the proud Prussian military. Big changes were needed. Prussia, although it was much smaller than France, would need a much bigger army. That meant a military draft of peasants. They would not be fighting for high pay or for revolution. Prussia needed to give them something and so promised reforms and a better life. By freeing the peasants from the burdens of the nobles, it would give them a stake to fight for. It was their country as well as the king's. King **Frederick William III** (ruled 1797–1840) set up a reform ministry under **Baron Karl Stein** and then **Karl von Hardenberg**. It abolished serfdom in 1807 and restored self-government in the cities. Townsmen could buy land and serve as army officers. Prussia remade and enlarged its army on the French model. Austria instituted the draft and promised freedom for serfs but did not fulfill its promise.

The Occupation of Iberia

Carlos III died in 1788. His son Carlos IV (ruled 1788–1808) pulled back in a conservative direction. Spain fought revolutionary France from 1793 to 1795, then allied with France despite the opposition of Crown Prince Ferdinand. In October 1807, after beating the Prussians and Russians, Napoleon concluded a treaty with Carlos against Portugal, which was Britain's sole entry point for trade after the Continental System took effect. The next month, a joint force including 100,000 French troops captured Lisbon. The Portuguese royal family fled to Brazil, carried by the British. In March 1808, there was a brief uprising against Carlos and his ministers. Ferdinand briefly became king, but the French intervened and installed **Joseph Bonaparte**, brother of the French emperor.

Joseph put in a French-style Constitution. The great Spanish landowners despised land reform, the clergy opposed tolerance of faiths other than Catholicism. In other areas, Napoleon and the French had appealed to middle-class reformers (Netherlands, Germany, Italy) or to nationalism (Poland). In Spain, there was no middle class to make a natural base of support for the Bonapartes. Provinces such as Andalusia, Catalonia, and Galicia were unhappy about French-style centralizing. Former Spanish soldiers and ordinary people organized attacks on French soldiers, installations, and supporters. They wore no uniform and after attacking would melt back into the general population. These new kind of warriors were called *guerrillas*.

The Spanish War of Liberation

After the *guerrilla* war broke out, Britain sent a force under Arthur Wellesley (later **Duke of Wellington**). A British army of 35,000 supplemented 125,000 Spanish regulars, levies, and irregulars. Napoleon came in with 194,000 troops and secured Spain by January 1809. The British force withdrew to Portugal and joined about 30,000 Spanish guerrillas. The French suffered 40,000 casualties each year from 1808 to 1813. In August 1812, Wellington took Madrid. By the end of 1813, Spain had been cleared of French troops.

In 1810, the free area around Cádiz chose a constituent assembly, which promulgated the Constitution of 1812. The leaders of this group called themselves **Liberals**, the first time this name was applied to a political movement. It called for progressive reforms, land reform, religious toleration, modernization, and a restoration of Ferdinand. The constitution called for a one-chamber parliament elected by all men. When Ferdinand VII (ruled 1814–1833) was restored, he promised to abide by this constitution.

The American Early National Period

The exercise of power in the early years of the American Republic was quite different than today. Congress was seen as supreme, as the Parliament was in Britain. The founders expected that in most presidential elections, the electors would fail to reach a majority and the House of Representatives would elect the President, thus ensuring Congressional control. The Congressional caucuses of the parties nominated candidates for the Presidency. By 1828, two states still had presidential electors picked by the state legislatures, not by voters. The Cabinet was not provided for in the Constitution, but Washington established a system of calling department heads together. Although one of Washington's two vetoes was a policy matter, it was expected that a President (like the British king) would only veto a bill for constitutional reasons. From 1789 to 1829, the President only issued ten vetoes. Congress did not override a veto until 1845.

The French Revolution deeply divided American opinion. The original United States Senate chamber had large portraits of King Louis XVI and Queen Marie Antoinette. When the king was overthrown, the U.S. did not consider the Convention to be the legitimate government of France. As the French West Indies flared in rebellion and the British attacked, France asked the U.S. to honor its commitment from the 1778 alliance to defend the islands. The U.S. refused. The French sent an agent to stir American opinion. This deeply irritated Washington. Both the French and British attacked American shipping. The faction dominant in government, led by Washington, Adams, Hamilton, and John Jay, leaned toward the British. Jefferson and his Congressional leaders James Madison and Aaron Burr were initially sympathetic to France and always suspicious of Britain. Jefferson also believed that Hamilton favored the rich and trading interests over farmers. This caused two factions to harden: Hamilton, Washington, and Adams as **Federalists**; Jefferson, Madison, and Burr in the **Democratic-Republican** party.

In 1798, the French tried to bribe U.S. officials, causing a sensation. The U.S. annulled the French alliance. Adams and the Federalists passed the Alien and Sedition Acts to give the President unilateral power to arrest and expel aliens in time of war and banned criticism of government officials. Hamilton dreamed of war across the Americas and taking over Canada, Mexico, and Latin America.

The Jefferson/Madison group soon reduced the Federalists to a regional party. The Jeffersonians did reluctantly accept some Federalist principles. The Federalists had used courts to persecute "seditious" enemies, and Adams had created new federal judges after losing the election of 1800. One appointment had been the Federalist **John Marshall** as Chief Justice of the Supreme Court. Marshall claimed a sweeping right for the Court that no British court ever had: the power of constitutional review. Marshall struck down one of these appointments and part of the law that enabled the Supreme Court to order the Secretary of State to give a commission in the famous *Marbury vs. Madison* case of 1803. The implications were enormous, but it would be more than fifty years before the Court dared to strike down an entire Act of Congress.

The independence of Haiti and the end of Napoleon's hopes for an American empire led France to sell Louisiana territory in 1803 to the US for $15 million. This accelerated the opening of the "West." Tennessee, Ohio, and Kentucky had already become states, and the West was becoming a region on an equal footing with the North and the South. The West's main interest tended to be Indian affairs, internal improvements, and land policy.

The War of 1812

The Continental System and a renewed British blockade angered Jefferson. From 1803 to 1812 the British impressed at least 5,000 sailors from American vessels. The U.S. responses were ineffective or backfired. Renewed battles with Indians and a lingering desire to conquer Canada led the western War Hawks in Congress to push the U.S. into the War of 1812 against the British. The British dominated the high seas. Canadians and Indians repulsed American attacks and captured Detroit and Fort Dearborn (later known as Chicago).

The Russian Disaster

At the end of 1810, Alexander I pulled out of the Continental System. He felt he had not gotten much out of alliance with Napoleon except Finland: Napoleon did not help in Russia's war against Turkey, married an Austrian princess, and supported Poland. For his part, Napoleon saw a conflict with Russia as inevitable. He tried unsuccessfully to win peace with Britain. A Grand Army of 611,000 assembled by Napoleon, consisted of one-third French, one-third German, and one-seventh Polish soldiers; the rest were Italians, Swiss, and Dutch. The Russians had 160,000 soldiers. Napoleon invaded in June 1812, carrying only three weeks of supplies. He fought his way to Moscow, which was abandoned and burned by the Russians. Almost half of his Grand Army had deserted by this time. Napoleon hesitated for a month, could not make winter quarters in the ruined city, and began a retreat. Russian irregulars and army harried the Grand Army. The weather turned bad and bitterly cold early.

400,000 died of cold, disease, and the enemy. The Russians took 100,000 prisoners. Perhaps 100,000 survived; only 30,000 troops returned home.

The End of the War

When things went sour, Napoleon abandoned his troops and rushed to Paris in thirteen days to raise another army. Things were falling apart. As the Russians reached the border with Prussia, the latter proclaimed an alliance as well as a War of German Liberation from France. Britain poured in £32 million for subsidies. Austria joined in August 1813, creating a **Quadruple Alliance**. At the **Battle of Leipzig** (October 1813), armies from four nations with twice as many soldiers overwhelmed and defeated Napoleon.

Revolts now followed Napoleon's retreat across Germany. Austrian Chancellor Metternich offered Napoleon a chance to keep his crown and the Rhine frontiers, but Napoleon refused. The forces of the Quadruple Alliance followed him into France. Finally, on March 31, 1814, the Allies marched into Paris, ending the Napoleonic Empire. France desperately wanted peace and would not rally to Napoleon. At the **First Peace of Paris** in May 1814, 1) Louis XVIII returned as king and restored the Bourbon family; 2) France lost all its acquisitions since 1792; 3) Napoleon was exiled to the Italian island of Elba.

In America, the British went on the offensive against the United States. They sailed up the Potomac river and burned the capital city of Washington. Peace restored things to prewar status. After the peace, **Andrew Jackson** beat the British at New Orleans and established himself as a war hero.

The End of the Slave Trade

The end of the European slave trade is one of the most curious events of the time. Economically, slave owners were making a profit and the volume of slave-produced goods—cotton, sugar, and coffee—was growing. Very few free workers would work under plantation conditions. The British plantations were thriving. Napoleon's takeover of Spain had the unintended consequence of opening the Cuban market to British ships. The anti-slave trade movement was both intellectual and political, sprang from the Enlightenment, and was centered in England. Montesquieu (slavery corrupts masters), Rousseau, and Adam Smith had condemned slavery. Quakers and nonconformist Protestants took up the call, giving it a strong religious flavor. In 1771, the Chief Justice had effectively ruled that there could be no slaves in Britain.

The belief grew that free labor was more productive than slave labor and that abolition would increase profits. In 1787, Britain paid a ship to take freed slaves to Sierra Leone in western Africa. Half of these settlers died in first year, and some became slave dealers. In 1788, Parliament placed the first limits on the manner of carrying slaves. New Jersey, Pennsylvania, Connecticut, Rhode Island, and Massachusetts abolished the slave trade. The Haitian revolution magnified the urgency. In 1792 Denmark said it would abolish import as of 1803. In 1799, the space requirements increased for slaves on the ships. Urged by President Jefferson (himself a slaveowner), the U.S. abolished the import of slaves in 1807. In Britain abolitionists in the House of Commons led by William Wilberforce pressed step by step until the trade was outlawed starting January 1, 1808. The majority in the Cabinet, King George III, and his sons opposed abolition, but Pitt, Burke, and Fox had all supported Wilberforce. The new Irish members joining the British House of Commons bolstered the anti-slavery forces.

TIMELINE

1798	Napoleon's invasion of Egypt ends in disaster
1799	Napoleon and Sieyès overthrow Directory; Consulate established
1800	Bank of France
1801	Thomas Jefferson becomes President French Concordat with Catholic Church
1801–2	Treaty of Lunéville and Peace of Amiens
1803	French franc established France sells Louisiana to the United States
1804	Haiti independent First parts of Napoleonic Code put out
1805–7	France defeats Austria, Prussia, and Russia
1806–13	Confederation of the Rhine Continental System
1808–13	*Guerrilla* war in Spain
1812–15	War of 1812 between Britain and U.S.
1812	Napoleon invades Russia
1813	Battle of Leipzig
1814	Quadruple Alliance occupies Paris; fall of Napoleon

KEY TERMS

Napoleonic Code
Battle of Trafalgar
Battle of Austerlitz
Confederation of the Rhine
Continental System
guerrilla
Quadruple Alliance
Battle of Leipzig

PRIMARY SOURCE DOCUMENTS

Napoleon Speeches to Troops, http://www.historyguide.org/intellect/nap1796.html
Remembrances of Napoleon, http://www.fordham.edu/halsall/mod/remusat-napoleon.html
Fichte, Addresses to the German Nation, http://www.fordham.edu/halsall/mod/1806fichte.html

Chapter 6

NATIONAL REVOLUTIONS AND ROMANTICISM

THE CONGRESS OF VIENNA

The Reconstruction of Europe

The Congress of Vienna began in October 1814. Czar Alexander I of Russia was a leading personality. **Lord Robert Castlereagh**, the British Foreign Secretary, sought a moderate peace but was willing to tolerate a reactionary mood. He came from the right wing of Conservative Party and was disliked by those who saw themselves as more progressive, such as the Romantic poet Percy Byssche Shelley.

> *I met Murder on the way*
> *He had a mask like Castlereagh*
> *Very smooth he looked, yet grim;*
> *Seven blood-hounds followed him:*
>
> *All were fat; and well they might*
> *Be in admirable plight,*
> *For one by one, and two by two,*
> *He tossed the human hearts to chew*
> *Which from his wide cloak he drew.*
> —From "The Mask of Anarchy"

Klemens von Metternich, the Austrian Chancellor, was the host and dominant influence at the Congress. His main goal was to restore a balance of power in Europe and to get Russian troops out of central Europe. He would become the main foe of liberal and revolutionary forces in Europe. He also wanted to ensure Austrian supremacy in central Europe against Prussia, the other great German power. The king of Prussia, Frederick William III, wanted to annex Saxony, which had aided Napoleon. That would make Prussia the supreme German-speaking nation.

Frederick William and Alexander teamed up against Metternich. Poland had supported Napoleon to the end, and the great powers had agreed to wipe it off the map of Europe. Prussia was willing to give its parts of Poland to Russia if Russia would support Prussia taking all of Saxony. Metternich desperately turned to France for help at the Congress. Napoleon was gone, but King Louis XVIII had kept his foreign minister the clever **Charles de Talleyrand**. Britain, France, and Austria only allowed Prussia a piece of Saxony. The rest remained an independent kingdom. Poland was theoretically separate from Russia but would have to accept Alexander as its king.

Territorial changes of the Congress of Vienna:

1. Austria gave up Belgium and its southern German possessions in exchange for Lombardy and Venetia in northern Italy. It recovered its Polish parts and lands in Tyrol and Illyria. The result was that Austria was more centralized but less German.

2. Russia had taken Finland from Sweden and Moldova from Ottoman Turkey during the Napoleonic wars. By taking control of a puppet kingdom of Poland, Russia had moved its effective territorial boundary west.

3. Prussia got half of Saxony, but lost three-fifths of its Polish lands. It also received Swedish Pomerania and Rhineland as a buffer against France. The result was that Prussia became more powerful within Germany and more German.

4. The South and North Netherlands were united. The House of Orange had dominated the North before the French Revolution and its leader now was king of the united area. The Allies wanted to create another strong power on the French boundary. The result was that it proved unworkable quickly.

5. Germany was divided into thirty-nine states. The result was a group of stronger middle states. The chances of German unification were much better than before Napoleon.

6. In Italy, the king of Piedmont-Sardinia and the Pope enlarged their territories. The Bourbon family regained the Kingdom of Two Sicilies.

7. Others provisions included the assurance of Swiss neutrality. Denmark lost Norway to Sweden. Britain received strategic islands including Helgoland, Malta, and Ceylon. After the Congress of Vienna, only Spain (below 10°N) and Portugal (below the equator) were left as European slave traders. However, the slave trade was increasing across the Sahara Desert to North Africa and in East Africa.

Waterloo

Just as the Allies were finishing the agreement, Napoleon got loose from Elba. He had heard of the dispute over Poland and Saxony and hoped his enemies were split. Louis XVIII sent the army to capture Napoleon, but it went over to him instead, and it was King Louis who fled. Napoleon again wore the imperial crown. Europe trembled: Britain had borrowed huge amounts of money to finance the Quadruple Alliance and now owed twice as much as the entire country's Gross Domestic Product. If Napoleon could inflict one solid defeat on the British, they might go bankrupt and the French would rule again. The British and Prussians defeated the French at Waterloo in June 1815. The **Second Peace of Paris** (November 20, 1815) exiled Napoleon to St. Helena in the south Atlantic as King Louis returned again. France lost some strategic posts and suffered an indemnity and an army of occupation for three years.

THE CONCERT OF EUROPE

The Concert

The five great powers of Europe would work together to uphold the international order. As long as no crisis required absolute commitment, the system could work. Henry Kissinger, a student of Metternichian diplomacy, in the 1970s also perceived five powers that could form a new concert: the U.S., the Soviet bloc, Western Europe, China, and Japan. There was an idea that the great powers should hold regular meetings even during peacetime. At the **Congress of Aix-la-Chapelle** (1818), the four powers admitted France into the alliance and removed their army of occupation.

Postwar Tensions

Metternich and his friends dreamed of turning the clock back to 1789, but the French Revolution had unleashed powerful forces. The most powerful was nationalism. A nation is a group of people with common language, traditions, culture, history, and sometimes religion. Nationalists insist that such a group needs its own government. Nineteenth-century governments tried hard to create these nations by imposing a language in education to replace local dialects. Some languages were practically invented in the nineteenth century to give people an identity. Many individuals had fluid nationalities and might pass back and forth between two or even three national identities. In existing areas, the governments imposed the dialect of a small area (Paris, London, Piedmont) upon France, England, and Italy. Fluid identities could lead to "checkerboards" of nationalities, as often happened in east-central Europe. To create a nation in these areas would automatically deprive another group of its nationhood. This led to instability, revolt, and war.

France

Louis XVIII had gradually moderated during his twenty years of exile in Vienna. He knew that he had to govern with some kind of constitution, so in 1814 he provided a Charter as a "gift." The king kept considerable authority but had to share power with a Parliament, which consisted of a Chamber of Peers appointed for life by the king and a Chamber of Deputies elected for five years; a Deputy had to be at least 40 years old and pay 1,000 francs in taxes. The voters were all men, thirty years or older, and had to pay at least 300 francs in taxes. Only 0.3% of the French population could vote, sharply down from the most democratic days of the 1792 Convention. All French were called equal under the law, which continued to be the Napoleonic Code. They were eligible for all civil and military positions and free from arbitrary arrest and imprisonment without due process. Although King Louis had become a moderate, the rich supported the reactionary political group called **the Ultras** that wanted to abolish the Charter and return to absolutism. The Ultras grew stronger in 1824 when King Louis XVIII died and was succeeded by his youngest brother **Charles X** (ruled 1824–1830), who was reactionary and not very bright. He decreed that he would not pay some of the interest on the government bonds held largely by the middle class and use the money to pay nobles compensation for lands lost during the revolution.

Britain

Tensions also existed with reformers frustrated and the social impact of the agricultural and industrial revolutions taking full hold. A very conservative government headed by **Lord Liverpool** (Prime Minister 1812–1827) and Castlereagh governed for the rich. The **Corn Law of 1815** kept out foreign (mostly Russian) wheat by imposing high tariffs. Workers would have to pay more for their bread even as a sharp reduction in armed forces put pressure on the job market. Violence flared as **Luddites** smashed industrial machines that threatened jobs, and British troops fired on protesters who demanded reform and their rights.

The German Confederation

After Napoleon, Germany had thirty-nine states including the Austrian Empire, and the five kingdoms of Prussia, Hanover, Bavaria, Württemberg and Saxony. The Confederation joined them together loosely and met in Frankfurt. Austria was its leader, and Metternich used the Confederation to carry out his will. Article XIII of the Federal Constitution called for states to grant constitutions and in the aftermath of Napoleon, five states put out constitutions that were all royal grants like the French charter. Prussia and Austria, the two biggest German nations, did not put out constitutions. Many young men had fought Napoleon and died for "German liberation." Student unions were formed in a number of universities by returning soldiers. The student union at the University of Jena held a big meeting at **Wartburg** Castle in 1817 to celebrate the anniversary of the Battle of Leipzig. Speakers complained about those princes who had not granted constitutions. Metternich convened the Confederation and put out the repressive **Karlsbad Decrees** (1819) that dissolved the student unions and imposed strict censorship over the press and universities.

The Revolutionary Ripple of 1820

The Greek War of Independence

The main problem for European security was the decay of the Ottoman Turkish Empire. This empire had been declining for over a hundred years and Austria and Russia had steadily forced it back. It had a corrupt administration and an inefficient economy. Large landowners and Muslim religious leaders foiled attempts by Sultans (Emperors) to reform the government. The French ambassador in 1807 said: "To make an alliance with Turkey is the same as putting your arms around a corpse to make it stand up!" The Serbs revolted in

1804 after the **Janissaries** (elite soldiers) began murdering prominent Serbs. Serbia won a measure of freedom in 1830. The Greeks joined the revolt in 1821. Greek intellectuals, inspired by French nationalism, led these revolts. The Turks responded savagely and Greeks were aided by people all over the world. The British provided a big loan to the rebels. Austria opposed this national revolution. When the Greek leader crossed the border, the Austrians imprisoned him in the grim fortress of Theresienstadt.

The Decembrist Revolt

In Russia, Emperor Alexander died in 1825 and was succeeded by his more autocratic brother **Nicholas I**. Younger officers, influenced by ideas of the West and some of whom had been in Paris after the defeat of Napoleon, backed Alexander's other brother Constantine, who they saw as more moderate. They rebelled in December after refusing to swear allegiance to Nicholas. Conspirators told the Moscow soldiers that Constantine was the real Emperor and started a cry of "Long live Constantine, long live the Constitution!" The soldiers thought that "Constitution" was Constantine's wife. Its pitiful failure met with very harsh punishments. This was the last of the revolts of the early 1820s. In Europe, only the Greek revolt succeeded.

Muhammad Ali Pasha

Sultan Mahmud III (ruled 1808–1839) turned to the semi-independent governor of Egypt **Muhammad Ali** (1769–1848) to crush the Greeks. Ali had been born to a mixed Turkish/Albanian family and had led an Albanian force to Egypt in 1798 when Napoleon invaded. In 1806, the Sultan named him governor of Egypt. Muhammad Ali consolidated his power when turmoil roiled the Empire for several years. Muhammad Ali modernized Egypt by planting cotton as a cash crop and using the money to bring in modern weapons and European training for his substantial army. The Sultans had always feared power in Cairo and had usually changed governors often. In 1825, Sultan Mahmud promised Crete to Muhammad Ali and the governorship of southern Greece for Ali's son if he would help. Muhammad Ali's forces quickly pushed the Greeks back, but there was disarray when the Sultan ordered the Egyptians to kill the Janissaries. This got rid of a troublesome element that had blocked reform but left Muhammad Ali as the supreme military power in the Empire. The Greek cause seemed lost, but France, Britain, and Russia now agreed to work for Greek autonomy.

British and Russian Intervention

The British destroyed the Turkish/Egyptian navy in 1827 at the **Battle of Navarino**, cutting off Greece from Egypt. The Russians declared war on Turkey in 1828. The Greeks brought in the former Russian Foreign Minister as President, but he was assassinated in 1831. Greek leaders then chose a Bavarian prince to be king. At the **Treaty of Adrianople** (September 1829) Greece gained its independence, but many Greeks were left in the Ottoman Empire. Turkish control of Romania became nominal, and Russia gained a little territory and payment from Turkey.

LATIN AMERICAN REVOLUTIONS

Continuing Unrest and the Influence of Revolution

While Ambassador to France, Jefferson was approached by a Mexican and a Brazilian sounding out the U.S. for help in their revolt against the European colonizers. Jefferson refused. The French Revolution inspired Latin America. Police found identical handwritten copies of French speeches in Mexico City and Bahia, 5,000 miles apart. The Haitian revolution and the French abolition of slavery caused unrest among blacks and mulattoes.

War in Mexico and South America

When the Bonapartes took over Spain in 1807, the Creoles saw their chance. They rejected Napoleon's takeover and proclaimed loyalty to the powerless King Ferdinand. They set up *juntas* (political committees) that were to serve as temporary governments until their king returned to the throne. In Buenos Aires, the local militia, not the tiny Spanish force, defended the city against British invasions in 1806 and 1807. In May 1810, a revolutionary *junta* in Buenos Aires was theoretically loyal to Ferdinand but ruled absolutely. It formed an **Army of the North** to liberate the rest of the colonies, but was defeated in Upper Peru in June 1811. Coup and countercoup rocked La Plata. Uruguay and then Paraguay broke off.

The Creoles in Paraguay and Venezuela formed their own governments. On July 5, 1811, Francisco de Miranda and **Simón Bolívar** (1783–1830) led the Patriotic Society and declared the independence of Venezuela. Bolívar had been in Paris when Napoleon became Emperor and was deeply impressed. They outlawed the slave trade, but not slavery itself. By the end of 1812, Spanish royalists had driven Bolívar out of Venezuela. He returned in 1813 and led a war in Venezuela of bloody slaughter. Bolívar also fought an uprising of blacks determined to wipe out European rule. Ferdinand sent 11,000 soldiers in February 1815 to crush the rebels in Venezuela. Many were sick of war and welcomed the return of the Spanish. Bolívar fled to Jamaica. In September 1815 Bolívar condemned Spanish rule, asked for assistance from Haiti, and vowed that independence would also mean abolition of slavery.

Then Ferdinand disavowed his promise to abide by the Constitution of 1812 and ruled without the Spanish Parliament. Liberals rose in anger, and there were frequent uprisings and conspiracies after 1815. By 1819, with British assistance and taking advantage of turmoil in Spain, Bolívar had conquered the northern region (Venezuela, New Granada, and Ecuador).

Spanish, Italian, and Portuguese Revolutions

In January 1820, the troops in Cádiz mutinied after receiving orders to go to South America. They marched on Madrid, and other garrisons rebelled. They demanded the restoration of the Constitution of 1812. Ferdinand agreed, but the rebels held him as a virtual captive to make sure he did not slide back. In August 1820, inspired by Spain, the Portuguese liberals expelled the regency established by Britain during King John's absence in Brazil. The return of the king touched off a civil war that lasted until 1834, when Britain's influence created a constitutional monarchy.

Metternich called the Concert of Europe to meet at the **Congress of Troppau** in October 1820 to respond to the turmoil in Spain, Portugal, and the Kingdom of the Two Sicilies. Russia and Prussia supported Metternich's anti-nationalist line, but Britain and France were more cautious. The Concert began to show strains. The conservative three signed the Troppau Protocol that revolutionary governments were outlaws and vowed to crush them.

This led to the **Congress of Laibach** in January 1821, which focused on Italian affairs. Many Italian soldiers had served under Napoleon and dreamed of a more liberal government. Southern Italy was ruled by a king who was the uncle of King Ferdinand of Spain. As a member of that royal family, he had vowed in 1812 to uphold the Spanish constitution. Italians in Naples demanded that he grant similar rights to them. In 1820, there had been a military revolt, and the king agreed to call a parliament. This alarmed Metternich, who feared that constitutions and Italian nationalism might take away Austria's Italian lands.

The Congress of Laibach authorized Austria to crush the revolt in the Kingdom of the Two Sicilies. The Austrian army would remain in Naples until 1827. A smaller liberal mutiny in Piedmont-Sardinia had called for the installation of the Spanish Constitution of 1812, and the Austrians crushed that as well.

When Italian liberals fled to Spain, Metternich identified that nation as the chief haven of revolutionaries. Castlereagh had committed suicide, and his replacement **George Canning** was not willing to support Metternich. At the **Congress of Verona** in October 1822, Metternich demanded action against the Spanish revolutionaries. France, which was becoming increasingly reactionary as the Ultras' power grew, was willing to do the job. Canning and the British Cabinet feared that Metternich would next intervene in Latin America. This would threaten a major British market. By 1840, the British cotton industry was shipping 35 percent of its exports to Latin America. The British withdrew from the Alliance. In April 1823 200,000 French troops entered Spain. Ferdinand took bloody revenge against the liberals when he regained power.

South American Freedom

The Spanish revolutionaries reached a truce with Bolívar. Bolívar was dependent on other generals and was forced to give them vast grants of land to keep the peace. In the south, **José de San Martín** (1778–1850) and Bernardo O'Higgins, an exiled Chilean patriot, put together a new Army of the Andes in Argentina to take Chile; half of the 3,700 troops were former slaves. It conquered Chile in 1817 but was forced to rely on local strongmen and notables in countryside. In 1820 a "private" British shelling of Valdivia erased the last Spanish holdout. Peru still feared independence with 140,000 whites surrounded by a million Indians and mixed-race persons.

After meeting with Bolívar, San Martín resigned his offices; he did not have political skill to run a government. They also had different visions: Bolívar dreamed of a United States of Latin America from Mexico to Argentina, while San Martín wanted monarchies. As Peru fell apart, the Creoles appealed to Bolívar to restore order; he entered Lima in September 1823. The Battle of Ayacucho in December 1824 decided the issue: Spain withdrew its remaining 23,000 troops. Bolívar's attempts to set up confederations in preparation for union failed.

During the Napoleonic wars, the British navy had brought the Portuguese royal family to Brazil. The kings then opened up trade, benefiting Britain. When the king returned to Portugal, Prince Dom Pedro (ruled 1822–31) remained behind and eventually declared himself as the independent Emperor of Brazil when Portuguese liberals tried to tighten the home country's control over Brazil and threatened to abolish slavery. Dom Pedro called on the aid of Thomas Cochrane, who had helped San Martín, and Portuguese attempts at reconquest were rebuffed in July 1823.

Once Ferdinand got free and disavowed the Constitution, he wanted to reconquer his American colonies. Britain foiled this by militarily backing the American **Monroe Doctrine** of December 1823. This statement told Europe to stay out of the Americas. Only the despised government of Haiti was declared outside the umbrella of American protection.

Reaction in Mexico and Central America

As Bonaparte took power in Madrid, the Mexican government called for solidarity between Creoles and *peninsulares*. Miguel Hidalgo y Costilla called for the independence of Mexico and equal rights for Creoles and Indians in 1810. Around 60,000 ill-equipped volunteers joined him. As the looting and violence grew, the Creoles deserted Hidalgo, and the Spanish defeated and executed him in 1811. Insurgents now rallied behind the priest José Maria Morelos. They tried to declare independence and appeal to the Creoles. That rebellion also failed and the Spanish shot Morelos in 1815.

Mexico then settled into small-scale guerrilla war. Reactionaries in Mexico feared that revolutionaries might take control in Madrid during the 1820 Revolution and impose land reform that would break up the big estates. The elites declared independence in 1821 and agreed to **Agustin De Iturbide's** Plan de Iguala which rested on three principles: 1) equality between the Creoles and *peninsulares*; 2) the supremacy of the Catholic church; and 3) an independent monarchy. They abolished slavery. In 1822, Iturbide was proclaimed Emperor Agustin I. Within two years, Mexican leaders would begin to quarrel over their vast land.

Central American states were at first in league with Mexico, then took independence as a Central American federation in 1823 (excluding Panama). In 1840, this federation dissolved into its components of Guatemala, El Salvador, Honduras, Nicaragua, and Costa Rica.

THE REVOLUTIONS OF 1830

France

King Charles X faced ever more opposition from liberals. In 1830, the liberals for the first time in France used a no-confidence vote against the king's chosen ministers. When the liberals won a parliamentary election, Charles X issued **Four Ordinances** (July 26, 1830) that suspended press liberty, dissolved the Chamber, took away the right to vote from the middle class, and set the date for a new election. Charles then left town. Liberal journalists led by the editor **Adolphe Thiers** (1797–1877) signed a letter of protest. The next day, the police demolished the presses. Liberal leaders, including the banker Jacques Lafitte, the famous Marquis de Lafayette, and the historian François Guizot all returned to Paris. Barricades went up as the mob of Paris pillaged gun shops and cut down trees. 8,000 armed men clashed with the Swiss Guards, who were the only reliable troops in the area for the king. On July 28, the barricades spread and the violence grew. About 800 civilians died and about 4,000 were wounded while about 200 troops died. The revolutionaries gained control of Paris. Parliament offered to mediate, but the king refused. Thiers and his friends put up posters urging that the Crown be offered to the king's cousin Louis-Philippe, son of Philippe Égalité (Equality), the Duke of Orléans and a Jacobin during the Terror. Lafayette and Louis-Philippe appeared together wrapped in the revolutionary tricolor flag. Charles left Paris again, fled to Britain, and on August 2 abdicated in favor of his grandson. Republicans called for Lafayette to accept the presidency, but the elderly liberal preferred that Louis-Philippe take the throne. On August 3, the Chamber revised the Charter. On August 7, it declared the throne vacant and two days later elected Louis-Philippe king. He agreed to uphold the Charter and embraced the tricolor flag. Voting rights were expanded slightly so about 0.5% of the people now had the right to vote.

Belgium

The Congress of Vienna's merger of Belgium with the Netherlands to the north had never worked well. There were different traditions, religions, and languages. As the news came from France of the overthrow of Charles X, unrest broke out leading to a full revolution on August 25. Delegates wrote a very liberal constitution with a sweeping bill of rights. Belgium would have a king, but he would share power with a two-chambered parliament elected by 1 percent of

Belgian men. Britain and France presided over the **London Protocol of 1830** that declared Belgian independence. Another German prince became king.

The German Confederation and Switzerland

The ouster of the French king provoked responses, and constitutions were given in Brunswick (where the Duke was deposed), Hanover, Saxony and Hesse-Kassel. When the German nationalists gathered in Hambach in 1832, Metternich again summoned the German Confederation to crack down on the liberal movement. The liberals did advance the idea of free trade, led by Prussia. In 1834, a number of smaller states plus Bavaria and Württemberg joined Prussia in a **Customs Union** that brought down the trade barriers. By the 1850s, most German states (except for Austria) belonged. In Switzerland to the south, some cantons began to allow representative government and press freedom in 1828. After a short war in 1847, all the cantons allowed every man to vote.

Italy

There were rebellions in Modena, Parma, and other areas. The Austrian army again crushed all revolts and occupied parts of Italy until 1838. Italian nationalists had varying reactions. **Giuseppe Mazzini** (1805–72) formed a group called Young Italy and, from his exile in France, tried to organize a movement for a united Italy rather than focus on the divided states. This excited a young man from Piedmont named **Giuseppe Garibaldi** (1809–82), who joined the Piedmontese navy to organize a revolt. He was discovered in 1834 and condemned to death, but escaped and lived for a time in New York and in South America.

Poland

Polish nationalists had been unhappy about the Vienna settlement. When Emperor Nicholas proposed attacking France and Belgium to crush the new governments, Polish officers saw their chance and drove out the Russian garrison in January 1831. Nicholas reacted with a massive force of 180,000 soldiers and defeated the Poles by September 1831. A wave of Polish nationalists fled west.

LIBERALISM AND REFORM IN BRITAIN

Liberalism

The name Liberal had begun in Spain with the leftist opposition to Napoleon and Joseph Bonaparte, but by the 1830s, it applied to a broad movement across Western Civilization. It was intellectually rooted in Enlightenment with its faith in progress, the perfectibility of humankind, and the social contract between the people and the ruler, aimed at realizing individual freedom.

The program of the liberals included:

1. Freedom of the individual, based on human or constitutional rights, including freedom of speech, conscience and thought. Liberals supported equality before the law, but this did not mean equality of education or property.

2. A constitutional state with a separation of powers. The constitution was the supreme law in a state of laws designed to protect the citizens. No one was above the law, not even a king. Nor would anyone be below the law, that is selected for legal prosecution when other people were not.

3. Political participation by a larger number of men to elect representatives to a parliament. Generally, the liberals did not call for universal manhood suffrage or for Rousseau-style direct democracy. They believed in votes only for the educated middle- and upper-class men who would elect representatives. There was a lingering fear of the radicalism that had happened in the French Revolution, when all men got to vote for a constitutional convention. In practice, the liberals supported opening the vote to more and more people until by 1920, most men and women had the right to vote in Western Europe and the United States.

4. A free economy with freedom of occupation, trade, entrepreneurial activity, coalition, competition and movement. They were influenced not only by the ideas of Adam Smith, but also the French economist Vincent de Gournay who had coined the phrase *laissez-faire, laissez-passer* ("let it be, let it pass") which effectively meant allowing businesses to do as they pleased. Smith had warned that this practice allowed businesses to grow too large and distort the market. Another influential liberal economic thinker was **David Ricardo** (1772–1823). Ricardo agreed with Malthus that population would always be near its maximum. He devised an "iron law of wages" that pay would always be low because there would always be more workers than jobs, therefore pay would not rise above the lowest level necessary for survival.

Liberals in the Italian and German lands had a priority: national unification. Liberals in areas such as Poland or Hungary saw their first goal as gaining independence from the dominant country that ruled them (Russia and Austria in these cases). Many countries continued to be absolutist or at least have some absolutist tendencies, such as a dominance by noble families and an established church. Thus the liberals often took on the nobles and the church as enemies, pushing for an end to tax money going to the church, religious toleration, and an end to any remaining noble privileges.

Liberal Reform in Britain

In Britain, the liberals gained some victories in the late 1820s. They reformed criminal law and removed the death penalty from more than a hundred trivial crimes such as petty larceny. They allowed non-Anglicans to hold public office and reduced the Corn Law tariffs somewhat. A major fight occurred over rights for Roman Catholics. Ireland had a strong majority of Catholics but none of them could serve in Parliament. The Irish Catholic **Daniel O'Connell** (1775–1847) established a Catholic Association and illegally ran for a seat, forcing the Parliament to consider the issue. Not wanting another John Wilkes-style debacle, the Parliament gave in and allowed **Catholic Emancipation** in March 1829. This was the first time a political association had forced Parliament to pass a law and gave the reformers new hope. Attempts at a similar Jewish Emancipation failed until 1858.

The First Reform Bill

The British political system was wildly uneven. The population shifts from the Agricultural and Industrial Revolutions had created even more rotten boroughs and pocket boroughs. The rottenest borough was Old Sarum, a deserted hilltop whose eleven voters all lived elsewhere but sent two members to the House of Commons. Meanwhile, the industrial cities of Birmingham, Manchester, Sheffield, and Leeds sent no members at all. There were no real elections for two-thirds of the seats in the House.

Catholic Emancipation, the overthrow of Charles X, and an economic recession built pressure for political reform. Reformers used riots, tax strikes, and a run on the banks to increase this pressure. The Parliament passed the **First Reform Bill** in 1832. It gave the vote to 20 percent of the men in England and Wales, 12.5 percent in Scotland, and 5 percent in Ireland. Altogether, about 3 percent of all people in Great Britain could vote as opposed to 0.5 percent in

France. It eliminated fifty-six rotten boroughs and moved more than one-quarter (143) of the seats from the rural south to the industrial north of England.

A more liberal government took power after the elections. It abolished slavery in the British colonies and passed a Factory Act in 1833. This limited work hours for children under age thirteen to nine hours a day and those under eighteen to sixty-nine hours a week.

THE JACKSONIAN BREAKTHROUGH IN THE UNITED STATES

An Era of Bad Feelings

One-party rule had effectively lasted since 1802 but began to break down in 1822. A succession system had been established where the Secretary of State succeeded the President after two terms. The next in line was **John Quincy Adams**, son of the former president. Many doubted his commitment to states' rights and disliked him personally. This spurred the ambitions of others: William Crawford, the Treasury Secretary from Georgia; **John C. Calhoun**, the War Secretary from South Carolina; **Henry Clay**, the House Speaker from Kentucky, and **Andrew Jackson**, a general and former Senator from Tennessee. The New York Senator Martin Van Buren, supporting Crawford, denounced President Monroe, and by extension Adams, for having abandoned Jeffersonian principles. Van Buren, a protege of Aaron Burr, was trying to reforge the alliance between the great landowners of upstate New York and the southern planters.

The Presidential Election of 1824

The Congressional Caucus nominated Crawford, but he suffered a stroke and was paralyzed. Partisans of the other candidates denounced the caucus nomination as undemocratic. Calhoun pulled out to run for Vice-President for both Adams and Jackson. The state legislature of Tennessee nominated Jackson. In a sense the election went as the Framers had intended: it was thrown to the House. But Jackson won a strong plurality of both popular and electoral votes and there was skullduggery: the Adams electors cast votes for the disabled Crawford to keep Clay out of the top three. This meant that members of the House could not vote for him. Nonetheless, Clay made a "Corrupt Bargain" with Adams: Clay would throw his support in the House to Adams, and Adams would appoint Clay to the "succession" job of Secretary of State.

The Democratic Party

The Jacksonians were outraged and began organizing the machinery of a party that would return to the true traditions of Jefferson: the Democratic Party. Jackson, another early ally of Burr, joined with Van Buren. Despite his influence, Burr was a political outcast because he had shot and killed Alexander Hamilton during a duel in 1804. The Jackson/Van Buren alliance swamped the Clay/Adams group in the mid-term elections of 1826 and trounced Adams himself in the presidential election of 1828. Voting participation rose markedly and the Democrats introduced the **political convention** to reach grass-roots partisans. While voting records are incomplete, it seems that participation as a percentage of population roughly tripled from 1824 to 1828 and would reach 10 percent by 1832 with a peak of 14 percent in 1840. Only a few parts of France had reached this level of participation in the vote for the constitutional convention of 1792. Clay had to follow suit by building a rival political party: the Whigs.

Jackson as President

Jackson opened the "era of the common man," to the dismay of many. Jackson's followers were rough westerners. Cheap newspapers became available based on steam presses in the 1830s. Candidates ran for the House as representatives of their local areas. Jackson saw himself as the direct representative of all the people and the embodiment of the nation. Jackson was at odds with Vice President Calhoun over states' rights, and he got into a bitter dispute with Clay. He vetoed the bill reauthorizing the national **Second Bank of the United States**, both because it was run by a supporter of Clay and because he thought it was an unreasonable enterprise by the nation. This shocked the Whigs because it was a rare policy veto. He ruined the bank by withdrawing the government deposits. The Clay-controlled Congress censured Jackson in 1834.

The Jackson period transformed the United States government as surely as the revolutions of 1820 and 1830 had in Europe. In 1833, the last state ended its official sponsorship of a church. The Presidency emerged as the supreme branch of government. Popular vote for presidential electors, political parties, and the abandonment of the last vestiges of "virtual representation" in House elections created more democracy and closer ties between the voters and their government. This did not mean necessarily better or fairer government, as the tragedy of the Cherokees showed.

Relations with Indians

Jacksonian nationalism and intense democracy victimized the Indians. Popular demand wanted the Indians removed in some fashion so that their land could be taken. Dislocation and forced transportation led to disease, distress, and death. When the Cherokee Indians sued the state of Georgia, the Supreme Court ruled that the state could not nullify Cherokee laws. Jackson refused to recognize the court ruling and retorted: let John Marshall enforce it.

SOCIALISTS AND REVOLUTIONARIES IN EUROPE

The Origins of Socialism

Liberalism mainly appealed to the middle classes. There was very little in the liberal political program for the lower classes. In the 1830s, another political movement called socialism began to take shape. **Socialism** believes in a fair distribution of property, a fair social order, equal rights, and well-being for the lower classes (usually this means industrial workers and the peasantry). Socialist ideas had been growing for a while. The Diggers during English Civil War in the 1640s had called for income redistribution. Rousseau had blamed private property for many of the ills of the world, and Jefferson had famously stricken Locke's enshrinement of property as a basic right in favor of the "pursuit of happiness" in the American Declaration of Independence.

The Hungry Forties

With the Industrial Revolution in Britain, many noticed that although national wealth was increasing, many people's conditions became increasingly wretched. Monarchs were more responsible in past, but nobles held most positions of leadership and much of the land, which was still the main form of wealth outside Britain. The "Hungry Forties" saw peasant revolts break out in Ireland, Wales, Russia, Galicia, and Silesia. While meat had been a main part of the diet in the sixteenth century, the typical peasant meal was now a lot of potatoes with a little milk or cheese and maybe some pork in the autumn months. An Irish working man of the time typically ate twelve pounds of potatoes a day. Winters were cold and hungry and hard liquor production skyrocketed as people tried to keep warm. In Antwerp, the Netherlands, a survey of the whole population (including children) in 1820 found an average consumption of two bottles of beer a day, one bottle of wine and one bottle of gin every month. 10 percent of all calories came from alcoholic drinks. A later survey of people over the age of fourteen in wine-loving France showed that the average person drank six bottles of wine, two bottles of beer and three shots of hard liquor every week. In reaction to the spread of alcoholism, temperance societies sprang up, starting with Ireland in 1818. Because alcoholism often led to violence against women, they took the lead in the movement to restrict or ban alcoholic beverages. Never before or after were things so tough for the common person as in the 1840s.

Socialist thinkers begin to carve out an ideology:

The **Count de Saint-Simon** (1760–1825) had been at the Battle of Yorktown with Washington and Lafayette and later fought in the French Revolution. He called on scientific and industrial leaders to reorganize the state based on the brotherhood of man. He considered economic progress to be the driving force of history. Science and technology would solve social problems. Social classes would collaborate guided by an elite of engineers and entrepreneurs. Saint-Simon is often known as the father of modern socialism. His followers called for the abolition of inheritance rights, public control of the means of production, and gradually giving women equal rights as men, including the right to vote.

Louis Blanc (1811–82), another French socialist, wrote *The Organization of Work* in 1840. This book attacked the competitive system. It is ruinous to common people and to the upper classes since it produces continual crises. Blanc believed that there should be a nationally-planned economy. In a democratic republic, the state would create national workshops in the most important industries; it would regulate production and allocate functions to prevent sudden booms and busts that hurt the workers. Because workers would get fair pay from the state, they would know that they were not being exploited by the owner and would have greater productivity and thus make the nation as a whole richer. Blanc tried to raise seed money in the 1840s to start a few experimental national workshops to prove his ideas, but not surprisingly, few banks or wealthy people were interested.

The Englishman **Robert Owen** (1771–1858) came at socialism from another direction. He was a rich factory owner and tried to build model industrial villages in which he provided education, housing, and insurance facilities for workers. Owen believed that this would make his workers more productive and loyal than workers at other factories. Owen encouraged the formation of the first big labor union in Britain to help gain workers' rights. Many other factory owners regarded Owen as a fool and refused to cut into their profits.

There were also writers and leaders who might vaguely endorse socialism, but their main aim was to have a violent Jacobin-style revolution that would overturn the political and economic order. Auguste Blanqui (1805–1881) wrote of a "duel to the death between dividends and wages." "Mechanized man" must wage war against a bourgeoisie with whom he shared no common interests. Blanqui supported the most hopeless of conspiracies and spent most of his adult life in jail. His political leaning was probably more **anarchist** (no government at all should exist) than socialist. Another French writer **Pierre-Joseph Proudhon** (1809–65) published *What is Property?* in 1840. He answered his own question: Property is theft! Profit is actually money owed to workers because their labor has increased the value of the materials used in the manufacturing process. He promoted the idea that small businesses paying workers fairly could build a network and compete successfully.

ROMANTICISM IN WESTERN CULTURE

The Origins of Romanticism

The Enlightenment began to decline in influence in the 1770s. There had been a strong reaction against rationality. New fads began to grow in quack medicine such as "mesmerism" that said that people could be hypnotized out of physical sickness. Fake sciences such as astrology flourished. Jean-Jacques Rousseau had called for a return of nature and emotion in two of his later novels.

The Romantics followed this. They believed in the superiority of nature and how it pummels works of man. An example of this is the poem "Ozymandias" (1817) by the Englishman **Percy Byssche Shelley**:

> *I met a traveller from an antique land*
> *Who said: "Two vast and trunkless legs of stone*
> *Stand in the desert. Near them on the sand,*
> *Half sunk, a shattered visage lies, whose frown*
> *And wrinkled lip and sneer of cold command*
> *Tell that its sculptor well those passions read*
> *Which yet survive, stamped on these lifeless things,*

> *The hand that mocked them and the heart that fed.*
> *And on the pedestal these words appear:*
> *'My name is Ozymandias, King of Kings:*
> *Look on my works, ye mighty, and despair!'*
> *Nothing beside remains. Round the decay*
> *Of that colossal wreck, boundless and bare,*
> *The lone and level sands stretch far away."*

His wife **Mary Shelley** (1792–1822), the daughter of Mary Wollstonecraft, wrote *Frankenstein* in 1818 about the limits and abuses of science.

Early Romantics

Rousseau's call struck deepest in cosmopolitan Germany with its tradition of Pietism from the late 1600s. This had emphasized a close relationship with God and living like a true Christian. Pietism's ideas came to England and were modified in 1738 as Methodism (its followers resolved to conduct their lives and religious studies "by rule and method"). Methodists believed that the official Church of England had cut people off from a true relationship with God, so they would have open-air services and try to reach the common people. Because non-Anglicans were not allowed full rights as citizens, the Methodist approach of open-air meeting and marches soon inspired political causes.

The first great German Romantic novel was **Johann Wolfgang Goethe** (1749–1832)'s *Sorrows of Young Werther* (1774) about a young intellectual who kills himself because he is madly in love with a married woman. As we saw earlier Goethe wrote positively about Napoleon. Napoleon in turn told Goethe that he had read *Werther* seven times. Romanticism reached England and began its rise in the 1790s with poems such as "The Tiger" (1794) by William Blake. In 1798, **William Wordsworth** (1770–1850) and **Samuel Taylor Coleridge** (1772–1834) published *Lyrical Ballads*.

There was Romantic music such as that composed by **Ludwig van Beethoven** (1770–1827). Beethoven was the first composer who was able to make a living just by selling his music to the public. He originally dedicated his *Eroica* (1804) to Napoleon but then became disillusioned. The orchestra tripled to a large size; musical geniuses become cultural heroes; people fainted on hearing some of the piano work of Franz Liszt (1811–1886). There were Romantic lifestyles: the English poet **Lord Byron** (1788–1824) was fired up by Greek cause, went there to fight for its independence, and (rather unromantically) died of a fever. Romantics scorned the eighteenth-century fashion of wearing powdered wigs.

They preferred long and uncombed hair. In the United States Edgar Allan Poe (1809–1849) wrote thrillers, mystery stories, and poetry that tried to evoke emotions. There was a new interest in historical novels. Prominent writers included Sir Walter Scott in Britain and the Frenchman Alexander Dumas who wrote *The Three Musketeers*. In the U.S., James Fenimore Cooper wrote on the French and Indian Wars of recent history.

Points of Romanticism

Romanticism was extremely diverse. There is still a lot of controversy as to who is in and who is out. The Romantics rejected flowery conventions for ordinary speech and endowed simplest subjects with great majesty. Wordsworth's "I Wandered Lonely as a Cloud" is typical:

> *I wandered lonely as a cloud*
> *That floats on high o'er vales and hills,*
> *When all at once I saw a crowd,*
> *A host, of golden daffodils;*
> *Beside the lake, beneath the trees,*
> *Fluttering and dancing in the breeze.*
>
> *Continuous as the stars that shine*
> *And twinkle on the milky way,*
> *They stretched in never-ending line*
> *Along the margin of a bay:*
> *Ten thousand saw I at a glance,*
> *Tossing their heads in sprightly dance.*
>
> . . .
>
> *For oft, when on my couch I lie*
> *In vacant or in pensive mood,*
> *They flash upon that inward eye*
> *Which is the bliss of solitude;*
> *And then my heart with pleasure fills,*
> *And dances with the daffodils.*

Most Romantics tended to follow these points:

1. They drew away from Man, the abstract, and looked for individuals. They had a new interest in history, especially medieval history. Many writers emphasized THE HERO who has honor, love, bravery, originality, and

genius. At first many Romantics worshiped Napoleon as a true model for heroes.

2. There was more attention to people outside of Western Europe.

3. They focused on emotion and characters rather than narrative plot.

4. In politics, they sought freedom, diversity, self-reliance, and opportunities for self-development. There were strong disagreements on how this could be achieved. Some supported renewed absolutism with a strong monarchy and established church. After 1820 especially, a new generation pushed for the opposite: a republic with voting rights for all men and maybe even women. Some believed a united Germany and Italy could fulfill the needs of those peoples. Others called for a return to the traditional groups of the pre-modern era.

5. The conflicts between nature and the spiritual, emotion and reason, finite and infinite can be dissolved by "subjective internalization": fantasy, dreams, and mystic visions. There was more poetry about nighttime because it is darker and less rational.

6. They tended to believe in an unconscious *Volksgeist* (National Spirit) that guides national language, literature and actions. In this way, Romanticism tended to feed nationalism.

Idealism in Philosophy

Like literature and music, philosophy also tried to get beyond the rationality of the Enlightenment. Some of these pieces were called idealist because they focused on the invisible and ideas of the mind rather than the physical that could be experimented upon and tested. The German **Immanuel Kant** (1724–1804) in his *Critique of Pure Reason* (1781) said that reason is only one of several elements used to grasp reality. There was no rational explanation for experiences of conscience, beauty, and religion. Locke and Rousseau had emphasized how people make up the state, but the German **G.W.F. Hegel** (1770–1831) saw the state as a natural organism that goes through a lifecycle. The power of the state lies in its cohesiveness, and individuals are submerged in the greater state. Politically, Romanticism gained as part of German national movement against Napoleon and hence was against anything that smelled of revolution or even liberalism. Influenced by Burke's *Reflections on the Revolution in France* (1790), many Romantics blamed the Enlightenment for the French Revolution.

"Neo-Romanticism" After 1820

By 1824, a majority of the population had been born after 1789 and did not remember the French Revolution first hand. Mazzini's Young Italy movement spawned a liberal Young Germany movement. Lord Byron fought for Greek independence. French romantics opposed royalists as Bonapartism revived. People forgot how many Frenchmen had died in Napoleon's wars. Neo-Bonapartism grew in France after the revolutions of 1830. Victor Hugo wrote an admiring poem. Adolphe Thiers, a writer and Prime Minister under Louis-Philippe not only wrote an admiring twenty-volume history of Napoleon's Consulate and Empire, but also completed the Arc de Triomphe in Paris, and named streets and bridges after Napoleon's victories. In 1840, he arranged to bring Napoleon's bones back from St. Helena. The growth of socialism was related to "Neo-Romanticism." Karl Marx would be part of a "Young Hegelian" movement much more leftist and radical than Hegel while taking some of his ideas.

THE REVOLUTIONS OF 1848

The Revolution in France

In August 1845, a fungus destroyed half of the potato crop in Ireland. This was catastrophic because most Irish lived on the potato and made their money growing the potato. Now they had nothing to eat and no money to buy other kinds of food. The colonial power of Britain was slow to help while Ireland shipped out wheat and meat even as people starved. At least a million Irish died, and millions fled the country after 1845 as the blight destroyed the entire crop of 1846 and 1847. Across Europe, the loss of the potatoes cause food prices to skyrocket. In Paris, the price of rye for bread and potatoes doubled. Soup kitchens opened up. In the Prussian capital of Berlin, people fought over scarce potatoes when they appeared. The crisis put a strain on the poor transportation and distribution system. Outside of England there were few railroads in 1848.

In the summer of 1847 the French opposition held great feasts to feed the hungry and talk politics since it could not hold meetings. Daniel O'Connell had used this tactic in rallying support for Catholic Emancipation in Britain. The government of Louis-Philippe and his Prime Minister François Guizot put in no reforms, took no action, but did ban meetings. The opposition planned a "monster banquet" in Paris for Washington's birthday, February 22, 1848. The government tried to ban it, then set up conditions. Students and workingmen assembled in the streets. Louis-Philippe turned on Guizot and dismissed him on February 22 in an attempt to save his crown. This did not clear the air, it only encouraged the revolutionaries. The crowd headed for Guizot's home on February 23. They were met by soldiers, and forty died in the confusion. News of this "massacre" caused the protesters to build 1,500 barricades. The National Guard proved unreliable. Louis-Philippe feared a repeat of the Terror and quit as king.

With the king, the Chamber, and the Charter discredited, power fell to the liberal newspapers. Their editors picked a temporary government of liberals and socialists headed by the poet **Alfonse de Lamartine**. The temporary government immediately proclaimed a republic, announced elections where all men would have the right to vote, recalled the troops from abroad, and made service in the National Guard compulsory for all males. It set up a mobile guard of 15,000 in Paris to keep the peace. Later, the government abolished slavery in all French territories.

Radicals wanted the state to intervene in the economy and clean out the bureaucracy. Louis Blanc, who was part of the temporary government, wanted nationalization and decentralization of industry. But Lamartine was a liberal defender of property. The government set up "national workshops" that resulted from a compromise between the two. An opponent of Blanc's with every incentive to cripple the National Workshops was put in charge. Unemployed workers could sign up on a sheet to get work in or around Paris. Those who got a job through the government were paid two francs a day for working. But what if you signed up for work and the government did not have a job that day? Should you get nothing and risk the starvation of your family? The government would pay 1½ francs (later one) franc a day for not working. People poured into Paris. Many ended up being paid for doing nothing. The National Workshops had been designed for 12,000; by the end, 120,000 were enrolled and 80,000 more were trying to join. Government needed a 45-centime tax to keep the budget in order. This caused anger in the countryside against Paris and the Lamartine government.

The Revolution in Austria

Excitement greeted the news from Paris. The nationalist **Louis Kossuth** called for Hungary to have its own constitution. Fighting broke out in Vienna, and Metternich was forced out on March 13. Two days later, the Hungarian Diet put out a constitution giving Hungary autonomy. Without Metternich, Austria did not have strong leadership and the Austrian emperor had a severe mental disability.

Austria gave in to the Hungarians on March 31. Then the Czechs demanded and gained their rights on April 8. A Constituent Assembly convened in Austria seeking a Belgian-model constitution. The Assembly ordered peasants freed from serfdom, and the Emperor signed the decree on September 7. This was the main demand of the peasants and they now had no interest in further revolution.

Revolution in Italy

Most of the Austrian troops were tied down in Italy as the provinces of Lombardy and Venetia rose and sought independence. The revolt had begun in the Lombard capital of Milan when news from Vienna reached it on March 17. Venice rose March 22, and the Austrian troops withdrew to strategic positions in forts. King **Charles Albert** of Piedmont-Sardinia (ruled 1831–49) invaded Lombardy and reached Milan on March 26. Lombardy, Parma, Modena, and Venice voted to join with Piedmont-Sardinia. The unification of northern Italy, at least, seemed likely.

Revolution in Prussia and the German States

The Prussian cities had already seen hunger riots and riots by artisans whose work was being threatened by cheap British industrial goods. When Metternich fell, Prussian King **Frederick William IV** (ruled 1840–61) promised to convene a Prussian parliament, grant a constitution, and sponsor reforms. On March 18, fighting broke out in Berlin after crowds clashed with troops. Over 250 died. The king ordered the troops out of Berlin and was essentially a hostage of the revolution. The king abolished lord-run local courts that were the last vestige of serfdom, satisfying the Prussian peasants. Especially in the overcrowded states of southwestern Germany, crowds with liberal petitions marched even as riots of the workers in cities smashed industrial machines. In the countryside, peasants destroyed landlords' records. Governments offered little resistance. In Bavaria, demands for reform combined with demands that the king and his mistress leave town. The revolutionaries were also German nationalists in many cases and saw their chance. All the states in the German Confederation agreed to choose representatives to meet in Frankfurt and draw up a liberal constitution for a united Germany. This **Frankfurt Parliament** started on May 18. Some say that Parliament should have declared its authority and acted dictatorially or at least employed revolutionary methods. It did enact agricultural reforms, including the abolition of all feudal dues. The artisans in the cities turned against the revolution because they were opposed to change and liberalization. The Parliament drafted the Fundamental Rights of German People. It voted to exclude Austria from united Germany and offered the crown to Frederick William IV of Prussia by a vote of 290 to 248. Twenty-nine of the remaining thirty-eight states approved the Constitution; that was more than the three-fourths that put the U.S. Constitution into effect. The Germans had to wait for Frederick William's decision.

The Failure of the Revolutions

France

The April 23 elections led to a great reaction in the countryside. 85 percent of the eligible voters participated. Many peasants voted for the first time under Church influence and were disgusted at free-spending Paris. The moderate republicans controlled the assembly and forced Lamartine to drop Blanc. On May 24, it ordered the dissolution of the National Workshops. The younger unemployed could join the army, those from rural areas were paid to go home, others could undertake public works outside Paris. Attempts to delay this action failed.

On June 23 when the army enlistments were supposed to begin, the workers met at the square where the Bastille had once stood and set up barricades. The Minister of War **Eugene Cavaignac** put down the revolt in four bloody days. The government killed 1,460, tracked down and executed 3,000, and arrested 12,000. These **"June Days"** represented a conflict of the middle class against the workers as well as a conflict between Paris and the French countryside. A dictatorship replaced the government's executive committee and got rid of social reform. Lamartine was completely discredited.

In October 1848, the Constituent Assembly agreed on a Constitution modeled upon that of the United States. There would be a strong president, but he was limited to a single four-year term. The president would share power with a National Assembly elected every three years. All men would have the right to vote, about 25 percent of the total population.

Lamartine and Cavaignac both ran for the presidency and received little support. The overwhelming winner was **Louis-Napoleon Bonaparte**. Napoleon I's only son had died in Vienna in 1832, and his nephew Louis-Napoleon had proclaimed himself the leader of the Bonapartes. He had been active in the Italian revolutions of 1831. He had tried in 1836 and 1840 to overthrow Louis-Philippe without success and had been exiled to the United States. After six months in New York and Philadelphia, he had returned to Europe and resumed plotting. He had returned to France with the Revolution of 1848. In 1839, the book *Napoleonic Ideas*, with Louis-Napoleon's name on it, appeared. It was a hodgepodge of liberal and socialist ideas, designed to appeal to the lower classes. Louis-Napoleon called himself a socialist, and his book seemed somewhat inspired by Saint-Simon. In his pamphlet "The Extinction of Poverty" (1844), he called for the government to move the unemployed out of cities and into special barracks where they would elect governors of twenty-year agricultural colonies.

In 1849, the voters chose a reactionary monarchist assembly that tried to remove universal manhood suffrage. This gave the President an opening and in December 1851, Louis-Napoleon and the army threw out the assembly. In 1852, a popular vote converted the republic into an empire and Louis-Napoleon took over as Emperor Napoleon III.

Bohemia

The Czechs called a pan-Slav Congress to transform the Austrian empire into a federation where Germans, Magyars, and Slavic peoples would have equal power. On June 13, a full rebellion broke out in the Bohemian capital of Prague. The Austrian military commander **Alfred von Windischgrätz** bombarded Prague, and it gave up June 17.

Italy

In July 1848, the Austrian forces rolled back in, under the command of **Joseph Radetzky**. At the **Battle of Custoza** (July 23–27, 1848) Radetzky defeated Charles Albert. The Austrian regained Milan on August 6. For six months things stayed quiet, but in February 1849 there was a new revolution in Rome that drove out the conservative Pope and proclaimed a republic. Mazzini was one of the leaders, and Garibaldi headed the defense squad. The United States was the only nation to recognize the Roman Republic. Charles Albert again attacked Lombardy and was defeated. Louis-Napoleon ordered French troops to retake Rome for the Pope in order to please conservative Catholic voters. The city of Venice held out for months against Austrian bombardment until August of 1849. The Revolution had failed in Italy and the divisions remained.

Events in Vienna

Vienna had begun its own version of the national workshops, and similar problems developed as in France. On October 6, 1848, revolt broke out in Vienna centered on a soldiers' mutiny when they were ordered to attack Hungary. Students and workers backed the mutineers. General Windischgrätz brutally suppressed the rebellion by October 30 killing and wounding about 4,000. The general installed his cynical brother-in-law **Felix zu Schwarzenberg** as chief minister. Schwarzenberg engineered a change in emperor. The mentally-disabled Ferdinand resigned in favor of his eighteen-year-old nephew **Francis Joseph** (ruled 1848–1916). The Emperor and Schwarzenberg dissolved the Constituent Assembly and issued their own very conservative constitution.

Hungary

The Austrians had been stirring up trouble in Hungary by encouraging the non-Hungarian groups such as the Croats, Serbs, and Romanians to try for their own independence. When Austria tried to send troops to Hungary, Kossuth's power grew. In December 1848, the Hungarian Parliament refused to recognize Francis Joseph as the new Emperor. The Hungarians defeated Windischgrätz in April 1849. The Austrians appealed to Russian Emperor Nicholas, who sent 140,000 troops in 1849 and crushed the revolt. There was massive retaliation by the Austrians starting with the execution of thirteen leading Hungarian generals. Kossuth escaped to the United States.

Prussia

In May 1848 the Prussian National Assembly split between the liberals and democratic radicals. It did not get control over the army and police. In November 1848 Frederick William IV, inspired by the crushing of the Vienna revolt, suspended the Assembly and called in the army. The king put out the **Prussian Constitution of 1850**. This established a bicameral legislature with an upper House of Lords and a lower house elected by universal manhood suffrage in a three-class franchise. This meant that the richest 17 percent of the male taxpayers elected two-thirds of the seats in the lower house. This would be a strong barrier to democratic and social reform legislation in Germany down to the end of World War I in 1918. Not surprisingly, few from the lower class bothered to vote.

Germany

Frederick William IV also dealt with the Frankfurt Parliament. He wanted to be the first German Emperor, but did not like being bound by a constitution or sharing power with an elected assembly or weakening the state of Prussia by breaking it into eight provinces. The king refused to "take the crown out of the gutter." In the southwest and Saxony, radical revolts broke out. Prussian troops crushed these small revolts. The German revolution was over.

Frederick William IV then tried to unite Germany on his own terms while Austria was still weak by forcing the smaller German states into an **Erfurt**

Union (1849–50). Austria, backed by Russia, forced Prussia to back down. Under the **Punctation of Olmütz** in November 1850, Prussia agreed to the reestablishment of the German Confederation with Austria as Chair.

General Causes of Failure of Revolutions of 1848

We may sum up the reasons for the failure of the revolutions as follows:

1. The middle class feared the revolutionary radicalism of workers.

2. The revolutionaries lacked political experience.

3. The army and bureaucracy remained loyal to established authority.

4. In some cases, foreign intervention made the difference (Russia in Hungary, France and Austria in Italy). Without this, Hungary would have gained its independence and northern Italy down to Rome would have united in 1849.

5. The peasants were satisfied with a few reforms and thereafter sat on sidelines or backed conservatives. This is very important because most soldiers were of peasant background. Not only were most people peasants, but boys growing up in the cities of the Hungry Forties were often scrawny and rejected for military service. As long as the army supported the revolution or at least the king doubted their support, the revolution could advance.

Results of the Revolutions of 1848

1. The national desire for the unification of Germany remained, but the politically disappointed middle class turned more to economic endeavors. Many would go into business in the 1850s.

2. Many emigrated from Germany, especially democrats from the overcrowded southwest; this weakened the democratic movement and helped ensure that when unity came, Germany would be united as an autocratic Prussian empire.

3. Unlike what Hegel had preached, reality proved stronger than ideas, and a more realistic intellectual era would begin. Romanticism faded after the failure of the Revolutions of 1848. The new mood would be realism as represented by Otto von Bismarck: The great matters of time are not decided by debates and majority votes but by blood and iron!

TIMELINE

1815	Congress of Vienna
1820	Revolutions in Spain, Portugal, southern Italy
1821–1829	Greek War of Independence
1821	Mexican elites declare independence from Spain
1822	Congress of Verona; Britain refuses to back intervention in Spain
1823	Monroe Doctrine
1825	Decembrist Revolt in Russia
1829	Andrew Jackson becomes U.S. President
1830	Revolutions in France, Belgium, Italy
1831	Revolution in Poland
1832	First Reform Bill in Britain
1845–1848	Potato famine in Ireland
1848	Revolutions across Europe
1850	Death of Wordsworth ends Romantic era

KEY TERMS

Congress of Vienna
Klemens von Metternich
Muhammad Ali
Simón Bolívar
The Greek War of Independence
Monroe Doctrine
The First Reform Bill
Andrew Jackson
The Hungry Forties
Louis Blanc
G.W.F. Hegel
Louis Kossuth
Frankfurt Parliament
"June Days"
Battle of Custoza

PRIMARY SOURCE DOCUMENTS

Klemens von Metternich, http://www.fordham.edu/halsall/mod/1820metternich. html

Lord Byron on Greece, http://www.fordham.edu/halsall/mod/byron-greece.html

Louis Kossuth, http://www.h-net.org/~habsweb/sourcetexts/kosswash.html

Simon Bolívar, http://www.fordham.edu/halsall/mod/1819bolivar.html

Monroe Doctrine, http://avalon.law.yale.edu/19th_century/monroe.asp

John Stuart Mill, http://www.wsu.edu:8080/~wldciv/world_civ_reader/world_civ_ reader_2/mill.html

David Ricardo, http://www.fordham.edu/halsall/mod/ricardo-wages.html

Frederick Engels, http://www.fordham.edu/halsall/mod/1844engels.html

Seneca Falls Conference, http://www.fordham.edu/halsall/mod/Senecafalls.html

Louis Blanc, http://www.fordham.edu/halsall/mod/1840blanc.html

Carl Schurz, http://www.fordham.edu/halsall/mod/1848schurz.html

Chapter 7

NATION-STATE BUILDING

THE CONCERT OF EUROPE 1831-1863

The First Egyptian Crisis

By 1831, Muhammad Ali had rebuilt his forces and wanted Syria from Turkey for his help in the Greek War. When Turkey did not satisfy him, Ali's son Ibrahim marched up the Mediterranean coast. In 1832, the Egyptians beat a big Turkish army and threatened Asia Minor. Ibrahim sought to depose the Sultan and pressed on. Russian ships moved to the Straits to "protect" Turkey and forced Turkey to come to an agreement in 1833. Ali gained all of Syria and Russia gained the right to intervene in Turkey when it wanted. The British feared that the Russians might be trying to gain control of the Straits and threaten commerce. This remained a cornerstone of their foreign policy through the century.

The Second Crisis

Ali declared independence in 1838, and the Sultan was determined to punish him. The Egyptians whipped the Turks again. Ali's forces pushed into Arabia as far as the Persian Gulf. France supported Ali, but the other four powers lined up behind Turkey. The British demanded that Syria be put between the Turks and Egyptians and grabbed the strategic port of Aden. Tensions mounted, British and Turkish troops landed at Beirut, and Ali's forces fell back. In a treaty of 1841, the Sultan and the five great powers recognized Muhammad Ali and his heirs as hereditary rulers of Egypt. He would have to pay a sum to the Ottomans. The Straits would be closed to all warships when the Ottomans were at peace. The Concert had again held and prevented war among the great powers, but the Turkish decay still threatened the peace.

The Weakening of the Concert

The Concert had never fulfilled Metternich's vision as a global policeman after Britain's refusal to work against revolutions, but it was a way of keeping general order, especially among the great powers. The Russian intervention in Hungary had proved the continued strength of the Concert. The three eastern powers (Prussia, Austria, Russia) were still strongly committed to the principles laid down by Metternich, even though Metternich was gone.

After 1848, weaknesses began to eat away at the security system:

1. The revolutions had exposed the weakness of the Austrian Empire. Its failure to reform and modernize would cause it to join the Ottomans as an underlying security problem.

2. Napoleon III believed in a Concert system of some sort but had imperial ambitions, wanted to support liberal and national causes, and drew closer to Britain. Until 1866, the French Emperor was the most important international figure.

3. The "Vienna generation" that included Metternich, Nicholas I, and Castlereagh, had gradually passed from the scene. The new generation featured ambitious national unifiers such as Camillo di Cavour in Italy and Otto von Bismarck in Germany.

4. Britain slipped more into "splendid isolation," especially after the Crimean War.

The Crimean War

The Causes of the War

The weakness of the Ottomans continued to threaten security. In June 1853, the Russians intervened in Romania to "protect" Greek Orthodox believers, who they had considered to be under their protection since the Greek War of

Independence. The Russians also wanted some revenge on the Turks who had refused to turn over Kossuth and other Hungarian rebels who had fled the wreckage of the 1848–1849 revolution. Russia also felt that Austria owed it for help against Hungary and Prussia.

The Turks declared war on Russia and were beaten badly. Nicholas I tried to force a treaty on the Turks as he had in 1833, but Britain and France declared war. Napoleon III saw the war as the way to an alliance with Britain. He was again trying to win over French Catholic voters by declaring France to be the protector of the Christian holy places and people in the Eastern Mediterranean.

The Conduct of the War

The war centered on the most important Russian naval base at Sevastopol on the Crimean peninsula, hence the name of the war. For the first time, London and Paris directed the war by telegraphed instructions. Piedmont-Sardinia's chief minister **Camillo di Cavour** (Prime Minister 1852–1861) brought that nation into the war on the side of Britain and France so that it could vent its grievances at a peace conference and win possible allies for the future. For the first time, Austria took a stand against Russia in the Balkans. The clever Schwarzenberg had died, and it has never been clear what Austria thought it would gain with this maneuver. Considering its growing problems with national groups, the last thing Austria needed was more non-German people. This move was of huge significance: it foreshadowed the Austro-Russian rivalry over the Ottomans' carcass. The Russians saw it as a deep betrayal: they had saved the Austrian empire in 1849 and 1850. Some said it hastened the death of Russian Emperor Nicholas I. Sevastopol finally fell. About 500,000 soldiers died, evenly divided between the two sides. Most died from disease and not enemy fire.

The Peace of Paris 1856

The Allies finally took Sevastopol, and the Russians agreed to peace talks. The terms 1) put Romania under international control; 2) affirmed the total independence of the Ottoman Empire and denied any Russian protectorate over the Greek Orthodox; 3) forced Russia to give up a little territory and cede the mouths of the Danube River to Turkey; 4) forced all to accept the authority of international commissions on navigation rights in the Straits; 5) neutralized the Black Sea and forbade warships from entering the Straits and naval bases on the Sea. These terms were against Russia, weakened the Russian fleet, and took away Russian territory.

The Future of the Concert

The attempts to put the Prussian army on a war footing had shown the woeful inadequacies of its forces. Prussia would soon call for military reform and modernization. Russia was unhappy and particularly angry at Austria. It plotted to regain its military rights in the Black Sea. Many doubted the ability of the British forces. The British grumbled that France had tricked them and retreated into isolation. Russia was shocked at its poor performance and would start to transform its economy and society. By contrast, Napoleon III came out as impressive.

The Polish Revolt of 1863 and the Alvensleben Convention

Polish unrest had grown from 1860 to 1862, and a full-scale revolt against Russia broke out in January 1863. Prussia and Russia then signed the Alvensleben Convention to suppress the revolt. Prussia agreed to return any fugitive rebels to Russia for harsh punishment. The significance was that Russia, angry at Austria for Crimean betrayal, was moving toward Prussia. Russia had backed up Austria in the 1849–1850 war of words over the Erfurt Union and could have blocked German unification.

The Last Congress of the Concert

Napoleon III tried to convene the great powers at Paris at the end of 1863 to bring a solution to the problems in Poland, Germany, the Balkans, Denmark, and Italy. He unveiled an ambitious program of compensation, but the British refused to go along. The Congress, and the Concert of Europe, fell through. The Crimean War opened a series of wars among the great powers that redrew the map of Europe and changed the balance of power. Metternich's Concert of Europe had kept the peace from 1815 to 1854, the longest period of peace in European history up to that point.

THE UNIFICATION OF ITALY

Piedmont-Sardinia and Cavour

After his disastrous showing against Austria, Charles Albert was forced to abdicate in favor of his son **Victor Emmanuel II** (ruled 1849–78). The new king shared his father's ambition of a united Italy dominated by Sardinia. His Chief Minister Cavour agreed. 1848 had proved that Sardinia could not take on Austria by itself. It needed a great power. Cavour began to woo possible allies. He carried out a number of liberal economic reforms to impress the liberal powers Britain and France, then he elbowed his way into the Crimean War on their side to win respect. Cavour was driven by the fear that Mazzini and Garibaldi were still out there in exile and determined to unite Italy as a republic.

The Plombières Agreement

On July 20, 1858, Cavour met with Napoleon III at Plombières les Bains, a French spa. The European elite men of the nineteenth were always going to rest at spas, and no one would be suspicious when they "accidentally" ran into one another. They agreed that if Sardinia and Austria went to war, France would support Sardinia. If Sardinia won, it would get Lombardy, Venetia, Parma, Modena and part of the papal states. An Italian confederation under the Pope would be set up. France would get Nice and Savoy, two Italian provinces sought by France for two hundred years. Napoleon III then secured Russian noninterference by promising to seek a revision of the 1856 peace treaty. The illness of King Frederick William IV and political uncertainty sidelined Prussia. The British were in the middle of an election campaign and then spent two months trying to put together a coalition government.

The War of 1859 and the Armistice of Villafranca

Austria quickly blundered into war. Sardinia had called for volunteer soldiers, and many who answered were draft dodgers from Lombardy. Austria used this as an excuse to attack Sardinia, not realizing the danger. In June of 1859, the French defeated Austria at the bloody **Battles of Magenta and Solferino**. The Austrians (as in 1848) fell back to their formidable "Quadrilateral" bases. Napoleon III concluded a ceasefire at Villafranca because he feared the ambitions of Sardinia and did not want to challenge Austria's powerful fortresses. Sardinia gained Lombardy, but Austria still held Venetia. Cavour regarded the agreement as a double-cross. Uprisings in Tuscany, Modena, the Romagna, and Parma led to calls for direct union with Piedmont-Sardinia. Napoleon III got Nice and Savoy, as Plombières had mandated.

Garibaldi's Conquest of Naples

Even though he had wanted a republic and not a monarchy, Giuseppe Garibaldi returned from exile to help the Sardinians in the war against Austria. After the peace, Cavour secretly prepared Garibaldi for an expedition to Sicily. The king of the Two Sicilies had just crushed a nationalist uprising and the prospects for success seemed low. Garibaldi landed in Sicily with a thousand red-shirted guerrillas. Sicily rose in June and July 1860, and Garibaldi won control as his force grew to 57,000. Naples fell in September. Cavour feared renewed republicanism and ordered Sardinian troops into the Papal States. This left the Pope with a small state protected by Napoleon III's troops. Perhaps following the example of José de San Martin, Garibaldi turned over his conquests to Sardinia rather than fight for an Italian Republic. In February 1861 an Italian Parliament gathered in Florence and declared Victor Emmanuel II King of Italy. Only Venetia (still under Austrian control) and the small Papal State around Rome were left out of the new kingdom.

The Completion of Italian Unity

Piedmont did not treat the rest of Italy, especially southern Italy and Sicily, well. It stamped out local customs and law codes and forced northern Italian dialects on them. There was great resentment in the south against the wealth and power of the north. It gained Venetia in 1866 when Italy allied with Prussia against Austria in the wars of German unification. Austria crushed the Italian armies in the fighting but when Prussia won, so did Italy.

Napoleon III reluctantly continued to protect Rome so as to make French Catholics happy. Garibaldi tried twice to take Rome but failed. When the Franco-Prussian war broke out in 1870, Napoleon III pulled the troops out, and the Italians moved in. Pope Pius IX refused to recognize new government and barricaded himself in his palace. His successors continued this policy until 1929. The Church moved in a very reactionary direction: the Pope issued the *Syllabus of Errors* in 1864 that condemned all modern movements. He also called the first church council in over three hundred years, which became known as the First

Vatican Council (or **Vatican I** for short). Controversially, and perhaps contrary to Church Law, the Council put through the **Doctrine of Papal Infallibility** stating that when the Pope speaks officially in matters of faith and dogma, God is speaking through him and thus cannot be in error. Since this doctrine was proclaimed in 1870, the Pope has only invoked this three times.

EUROPEAN INTELLECTUAL TRENDS 1850–1900

The diplomacy of Cavour and Napoleon III during the Italian unification was typical of *Realpolitik*, the politics of realism. You do whatever must be done to get your goal. If you have to lie, cheat, break promises and treaties, cause death, then so be it. The end of Romanticism with the failure of the revolutions of 1848 had opened a general age of realism.

The Rise of Realism

In European literature, realism supplanted romanticism. Prose became more important than poetry. The social function of a realistic novel was to analyze society and criticize; it replaced printed sermons for the humanitarian public. In 1852, both **Charles Dickens'** (1812–70) *Bleak House* and **Harriet Beecher Stowe's** (1811–96) *Uncle Tom's Cabin* appeared, focusing attention on miserable living conditions in London and slavery in the United States. Older writers such as Victor Hugo (1802–85) adopted the new style for *Les Misérables* (1862). The writings of Karl Marx persuaded Heinrich Heine (1797–1856) to abandon the sufferings of passionate lovers and look to the suffering of the oppressed. Ivan Turgenev (1818–83) wrote *Sportsman's Sketches* to focus attention on the problem of Russian serfdom. Later in *Fathers and Sons* (1861) he looked at the philosophy of nihilism. Realism flourished in England (George Eliot, Thomas Hardy, Elizabeth Gaskell, Anthony Trollope), France (Emile Zola, Honoré de Balzac, Gustav Flaubert), Russia (Leo Tolstoy, influenced by Turgenev), Sweden (Frederika Bremer), United States (Theodore Dreiser). Writer after writer focused on the evils of factories and law courts, the problem of legal equality for women, the inhumanity of war, and a vision of future society.

The development of a reading public beyond the upper middle classes spurred much of this. For many in the middle class who were educated but not cultivated, culture was just another material item for them to consume. The word "realism" was applied to **Gustave Courbet** (1819–77)'s painting in 1850 in France and spread from there. The *Westminster Review* used it to describe

Bremer's work in 1856; then Eliot's *Scenes of Clerical Life* (1857); in German to describe Gustav Freytag's *Soll und Haben* (1855). Flaubert's *Madame Bovary* (1855) seemed to crystallize the entire movement. Love was conspicuous by its absence. Realism moved to drama with Alexandre Dumas' (fils) (1824–95) *La Dame aux Camélias* (1852); he was the son of the romantic author of *The Three Musketeers*. Stage scenery became realistic. Writers knew each other, scientists, and political figures. Tolstoy's experience in the Crimean War and his reading of Proudhon moved him to write *War and Peace* (1865–69).

At this time, popular literature was not far divorced from great literature, a situation not seen before or since. Press circulation boomed. England had abolished duties on paper in the late 1850s. The steam-driven rotary press and popularizing editorial policies drew readers. *Lloyd's Weekly* appealed to artisans and tradesmen and sold 350,000 copies a week in 1863. Serialization of stories broke down barriers among newspapers, magazines, and books. Wider circulation attracted advertisers and stimulated new forms of business. The department stores first opened in Paris during the time of Napoleon III. A treaty on copyright law between England and France in 1851 increased the security of authors. Books grew cheaper in Western Europe, and libraries became less necessary. A merger of literature with science led to **science fiction**, starting with **Jules Verne** (1828–1905) who wrote *5 Weeks in a Balloon* (1863), *A Journey to the Center of the Earth* (1864), *From the Earth to the Moon* (1865), and *Twenty Thousand Leagues under the Sea* (1870).

Realistic Art

Courbet and Manet

Courbet was the son of a peasant. He learned by copying art at the Louvre Museum. He wanted to focus on common people and used thick daubs of paint to create a rough and crude surface. Said Courbet:

> *The art of painting can consist only in the representation of objects visible and tangible to the painter. I also hold that painting is an essentially concrete art, and can consist only of the representation of things both real and existing... An abstract object, invisible or nonexistent, does not belong in the realm of painting. Show me an angel and I'll paint one.*

When critics called this socialistic he became a political radical. Romantic and classical schools attacked and viciously satirized him. Aside from Courbet, other realists were kept out of high art. Classical themes continued to predominate. The radical artistic protest against exclusion grew so loud that Napoleon III set up a special *Salon des Refusés* where their art could be displayed. **Eduard Manet's** (1832–83) art had scandalized the public by showing off nude women while men were in modern garb. Manet used a new kind of technique inspired by flash photography: a harsh light as if a flashbulb had just gone off. Manet's art was more impersonal; its focus was on paint, light and theme. It dispensed with the idea of painting as a "window."

Impressionism

Claude Monet (1840–1926) followed Manet and introduced a new style by juxtaposing small dabs of contrasting pigments to create new colors and greater contrasts. He did not need black to paint shadows. Monet displayed an extremely sophisticated use of light and darkness. **Edgar Degas** (1834–1917) became a recruit to impressionism in 1866. **Auguste Rodin** (1840–1917) displayed his realistic "Man with a Broken Nose" in 1864. After 1867, the word Impressionist came to be used to describe this school. Its duty was to the truth: horses were of stables, not battlefields; women were laundresses, ballet-dancers, and prostitutes, not nymphs and goddesses. It featured more outdoor landscapes and made better use of light. Complementary colors used side-by-side in large enough areas intensify one another. In small quantities, they mix. More use of primary colors (red, blue, yellow) next to each other created the desired effect.

Karl Marx (1818–83) and Marxism

Background

Marx was born in the Prussian Rhineland. He attended the University of Berlin in the late 1830s and early 1840s when Hegel's thought was still dominant. There he picked up Hegel's Dialectic: Thesis meets Antithesis to form Synthesis, which meets a new Antithesis to form a new Synthesis, and so on. This was a form of evolutionary theory used in philosophy from the time of Plato and the ancient Greek philosophers more than two thousand years ago. Hegel saw it as leading to higher forms of reason and freedom and suggested that everything is predetermined.

Marx combined Hegel's dialectic with the classical liberal economics of Ricardo and his Iron Law of Wages along with earlier socialist writers. He scorned these earlier socialists such as Saint-Simon, Owen, and Blanc as "Utopian" socialists who believed that socialism could come by gradual change. Marx claimed he was putting socialism on a realistic and scientific basis and that the ruling class would never surrender anything important. A violent revolution was the only thing that would lead to **communism**, which Marx said was true socialism.

Marx saw the dialectic as leading to successively higher economic stages. Everything, including art, science, religion, law and the state, is just a superstructure resting on the mode of production and who controls the means of production. Previously, the means of production had been used to work the land, and feudal lords controlled the land. Now the "feudal" stage is passing, overthrown by the "bourgeoisie" that controls the means of production in factories as the Industrial Revolution spreads. This synthesis is the capitalist stage. When the capitalist stage is complete, there will be only the bourgeoisie and the proletariat (workers). The struggle between classes is the engine that drives history.

Capitalism and Revolution

The first major work was the *Communist Manifesto* published in 1848 by Marx and **Frederick Engels** (1820–95). Marx expanded on his views in *Das Kapital* (1867). Engels had already written on the wretched conditions of the English working class. Capitalism exploits workers and does not pay them full value so that the rest of their labor's value becomes the capitalist's profit (Proudhon had first made this point). Only the accumulation of profit made technological and industrial progress possible. This progress throws people out of work. Competition among capitalists drives the weakest ones out and concentrates capital in even fewer hands showing up in monopolies. Marx sharply disagreed with Smith, who felt that productivity drove economic growth and progress and ultimately created jobs. Marx said that capitalism is marked by recessions caused by overproduction to increase profits or to lessen buying power of workers. These recessions cause misery when more people are thrown out of work. Eventually, this will lead to the socialist revolution with a fairer system of distribution. After the revolution will be a period of transition. The capitalists will try to recover their power, and there will have to be a "dictatorship of the proletariat" until the last elements of coercive power, all social classes, and the state itself withered away. Marx was vague on the form of government although it seemed close to Rousseau's ideas of consensus and the General Will.

Marx made a number of key errors. He was totally wrong about progress throwing people out of work permanently. Smith has had the better of the argument as productivity gains have meant enough wealth and employment to support more than six billion people on earth. Marx knew nothing of prehistory or ancient history and little of medieval history, though he tried to construct a grand theory based on history.

Promoting socialism

In 1864, the International Workingmen's Association (also known as the **First International**) was founded to promote labor unions and socialist politics. Marx fought a battle for leadership with the more liberal Mazzini. Marx fell into a bitter dispute with the Russian exile **Mikhail Bakunin** (1814–76), the father of modern anarchism. Bakunin believed in causing chaos with mass assassinations carried out by a conspiratorial revolutionary elite. He opposed Marx's centralization and believed that the state was "the most flagrant, most cynical, and most complete denial of humanity." Bakunin set up a secret society in 1866 to work for conspiracies. While Marx had said that a violent revolution was necessary, the authorities would outlaw the International if it organized violence. The expulsion of Bakunin led to the collapse of the International in 1872. In 1889 labor and socialist leaders from around the world set up a **Second International**. By the 1890s, socialist parties were concentrating more on winning elections, moderating policies, and abandoning revolutionary rhetoric.

Charles Darwin (1809–82)

The idea of evolution went far back but was popularized during the Enlightenment. Jean Baptiste Lamarck (1744–1829) suggested that adjustments to the environment and heredity of acquired traits are factors of biological development. The Transportation Revolution's digging of canals, roads, and railroads exposed layers of earth and rock to the light of day. **Charles Lyell's** (1797–1875) *Principles of Geology* (1830–33) showed that the layers of rock told the history of the earth: he found marine animals at the top of high mountains and animals that no longer existed. Lyell proposed that the earth is very old and has gradually developed over time with small changes. What has happened before is still happening today. Another early geologist, Louis Agassiz (1807–73), studied glacial remains and fossil fishes.

Darwin was born in 1809 and traveled around the world in the 1830s with Lyell's book while observing species. He also drew conclusions from the fossils revealed by railroad, canal, and port construction. His data on selective breeding came from modern agriculture. He seems to have formed his ideas by the middle 1840s, but withheld from publishing for a long time because he knew they would be controversial. By the late 1850s, other scientists were coming to the same conclusions, and in 1859 Darwin published *The Origin of Species*. Darwin's original contribution was to provide a mechanism for evolution: 1) more of a species are born than can survive, causing fierce competition (Malthus); 2) the differences or variations within a species make some better suited to survive in a particular environment than others; 3) those best suited survive and thus strengthen the species. Dispute soon grew as to whether Darwin implied that human beings were also the results of evolution. In 1871, Darwin settled the issue by publishing *The Descent of Man*: human beings are descended from the same common ancestor as apes such as gorillas, chimps, and orangutans. This brought Darwin in conflict especially with fundamentalist Christians who believed that the Bible said humanity started with Adam and Eve. Many others were uncomfortable because Darwin's work implied that there was no progress or direction to the existence of humanity. Random chance and constant struggle determined the course of the world. After 1900, biologists learned of the work of **Gregor Mendel** and the study of genetics began.

Richard Wagner (1813–83)

Opera was profitable and accessible to most social classes and could have considerable influence. The German composer Wagner enjoyed his first big success with *The Flying Dutchman* (1843). He participated in the revolutions of 1849 in Saxony joining Bakunin on the barricades. His career culminated in the massive *Ring of the Nibelung* (1864–76): four operas totaling fifteen-and-a-half hours combining music and drama. Wagner's goal was "a complete work of art" where the music tells as much of the story as the words with the use of many themes. The last part *Götterdämmerung* (*Twilight of the Gods*) ends with the destruction of the world in a fiery Bakuninesque fashion. Wagner was an ardent German nationalist but was disappointed by Prussia's unification of Germany to the point of where he talked of emigrating to the United States.

While certainly a romantic, Wagner differed considerably from previous generation of German romantics. His heroes achieved redemption through Christian love and death. Unlike Goethe's Werther, death was not a tragedy but a way to self-fulfillment. In the modern world, materialistic man has lost his soul and must reject his inner desires and outward riches. Those with power and riches were forever deprived of love. Wagner focused on great leaders and individuals: the Dutchman, Lohengrin, Tannhäuser, Siegfried, Brunhilde, Parsifal, Tristan and Isolde.

Wagner was anti-Semitic, yet some of his greatest patrons were Jews and his views were not very out of line with general European anti-Semitism of the nineteenth century shared by most of the upper classes. The works of Dickens and Trollope are full of casual smears and caricatures of Jews. Wagner was socialistically inclined, and certainly Hitler resembled no character as much as Alberich, the evil dwarf in *The Ring*.

Other Music

The other major figure was **Giuseppe Verdi** (1813–1901). An ardent Italian nationalist, Verdi first came to fame in 1840s with nationalist operas that enraged the Austrian authorities in Venice and Milan. He fled after the failure of the revolutions of 1848 and was better received in Paris than Wagner. Verdi greatly admired Shakespeare and based three operas on Shakespeare's plays. For many in high society, the music of Wagner and Verdi was too heavy. Much lighter classical composers dominated attention and performers playing older classics to large audiences. People would take sheet music home; the piano factory was a standard by the 1860s with 73,000 pianos produced in 1884 in Germany.

The Inheritors: Nietzsche and Spencer

Wagner and Nietzsche

One man most excited by Wagner's portrayal of heroic individuals was **Friedrich Nietzsche** (1844–1900), a German who published influential books in the middle 1880s after Wagner's death. He believed that a group of "supermen" would lead the world away from the "slave morality" of Christianity to a heroic morality that affirmed life and life values. The Superman represents highest creativity and passion and would live at a level of experience beyond good and evil. His creative "will to power" would set him off from rest of humanity. Because he was most fit in the Darwinian way, he would survive. Nietzsche was often accused of paving the way for Nazis (Hitler as superman, the Nazis as a race of supermen) but he backed individualism and despised the state, especially the German state. He explicitly criticized racism and anti-Semitism. His sister edited some of his later works and inserted racist ideas.

Social Darwinism

The Briton **Herbert Spencer** (1820–1903) helped formulate Social Darwinism, a perversion of Darwin's theories, and coined the phrase "survival of the fittest." Spencer opposed state intervention for poor because it just helped the unfit continue their inferior genes. He opposed all restraints on business. Spencer believed that once all the weak were eliminated and the survival of the species was assured, humans could band together and cooperation would replace conflict.

Spencer and others tied Darwin's ideas to ideas that one or several races are superior. They justified western imperialism in the late nineteenth century by saying that the white race was biologically superior to the darker races and thus deserved to rule. Others would say that the rich are biologically superior and should not be deprived of their wealth. A movement called **eugenics** developed to "improve" the human race. On the one hand, it encouraged the "best" to have children. It also frowned on sexual relations between races. Worst of all, it tried to identify those as "racially inferior" and prevent them from having children by locking them up or sterilizing them against their will. Many European countries and states of the United States had eugenic laws by the 1920s. Racist misinterpretations of Darwin and Nietzsche glorifying a superman leader and superrace would shape Fascist ideology in the 1920s and 1930s.

THE UNIFICATION OF GERMANY

The Industrial Revolution had spread to western Germany after 1850. Prussia had established a customs union in 1834 to make trade easier in parts of the German Confederation, although Austria refused to join. Vast iron and coal reserves existed in the valleys of the Rhine and Ruhr rivers. By 1860, the German customs union had become the second-largest coal producer, far behind Britain. Big private banks were founded and provided capital for new businesses. Many of these businesses were established by liberals, a few of whom had been leaders in the 1848 revolution and retained their nationalism.

The Constitutional Conflict

The significance of the economic shift became clear in the Prussian elections of December 1858. Frederick William IV had suffered a series of strokes and gradually went insane. His younger brother **William I** (ruled 1861–88) became regent and then king in 1861. The peculiar Prussian electoral system from the Constitution of 1850 gave great power to the rich. Frederick William and his advisers had assumed that the richest men in Prussia would always be the great landowners, especially those who lived east of the Elbe River. This was little more than absolutism with a mask. But by 1858, the richest men were liberal industrialists. The liberals won about 210 of about 300 seats in the Prussian

House of Representatives. They were cautious, and the few reforms they passed were easily voted down by the Prussian House of Lords.

Frederick William's mobilization of the Prussian Army during the Crimean War had been disastrous, and preparedness during the Italian War of 1859 was hardly better. Clearly, there was a need to reform the armed forces. In February 1860, William proposed a bill that would 1) double the size of the regular army; 2) lengthen the term of service to three years, followed by reserve service for another four to five years; 3) diminish the role of the independent civilian militia; and 4) increase the military budget by 25 percent.

The House of Representatives tried to reduce the level of military increase, but William misused the money and claimed total control over the army's organization. The left wing of the liberals now formed an American-style political party called the **Progressive Party**. In the elections of 1861, the Progressives won more than a hundred seats, the moderate liberals had about 150 seats, and the conservatives had been virtually swept out of the House of Representatives. The House refused to grant any money for the military unless William conceded. William called for early elections in 1862, but the Progressives gained even more seats. The conservatives clamored for William to repeal the constitution but he knew that this could cause a great uproar. He even contemplated abdicating in favor of his more liberal son Frederick.

Bismarck Comes to Power

Otto von Bismarck was born in 1815 in the East Elbian lands of Prussia. He came to prominence in 1848 as a bitter opponent of revolution in Prussia and the Frankfurt Parliament. Unlike most conservatives, he was a German nationalist. William called him in as a hard liner and his last hope. Bismarck considered how to outmaneuver the liberals. He had a series of secret conversations with German socialist leader Ferdinand Lassalle, a moderate who had disagreed with Marx. Bismarck thought that perhaps he could win over factory workers and miners to an alliance with conservatives against the factory-owning liberals. They reached no agreement, and Lassalle died in a duel in 1864. Bismarck formulated a theory of a "constitutional gap": government employees collect and spend money and can theoretically do it without legislative approval if so ordered. Bismarck appropriated the money to the military as the king wished. He could maintain this policy as long as economic times remained good, and he did not have to ask the parliament to raise new taxes. Bismarck looked to war and foreign affairs to break the deadlock.

What could the Progressives have done? They could have tried calling a tax strike, but that probably would have failed. They feared the rise of the radicals from 1848 who in their view had destroyed the revolution. They made no attempt to organize the people or call for universal voting rights. Out of 17 million people in Prussia, only 340,000 (2%) voted. That was not sufficient to claim a mandate. They were happy with the three-class franchise system.

The Danish and Austrian Wars

Schleswig and Holstein

Lord Palmerston, the British Prime Minister, once said there were only three men in all Europe who understood the complexities of the Schleswig-Holstein question: one was dead, one went mad, and Palmerston himself was the third but had forgotten all the details. The province of Holstein was almost entirely German, so a representative of the king of Denmark sat in the German Confederation. Schleswig was two-thirds German but not in the Confederation. In November 1863, Denmark put out a new constitution that took full control of Schleswig contrary to treaties it had signed. Prussia and Austria declared war on Denmark and crushed the small country in a short war. Austria wanted a separate independent state because it was too far from Vienna to control. Bismarck instead got Austria to agree to the Convention of Gastein (August 1865): Austria received Holstein, and Prussia took Schleswig. Bismarck had lured Austria into a trap.

Bismarck met Napoleon III at Biarritz in October 1865 and hinted at concessions to France in the Rhineland and maybe Luxemburg. In April 1866, Prussia made an alliance with Italy against Austria. Bismarck appeased liberals by calling for a democratic reform of the German Confederation and election by all men. Bismarck always championed universal manhood suffrage because he saw that as things stood, the liberal middle class could outvote the conservative elite. If conservative peasants and artisans and the petty bourgeoisie were given equal voting rights, they would overwhelm the liberals. He saw how Napoleon III had used universal manhood suffrage to bolster his power. Bismarck's miscalculation was that he did not see the rising numbers of socialist industrial workers. Austria also gained Napoleon III's neutrality. Napoleon III hoped that Austria and Prussia would wear each other out in a long war, and he would be stronger as a mediator. The smaller states tended to support Austria because they feared Prussia more, but they could contribute little to the struggle.

The Seven Weeks' War

The war went badly for Austria. Its military staff was behind the times. The Prussian breech-loaded "needle gun" could fire five to seven rounds a minute with the solider lying down, while the Austrians could only shoot three to five rounds a minute and had to stand exposed. Because Austria had not built enough railroads, it could not move its troops fast enough to face the Prussians. At the **Battle of Königgrätz** (July 3, 1866), Austria lost badly on the same day that Prussian conservatives gained almost half the seats in the House of Representatives. Half a million fought in this battle and one-quarter were killed or wounded, a warning of the growing bloodiness of modern warfare.

Bismarck wanted a quick peace and lenient terms before Napoleon III could stick his nose in the situation. The **Peace of Prague** (August 1866) separated Austria from the rest of Germany and gave Venetia to Italy. The rest of the German Confederation suffered more. Prussia annexed some territories such as Hanover entirely. William felt badly about taking Hanover from a king who was blind and whose family's nobility was older than William's Hohenzollern family. The Confederation itself came to an end. Bismarck oversaw the creation of the **North German Confederation**: the twenty-two states north of Main River joined together under Prussian pressure. The president of this confederation would always be the king of Prussia. It had a bicameral legislature: the Reichstag elected by universal manhood suffrage had budget powers and the right to approve or disapprove all laws but could not initiate laws. The Upper House (the Federal Council) was appointed by princes and effectively controlled by Prussia. It could veto laws and had to approve amendments. The king would pick the ministers, and they were not responsible to Reichstag control.

Effect on Austria

After the 1859 defeat in Italy, Austria had considered reforms. When Austria's domination of Germany ended once and for all on the field of Königgrätz, it needed to make peace with the Hungarians and set up a "Dual Monarchy" in the *Ausgleich* (Compromise) of 1867. There would be one imperial and royal army and joint responsibility for foreign policy, military affairs, and financial matters. Each half (Austria and Hungary) would have its own parliament and control over domestic affairs with its own cabinet of ministers. While this finally liberated the Hungarians, it was worse for the smaller nationalities, who now were caught under two layers of government and began to agitate for independence.

Effect on Prussia

If 1848 was one "turning point that failed to turn," 1862 to 1866 was another as Bismarck foiled the liberals. The Progressives split in October 1866 as the moderates joined others to form the National Liberal Party which became Bismarck's main support until 1879. They joined the conservatives in retroactively approving the illegal budgets that Bismarck had used from 1862 to 1866. The remaining Progressives still opposed Bismarck. The middle class, rather than asserting its own values as it did in other countries, instead sought to imitate the great aristocrats. Democracy was stunted. Bismarck's strategy was proved when elections were held under the new laws in 1867. The Progressives won only nineteen of 297 seats in the Reichstag.

Problems of Unification

The three southern German states (Bavaria, Württemburg, and Baden) refused to join the North German Confederation. Bismarck had to create a situation where the other states would willingly ally with the Confederation against another threatening power. Napoleon III had been disappointed by the 1866 result and sought compensation if Germany united because he realized that the new power would be a colossus. He sought Luxemburg, Belgium, or parts of the Rhineland. This came to nothing. The Austrians were still weak, and Hungary would not support a new war. Italy declined a French alliance. Bismarck kept Russia neutral by promising help in the growing disputes in southeastern Europe and in revising the 1856 Peace of Paris.

The Franco-Prussian War

As late as May of 1870, a French plebiscite gave Napoleon III 83 percent approval as he completed the transformation of the French Empire into a constitutional monarchy. Bismarck decided it was time to move. Spain had been suffering unrest since the 1820s, and there was a feeling that it should start over with a new king. Spanish leaders offered the Spanish throne to William I's Catholic cousin, much to France's alarm as it feared encirclement. At spa of Ems, the French ambassador Benedetti spoke with the vacationing William I and got him to drop the plan. But in Berlin, Bismarck edited the text of king's telegram (**Ems Dispatch**) to make the words look much harsher and make it appear that William had insulted Benedetti. France declared war on Prussia on July 19, 1870.

The southern German states joined the Confederation troops, giving Germany a two-to-one advantage in troops with better supplies and better administration. The Germans captured Napoleon III and an army of 100,000 at Sedan. When the news reached Paris, revolutionaries overthrew the government and proclaimed a republic. The new leaders called on the people to resist the Germans. After a long siege, the Germans took Paris. France lost 580,000 killed, wounded, or taken prisoner. Bismarck demanded and got elections which resulted in the monarchist Adolphe Thiers as President.

The German princes gathered outside of Paris at the old palace of Versailles and proclaimed William I as first emperor of Germany. In another show of *Realpolitik*, Bismarck bribed the king of Bavaria so he would go along. The Empire's constitution was just the North German Confederation's constitution extended to more states. Bismarck became the Chancellor of the Empire. The **Treaty of Frankfurt** (May 1871) was a very harsh peace because unlike Austria, France would be irreconcilable, and Bismarck wanted to keep it down. Under the Treaty, Germany took the rich provinces of Alsace and Lorraine from France along with 5 billion francs of indemnity. There would be a German army of occupation until France paid. Bismarck figured it would take the French many years to pay this off. Russia got the straits clause of 1856 nullified so it could finally send its warships through the Bosporus and Dardanelles.

NATION-STATE BUILDING IN NORTH AMERICA

Civil War in the United States

Coming out of the Revolution, the United States had split along lines drawn during the mercantilist era by the British: the northern states depended on trade and manufacturing, while the southern states focused on growing slave-dependent cash crops such as cotton and tobacco. The invention of the cotton 'gin caused a great expansion of slavery across the South in cotton plantations. The abolition of slavery by Mexico caused a revolt by the Texas slaveholders, who first won independence from Mexico in 1836 and then joined the United States in 1845. The South kept a balance in the Senate through the 1840s: for each free state admitted, a slave state was admitted. The South was overrepresented in the House of Representatives, because the Constitution considered each slave to be three-fifths of a human being though the states did not permit slaves to vote. For the same reason, the south dominated presidential elections. Every president elected before 1860 was from a slave state or supported slavery.

By 1850, slavery was in trouble. The North grew harsher in condemning slavery as it began to build industry and immigrants swelled northern numbers. In 1853, the New York to Chicago railroad opened, shifting trade away from the Mississippi River. The newer states were not well suited to cotton farming: the South had taken what it could. A battle over free trade grew as the new northern factories wanted protection from British industry with high tariffs while the south feared a retaliatory tariff against cotton and other products.

In the **Mexican War** (1846–48), the U.S. defeated Mexico and took the area of California, Nevada, Arizona, New Mexico, and part of Colorado. Unexpectedly, gold was discovered in California and hundreds of thousands of "Forty-Niners" swarmed in hoping to get rich quick. It became apparent that the population was large enough for California to apply for statehood. Outnumbered at the polls, the slaveowners unleashed murder and terror to try to win their way, but the majority of Californians banned slavery in their state. The bitter fight shifted to Congress. California came in as the sixteenth free state, breaking the balance with the slave states, but the **Compromise of 1850** gave southern slaveowners greater rights in tracking down runaway slaves. Fighting broke out over whether Kansas would be a free or slave state. The Republican Party was founded as an anti-slavery party. The Supreme Court failed to resolve things by issuing a pro-slavery ruling in the **Dred Scott Case** (1857) and lost credibility. In the 1860 presidential election, the Democrats split and nominated northern and southern candidates. The Republicans nominated **Abraham Lincoln** (President 1861–65) on a platform of no extension of slavery.

The South realized that if Lincoln were elected, more free states would be admitted, and the North would become stronger and stronger. The southern states had promoted the theory that individual states made up the union in 1787 and could leave when they wanted. When Lincoln won, South Carolina seceded from Union, followed by ten other slave states. They proclaimed the **Confederate States of America** (C.S.A.) that asserted in its constitution that slavery was a basic right.

In those days, there was a five-month lag between the election and the inauguration. This gap allowed the C.S.A. to seize most federal armories. When South Carolina bombarded one of few forts that had not surrendered in April 1861, Lincoln called for volunteers and the **Civil War** was on. The North had 23 million people against 5 million whites in the Confederacy. The North had better industry and finance. The North blockaded the Confederacy so cotton could not get out. The North made little progress in the first year. Lincoln decided that the soldiers needed a moral cause to fight for; the abstract of preserving the Union was not enough. Lincoln issued the **Emancipation Proclamation** (1863) setting slaves free without compensation to the owners. After four bloody years of fighting, the North wore down the South and defeated it at a total cost of 600,000 killed and 400,000 wounded on both sides.

While the South was out, the Congress outlawed slavery in the **Thirteenth Amendment** to the Constitution. Congress passed tariffs to protect new industries up to 47 percent of the value of manufactured goods and encouraged settlement of West in the **Homestead Act**. It granted land at 30,000 acres per member of Congress to support state agricultural colleges. It subsidized a transcontinental railroad, which was completed in 1869. In 1867 Russia sold Alaska to the U.S. for $7.2 million. The Fourteenth Amendment added American citizenship to state citizenship and defined it. The U.S. emerged as a solid nation-state that was industrializing rapidly.

The Dominion of Canada

70,000 loyalists had left the United States after the Revolution, more than the total of émigrés who left France permanently in the 1790s. Half were granted land in Nova Scotia, about ten to twelve thousand settled in Québec. The Constitutional Act (1791) granted a House of Assembly to be elected in Upper and Lower Canada every four years; it was supposed to govern its own taxation so there would be no complaint of "no taxation without representation." An 1837 political rebellion by Ontario and Québec against Britain led to the governor's recommendation in 1839 that Canada be granted more rights as one nation with Britain keeping only foreign policy, trade, and land distribution rights. The 1840 **Act of Union** forced the two Canadas together but did not reform the system. The Governor would name the executive council and legislative council and ignore the elected Assembly.

In 1848, as revolution swept Europe, the governor allowed reformers to form a cabinet that had a majority of the Assembly supporting it. In 1849 Britain abolished the mercantilist Navigation Laws that had restricted Canadian trade. In the 1850s telegraphs and railroads began to link the Maritime Provinces to the Canadas. In the 1850s and 1860s British North Americans adopted a decimal currency in place of the British system. The Crimean War stimulated the Canadian grain industry as Britain was cut off from the Russian supply. The American Civil War meant even more demand for Canadian goods.

The 1860s saw sectional differences accelerating. Railroads had created enormous public debts with little tax revenue. This revived the earlier suggestion of a union. Ambitious politicians supported the idea. The British government, withdrawing into isolation, saw colonies as needless financial drags. The U.S. Civil War also raised issues of defense because Lincoln had created a massive army of 2.2 million. What if the U.S. next invaded Canada, as some American officials were urging? Britain had neither the soldiers nor the money to defend Canada. It put heavy pressure on the colonies to accept union.

The 1867 **British North American Act** established the Dominion of Canada, which would have elected provincial assemblies and a national parliament with an appointed Senate giving Ontario, Québec, and the Maritimes equal representation. The Hudson's Bay Company turned over its western lands in 1869. A Canadian Pacific Railway linked the Atlantic to the Pacific in 1885. This was the first peaceful granting of liberty to a colony.

TIMELINE

1846–48	U.S.-Mexican War
1848	Marx and Engels, *Communist Manifesto*
1850	California admitted to the United States
1852	Dickens, *Bleak House*
1854–56	Crimean War
1859	France and Sardinia defeat Austria
	Darwin, *Origin of Species*
1859–67	Constitutional crisis in Prussia
1860	Garibaldi takes southern Italy
	Lincoln elected President
1861	Kingdom of Italy proclaimed
1861–65	U.S. Civil War
1862	Bismarck becomes Prime Minister of Prussia
1864	Austria and Prussia defeat Denmark and take Schleswig and Holstein
	Wagner, *Das Rheingold*
1866	Prussia and Italy at war against Austria and most of the German Confederation
	Prussia gains Schleswig, Italy takes Venetia
1867	British North American Act creates Dominion of Canada
	Compromise reforms Austro-Hungarian Empire
	Marx, volume 1 of *Das Kapital*
1870–71	Franco-Prussian War
	Italy takes over Rome
1871	German Empire proclaimed
	Darwin, *The Descent of Man*
1872	First International collapses
1883	Death of Marx

KEY TERMS

The Crimean War
Louis-Napoleon Bonaparte (Napoleon III)
Camillo di Cavour
Giuseppe Garibaldi
Karl Marx
Charles Darwin
Charles Lyell
Richard Wagner
Friedrich Nietzsche
Herbert Spencer
Otto von Bismarck
Treaty of Frankfurt
Abraham Lincoln
Emancipation Proclamation

PRIMARY SOURCE DOCUMENTS

Charles Dickens, http://www.mtholyoke.edu/acad/intrel/hardtime.htm
Charles Darwin, http://history.hanover.edu/courses/excerpts/111dar.html
Herbert Spencer, http://www.fordham.edu/halsall/mod/spencer-darwin.html
Karl Marx and Friedrich Engels, http://www.wsu.edu:8080/~wldciv/world_civ_
  reader/world_civ_reader_2/marx.html
Giuseppe Garibaldi, http://www.fordham.edu/halsall/mod/1860garibaldi.html
Alfred Tennyson, http://www.fordham.edu/halsall/mod/1880tennyson.html
Otto von Bismarck, http://history.hanover.edu/texts/bis.html
Emancipation Proclamation, http://odur.let.rug.nl/~usa/P/al16/writings/emancip.
  htm

Chapter 8

MASS MOVEMENTS AND DEMOCRACY

A NEW SOCIETY

Europeans and World Population Growth

After 1650, the population of Europe grew rapidly. The history of population had generally been a slow and unsteady growth marked by sudden disasters of hunger and disease. From 1650 to 1750, the European population grew 50 percent. From 1750 to 1850 it grew another 75 percent, and in the next fifty years it grew another 51 percent. This is even more astonishing when one considers that more than 10 percent of the Europeans left the continent. In 1900, the percentage of world population living in Europe reached its all-time high at 24 percent. Today, it is about half that. 1900 marked the high noon of European domination in part because of the number of people and in part because of economic domination. Europe without its colonies controlled a little under half of the Gross Global Product. This domination becomes even more pronounced if one includes the United States and Canada as branches of Europe. Western civilization directly controlled 29 percent of the people in the world and about 60 percent of its economy. Indirectly, the numbers would be even higher. Around 1889, the United States surpassed China as the world's largest economy. We have seen that much of the rise in population before 1850 was due to the Agricultural Revolution and especially the introduction of the potato. The Transportation and Industrial Revolutions in Western and Central Europe made local famine a thing of the past. Birth rates shot up, but death rates also rose as people crowded into cities and filth became overwhelming. Starting in the 1840s a public health movement began to sweep England, which established a Board of Health in 1848 and consolidated it in 1875. The movement then spread to France, especially Paris in the 1850s, then Germany with leaders such as Pettenkofer in Munich and Virchow in Berlin. It then spread to the U.S. and other countries. The idea of public health was that people needed clean water, clean air, clean living conditions, and more living space. Governments accepted their responsibility to safeguard health. Those that shirked their duty, such as the German city of Hamburg, suffered terrible epidemics when cholera swept through in 1892.

Louis Pasteur (1822–95) and **Robert Koch** (1843–1910) developed the **germ theory of disease** by using the microscope to identify various diseases and bacteria. Pasteur started by investigating fermentation in the beer and wine industry. He found that fermentation is the result of microorganisms and that activity could be retarded by heating milk and other liquids—"pasteurizing." By the 1860s, Pasteur was identifying specific germs. Darwin's mechanism of evolution created an understanding that germs can also evolve, and these researches make up the foundation of modern medical science. Hospitals were disinfected on the advice of **Joseph Lister** (1827–1912). This would end some of the aerial bacteria floating through the air. Germans would disinfect everything that came into the operating room: hands, instruments, clothing. Diseases began to vanish: diphtheria, typhoid, typhus, cholera, yellow fever. Death rates plunged, first in Europe and the U.S., then in the rest of world. This accounted for the big rise in the population in late 1800s.

The birth rate then began to fall, starting with France in the 1830s. As government gradually limited and banned child labor, there was less incentive to have them. An 1802 Act in Britain forbade the hiring out of pauper children to work in cotton mills until they were nine years old. The Act limited a child's work day to twelve hours and prohibited night work. The 1833 Factory Act in Britain prevented children below age nine from working in textile factories; between age nine and thirteen, they could only work forty-eight hours a week or nine hours a day; from age thirteen to eighteen they were limited to sixty-nine hours a week or twelve a day. Children under age thirteen were to have two hours of schooling a day. In 1841 France established child labor laws in industry prohibiting children under age eight from working. In 1839 Prussia prohibited employment of children under age nine in factories, and those under sixteen could not work more than ten hours a day. Prussia in 1853 prohibited children under twelve from working in industry. In 1890, Germany mandated Sunday rest for all workers and restricted weekday work hours for women and children. In 1908, Germany banned children under thirteen in factories and allowed a six-hour day for those age thirteen and fourteen and a ten-hour day for those age fourteen to sixteen. In the United States, the states handled child labor legislation: Massachusetts led the way by restricting the work of women and children to ten hours a day; by 1930, thirty-seven states had established a forty-eight-hour workweek for children in factories. The fall of the birth rate and the resulting **Demographic Transition** was linked to education, especially the education of women. France began the trend and had an education rate second only to Switzerland, with 74 percent of children aged five to fourteen attending school. Children had become an expensive burden rather than being a help on the farm from the time they could walk and in later life the sole support for parents. Birth control and abortion became more common.

Even though European-origin areas grew from 200 million to 700 million, productivity and the economy grew at an even faster rate, so there was no overpopulation. Wages and living conditions grew for the average person in western civilization. Society rebounded from its low point of the "Hungry Forties." This helps explain why the predictions of Marx and Engels failed to occur. The global economy became much more tightly integrated, and industrialism grew. Differences and inefficiencies were breaking down as much larger companies appeared and much larger organizations of workers grew to cope with them. This was related to the rise of mass politics: millions of people organized together in political parties and movements voting for their chosen candidates. Even culture started to integrate as regional differences faded and newspapers dictated taste for many.

The Spread of Industrialism in Europe

Britain

The spread of industrialism was slow, even in Britain. Between 1811 and 1821, a plurality of economic product (and probably employment; there are no statistics until 1841) shifted to industry. As late as 1870, half of all the total steampower in manufacturing was confined to textiles. The great majority of industrial workers in 1851 were still craftsmen in small shops. British exports grew 142 percent from 1814 to 1845. British firms mostly financed themselves with their own profits and overdrafts from banks that equaled 20 to 39 percent of the firm's total assets. The British savings rate barely rose from 6½% to 8% in that time from 1770 to 1815. Then it increased to 11 percent in the 1840s. Industry never absorbed more than 10 percent of the available capital in Britain. By 1875, factory workers made up half of the British workforce. They worked at a variety of tasks and machines. Layers of supervisors monitored their work. They enforced the discipline of the clock that the workers had never had in cottage and shop manufacturing. Drunkenness had been common in cottage industry but now merited punishment or dismissal. Factories needed clerks, accountants, and secretaries to deal with the ever-growing mountain of paper. Businesses needed a sales staff to market their products. A large group of "white-collar" workers appeared with better conditions and generally better pay than the "blue-collar" workers in the mines and on the factory floor.

The Continent

The wars of the French Revolution and Napoleon meant that Europe fell behind Britain by 1815. British goods were very cheap and undercut continental goods. This competition had caused constant urban riots in France and western Germany and had been a contributor to the revolutions from 1815 to 1848. It was hard to understand industrial technology, and the British did everything possible to prevent its spread. Before 1825, skilled mechanics and artisans could not leave Britain. Britain forbade the export of textile machinery and other equipment until 1843. Capital investment in steam power was very expensive.

Belgium

Belgium (known then as the Austrian Netherlands) had been the first area on the continent to install a Newcomen engine in 1720. It used the coke process in the latter 1820s. Until 1850, despite its small size, Belgium produced more coal than any continental country. It outstripped Britain as a supplier of coal to northern France and used canals and waterways. A cotton industry grew up in Ghent. Power looms appeared in the 1830s. Under Dutch rule from 1815 to 1830, Cockerill (an Englishman who slipped out illegally) built a massive iron and steel works. By 1880, a plurality of Belgian workers were in industry.

France

France followed a very different path of economic development. Its industrial growth was slow but more diverse than other countries. In the first part of the century, not only did the cotton and coal industries grow, but so did sugar refineries, chemical, glass, porcelain, and paper. New industries included gas lighting, matches, photography, and vulcanized rubber. Slow population growth and slow industrialization meant that the rate of urbanization was slower in France than elsewhere with less overcrowding and miserable conditions. Manufacturing remained widely dispersed, and luxury manufacturing that added much value remained important. Since France did not have much coal, it was more dependent on water power. In the early 1860s, water still produced twice as much horsepower in France as steam. France would later jump directly to electricity. France was not industrialized until 1954, and just fourteen years later a plurality was working in the service sector.

The Spread of Railroads

France, Belgium, and the German states quickly followed Britain's railroad lead. In 1840, just eleven years after Stephenson's *Rocket*, Britain (excluding Ireland) had 2,390 kilometers of track, France 410, Germany 469, Belgium 334. By 1860, Britain had 14,603 kilometers of track, France 9,167, and Germany 11,089. By 1862, Britain had built half of all the railroad track it ever would. Belgium reached this mark in 1867, Germany in 1876, France in 1877, the U.S. around 1884, Italy in 1886, and Russia in 1898. Others hit this railroad mark after 1900, including Japan around 1920 and China around 1960.

Urbanization

As the population grew, there were not enough (and never had been enough) jobs to support all the new people in farm work. In earlier times, this would have led to a grim death for many, either a fast death from hunger and disease or a slow death among the underclass in the cities. In Early Modern Europe, there was typically a hard core of 20 percent always without work, and the streets were even meaner in those days. As the Industrial Revolution created jobs, this permanent underclass began to shrink and in some places, disappear entirely.

The railroad had created a national labor market and greater mobility. If there were no jobs in one place, you could easily move to a more promising area. The railroad made it possible to transport bulky food and fuel into the city, while the new water and sewage system played an equally important role removing waste. Refrigerated cars in the 1880s made the transport of perishable goods such as meat and milk and vegetables widespread. The number of cities with over 5,000 persons more than doubled from 1800 to 1870. England again led the way in urbanization. In 1700, about 15 percent of all English lived in cities of 5,000 or more. This rose to 22 percent in 1750, 30 percent in 1800 and 50 percent in 1870. By 1891 more than half of all the English lived in cities bigger than 20,000. In 1840, only London and Paris had over a million people; by 1914, Berlin, Vienna, St. Petersburg, Moscow joined them. London invented sidewalks in the 1760s and installed gaslights starting in 1807. It developed a horse-drawn bus, then an urban railroad, culminating in the first subway opening in 1863.

The cities became much cleaner and better lighted with the public health movement. Cities used natural gas to light streets at night. Public transportation in cities also grew as the size of the city grew beyond walking distance. Traditionally it did not take more than forty-five minutes to walk directly from one side of the city to the other. In the 1870s, many cities authorized private companies to operate horse-drawn streetcars. In 1883, John Roebling designed the Brooklyn Bridge, a perfected steel cable suspension bridge. After the 1890s, U.S. cities adopted electric streetcars. European cities would follow. Public transportation made it possible to expand the city and have less congestion. By 1901, only 9 percent of the urban population lived in more than two persons a room. Urban planning also came into use. Previously, cities had used every scrap of land for maximum effect; unsafe buildings were crammed together with no air or light. France led the way in demolishing overcrowded Parisian neighborhoods in the 1850s under Napoleon III. Massive boulevards replaced them. There were new houses, neighborhood parks, and open spaces. **Zoning laws** allowed the majority to impose major street or sanitation improvements on a reluctant minority. Cities built schools, libraries, parks, and playgrounds.

The move from country to city was not simply a change of address. City life in western civilization was probably most different from nonurban life in the time from 1780 until 1945, before radio and television broke down cultural barriers, the last pieces of the old social order vanished, and new suburbs blurred the line between urban and rural. The nineteenth-century countryside was still dominated in many areas by the local aristocracy: one family or a small group of families that dominated economic, social, and cultural life and usually was tied closely to the church. Communities were small enough that everyone knew everyone else's business. The community punished deviations harshly, be they sexual, political, or religious. Outcasts served as living (and occasionally dead) examples to the rest. Resentment existed: the peasant revolts and rural violence during the French Revolution proved that. A person moving to the city broke his ties to the old families and church. While city neighborhoods substituted in many ways for town communities, the level of monitoring was much less. No one cared which church he attended or if he attended church at all. Except for some nosy building residents, no one cared with whom he slept. As general elementary education became widespread in the later 1800s, city-dwellers became avid newspaper readers. New ideas such as socialism were acceptable.

European Migration

Many left their home countries entirely including more than 13 million from England, Wales, and Scotland, 10 million from Italy, 5 million each from Germany and Ireland, 4 million each from Austria-Hungary and Spain. More than half of the migrants went to the United States, with other favored destinations being Argentina, Brazil, Canada, and Australia. The pattern was not constant: while the British and Irish rate was pretty steady, the German rate hit two peaks in the 1850s and 1880s, then declined as German industrialization provided jobs. Italian immigration accelerated up to 1914. Up to 33 percent worked abroad for just a time, sending money back home and then returned themselves. The level of return depended on national origins: only 10 percent of the Irish and 5 percent of Eastern European Jews returned home, while 88 percent of those from the Balkans returned. A number of Italians were migrant workers in Argentina from December to April saving $250 to $300 while passage could be had for as little as $16. In 1914, 30 percent of the Argentinean population was foreign born, the highest of any major country in the western hemisphere.

Better living standards made it possible to buy passage. Improved communication and transportation played a role. Britain introduced a new postal system in 1840 where senders would affix one-penny stamps to the letter. At the height of the system with morning and afternoon deliveries, one could post a letter to another city and receive a reply by the afternoon. In the 1840s, it took ten weeks for a message to travel from London to Bombay. By the 1870s, a telegraph message could travel the distance in four minutes. Communication enticed others to follow the trial-blazing migrants, often to the same town or factory. The *Royal William* made the first trans-Atlantic steamship crossing in 1833. After 1864, most British migrants came by steamer. Many were peasants and small artisans hurt by the Agricultural and Industrial Revolutions. Many were young: 67 percent of those coming to the U.S. were under age thirty-one, 90 percent were under age forty. Serfdom regulations and other rules binding certain workers to villages were also abolished in the 1800s; people were allowed to bring their savings and belongings. Some came for economic reasons, others to avoid the military draft, Russian and Polish Jews to avoid persecution. Some felt oppressed by the dominance of small, privileged classes; this migration slowed when basic political and social reforms were enacted.

There was also a substantial but smaller Asian migration at the time, especially from China, Japan, India, and the Philippines. Up to 3 million Asians migrated, far less than the almost 60 million Europeans. Many Asians worked in the mines or plantations of Latin America, southern Asia, Africa, California, Hawaii, and Australia.

The Impact of Immigration

By 1913, people in Australia, Canada, and the U.S. had higher average incomes than those in Britain, which was still the richest European nation. After World War I, nations would tighten restrictions on immigration. The late nineteenth century was probably the freest time for people to move. Travelers rarely had to show passports or obtain visas to travel to other nations.

CAPITAL AND LABOR

The Second Industrial Revolution

Capitalism and industrialism changed in the late 1800s. The steam engine had improved even more, but electricity and internal combustion engines grew after 1900. The first electromagnetic generator was built in 1866, Edison and others invented the light bulb in 1879, and alternating current was developed in the 1880s. The commercial exploitation of petroleum began in 1859 with a well in Pennsylvania. The key was cracking petroleum and finding uses for various the distillates: heavy heating oil, kerosene, and lubricants. At first, the main product was kerosene used for lighting. This gave way to electric light. Standard Oil of Cleveland headed by **John D. Rockefeller** (1839–1937) emerged as the chief oil company; Rockefeller himself was worth $800 million by 1892. There was a huge impact from chemical fertilizer, which depended on oil and natural gas. Farm yields quadrupled, allowing for the twentieth-century population explosion. Before 1914, Europe and the U.S. were able to supply their oil needs from their own fields, although there was growing interest in the fields of the Middle East. The United States was the oil superpower after 1920 and remained a net exporter of oil until 1948.

The most volatile products of petroleum cracking, naphtha and gasoline, were used for the internal combustion engine. This allowed oil to show its full power. Steam-driven cars had been devised by 1800, but they were too complicated. In 1885, the German engineer **Karl Benz** devised a three-wheeled car powered by the engine of **Gottlieb Daimler**. In the 1890s, people began to make car trips out of the city, although bicyclists, pedestrians and horse-drawn carriages crowded the streets. The airplane was invented in 1903 by a pair of bicycle mechanics from Dayton, **Orville and Wilbur Wright**. Submarines (U-boats) with internal-combustion engines would play an important part in World War I.

The urban landscape changed as improvements in iron and steel production caused great expansion. Aluminum and other metal alloys changed architecture. Great "skyscraping" buildings rose. In 1889, the Eiffel Tower in Paris surpassed the Great Pyramid in Egypt that had stood unchallenged for forty-four centuries as the tallest manmade structure in the world.

In the 1820s, the French physicist Louis Ampère had theorized about a telegraph. **Samuel Morse** learned of these theories in 1832, but did not construct a set of wires and send a message from Baltimore to Washington until May 1844. The coded message was based on signals from the long-standing semaphore system. By 1850, most major cities in Europe and America had links. In 1851 came the first successful underwater cable under the English Channel. Europe and America enjoyed nearly instantaneous communication in 1866 with a cable under the North Atlantic ocean. Transport improvements caused the price of commodities to fall as goods became cheaper. The telephone was invented by **Alexander Graham Bell** in 1876. Soon there were too many subscribers to phones to list by name; they had to have numbers.

The Export of Capital

Free trade had gradually spread across Europe. Britain had taken the first steps in the 1820s, then in 1846 repealed the Corn Laws. France made a free trade treaty with Britain in 1860, and this opened the way to more treaties. Some nations were hesitant: the United States imposed high tariffs to protect its infant industries during the Civil War and from the 1880s until 1914 it went back and forth on free trade according to the political party holding power. Germany also wavered. From 1830 to 1929, the volume of global trade roughly doubled every twenty years: it was thirty-two times greater in 1929 than it had been in 1830.

In 1854 France and Austria were the first nations to offer their bonds to the general public. Nations had been reluctant after France's disastrous experience with the *assignats*, but the governments kept the denominations high so only wealthy people could buy them and would not use them like paper money. Cavour paid for Sardinia's 1859 war with this form of public finance. Another form of finance grew as private companies began to sell bonds to investors. The first major issue was in 1842 when Baring Brothers offered bonds of French railroad companies to British investors. Corporate bond issues rose rapidly after 1866 and became another source of money for companies.

European capital followed people. Investors bought foreign stocks and bonds. Banks lent money to foreign banks. Owners took profits and reinvested them in domestic or foreign concerns. Industries now opened foreign branches. By 1914 Britain had $20 billion in foreign investment, France $9 billion, and Germany $6 billion. Foreign capital first built railroads in Europe (such as the Baring Brothers' French railroad bonds) and the Americas, then expanded from there. In 1914, American companies owed $4 billion to the Europeans; this was three times the size of the government's national debt.

The late nineteenth century saw an international system of currency values, with the gold standard at its base. An 1867 international conference in Paris had agreed on a gold standard. England adopted a gold standard at 113 grains of gold to one pound sterling. Other countries set the value of their currencies relative to gold so that the United States set the dollar's value at about twenty-three grains. This fixed for many years the value of the British pound at about $4.86. The long-term effect of the gold standard was to limit the growth of the money supply and depress prices, causing a depression that lasted on and off from 1873 to 1896. California and Australia added as much gold as the Europeans had mined from 1500 to 1850. In the 1890s new gold supplies were discovered in South Africa, Australia, and Alaska. The world gold supply tripled in this short time but even so could not keep pace with economic growth. Grain prices fell by two-thirds from the 1860s to the 1890s. This deflation forced large numbers of farmers off the land and into the industrial workforce.

A true world market developed as distant areas competed directly for the first time. As early as the 1820s one can find global trade relations affecting the British economy as a whole. By the 1830s, the British Industrial Revolution sent out shock waves not only in nearby Europe, but as far away as India, where cotton manufacture in Bengal collapsed from 1813 to 1833 and threw millions of Indian men and women out of work. Britain had previously imported Indian cottons; after 1833, cheaper British cottons would overwhelm India.

This was a very uncertain period of laissez-faire, where governments did not want to intervene. Panics could set in and cause crashes. Boom and bust cycles were violent and unexpected. Changes in faraway industry or agriculture could be ruinous and were little understood by the farmer or worker. The crash of the Vienna market and the "Panic of 1873" when many corporate bonds defaulted opened a long world depression from 1873 to 1896. Governments responded by cutting back on free trade and then Germany led the way in providing more comprehensive social programs. Demands grew for government intervention in the economy, and this increased the popularity of the socialist parties.

The Birth of the Modern Corporation

In the 1830s, the Belgians innovated the **joint-stock investment bank**. These banks would sell stock to the public like other companies but rarely accepted ordinary deposits or made ordinary loans. Instead they would direct their capital to a few companies with which they kept close relations. They mobilized money from small investors to create huge companies. Four major banks in Germany dominated corporate finance to a degree that companies would cooperate on all things by forming **cartels**. They agreed to fix prices, limit output, and divide markets. Britain and the U.S. banned cartels, but they flourished in Germany where firms could maintain high prices thanks to trade protection (after 1879) while selling at low cost abroad.

Britain had banned joint-stock companies after 1720 unless they had special permission from Parliament. Not until 1844 could companies simply register. This left another barrier to massive sales of shares of stock: liability. Under the law, an individual was responsible for all debts of the company no matter how small his stake in the company or responsibility in incurring debts. Britain passed laws from 1856 to 1862 limiting liability, with France following in 1863. Company capital in Britain doubled from 1856 to 1885. Starting with the railroad corporations, large corporations were born, financed by massive bond and/or stock issues. The banks' influence became much greater as they managed these issues. Stock ownership became too diffuse in many cases for the owners to exercise real leadership. **Indirect ownership** grew with the boards of directors drawn from banks or other corporations supervising management on behalf of the stockholders. Often the management chose the boards and stacked them with friends so they could all award themselves huge salaries and bonuses and enjoy giant expense accounts. Many companies collapsed because of this legal theft. Adam Smith had warned of this and had urged government to ban this form of organization permanently.

Companies used money raised from sales of stock and bonds to grow. Sometimes this meant opening more factories to increase production. Often it took the form of vertical and horizontal integration. Integration reduced production costs: the savings went into higher wages, lower prices, or higher profits. **"Vertical" integration** was the control of the process from raw materials to final manufacturing and distribution. **"Horizontal" integration** would be an attempt to dominate a market and drive out competition. The goal was to achieve a **monopoly**. This word is a combination of two Greek words meaning "one" and "all." One company would get a near-total stranglehold on materials or a product and could force all buyers to pay the price demanded. Monopolies and the drive for monopolies could violently distort the free market and injure many people. Countries have made some attempt to prevent monopolies. In

1901, the merger of leading American steel firms created the **United States Steel Corporation**, the first billion-dollar-corporation in the world. The deal was overseen by the New York banker **J.P. Morgan** (d.1913), who served as U.S. Steel's first chairman of the board of directors.

Corporations in industrialized countries began to assume some of the same role and power that nobles had once had. By bribing voters or elected representatives, they could create virtual "pocket boroughs." In the U.S. Senators and Representatives handed out bribes to their colleagues. Certain rich individuals such as Morgan and Rockefeller also had enormous personal influence on the government, mainly to protect their riches.

Growth in Labor Unions

Even as corporations grew in size, the workers had to organize to meet this challenge. Labor unions had grown first in Britain, which tacitly allowed them after 1825, explicitly recognized them after 1871, and allowed them to picket in 1875. French unions were recognized after 1864, suffered for a while after the fall of Napoleon III, and gained full legal rights in 1884. The skilled unions organized first; unskilled labor organized after the 1880s. The unions' main interests were higher wages, shorter hours, better benefits, and improved conditions. They did not care about ideology. In 1900, there were 2 million union members in Britain, 850,000 in Germany, and 250,000 in less-industrialized France. This grew over the following ten years and then from 1910 to 1913, when leftists broke through in a number of countries. Union membership boomed 60 percent in Britain, 25 percent in Germany, 20 percent in the U.S., and 12 percent in France. Put another way in 1913, 5.7% of the British population belonged to unions, 3.7% in Germany, 3 percent in the U.S., 2.5% in Sweden, 1 percent in France and Austria-Hungary, and 0.08% in Russia. Unions began as carefully nonpartisan organizations, but this changed when the ruling elite used police, sheriffs, mayors, and elected officials to destroy the unions. This often included violence and murder. Unions realized that they had to become involved politically and put favored candidates into office, who would at least give them a chance to organize workers. The real wages for British workers doubled from 1850 to 1906.

MASS POLITICS

Democratic Socialism

As the Industrial Revolution grew and spread, many workers supported socialist parties. Socialists established parties in Germany in 1875, Belgium in 1879, Russia in 1883, and France in 1905. Although it was the first industrialized country, Britain did not have a socialist party until 1900, when leaders formed the Labour Party. Some Socialist parties were originally Marxist, but by the 1890s, the socialist parties were concentrating more on winning elections. One key figure in the democratic socialist movement was **Eduard Bernstein** (d.1932) in Germany, who said that Marx's theory of revolution was "a mistake in every respect." During World War I, socialists entered some governments for the first time. The rise in real wages took the edge off of revolution. The greater productivity through mechanization, the growth of the world economy, the accumulation of capital wealth, and a gradual fall in the prices of food and other items all caused an improvement in living standards for the average man and woman in western civilization.

Syndicalism

Some were unhappy with the turn away from revolutionary rhetoric. A movement grew on the left after 1900 protesting the moderation of trade unions and socialist parties. The movement was known as Syndicalism. It was strongest in the "Catholic Arc" of France, Spain, and Italy. In France and Italy, it could not become dominant on the left because of the strength of the socialists, but it and anarchism became the main force on the left in Spain with the absence of Marxist or socialist groups. Georges Sorel (1847–1922) called for direct action to maintain class consciousness with acts of violence while weakening the capitalist system. After World War I, the right led by Mussolini and Hitler would pick up this call for direct action.

The Gilded Age in the United States

Lincoln had intended a moderate policy for the defeated South. Once a number equal to 10 percent of those who voted in the 1860 Presidential election swore allegiance to the U.S., it would readmit the state. The state would have to recognize the permanent freedom of blacks and provide for black education, but it did not have to give blacks the vote. The assassination of Lincoln gave the upper hand to the Radical Republicans. They wanted to punish the South more harshly and provide greater rights to freed slaves, although Republican moderates stopped short of full political and social equality. Southern states showed little sign of reforming their ways. Lynchings became common. The mass politics that had existed in the U.S. since the Jackson era combined with nationalist injury in the South. This mix is fertile ground for the fascism that would blossom in twentieth-century Italy and Germany. Proto-fascist movements grew in the American South. The **1866 Civil Rights Act** denied states the power to forbid blacks the right to hold property or sue in court. Enforcement would be on a federal basis. However, northern states still refused to give blacks the vote.

The South refused to ratify the Fourteenth Amendment, which provided for national citizenship, banned any former official who had turned to the Confederacy, and repudiated Confederate debt. Congress imposed the **Reconstruction Act** (1867) that divided the Confederate South except for Tennessee into five military districts. To lift military rule, a state would have to write a new state constitution giving the vote to African-Americans and taking it away from the former federal officials who had served the Confederacy. They also had to ratify the Fourteenth Amendment. The southern states continued to resist but fulfilled these minimal requirements and were readmitted to Union by 1870.

When the Republicans nearly lost the Presidency in 1868 because of northern states' refusal to let blacks vote, the **Fifteenth Amendment** (1870) forbade voting discrimination on the basis of race or color. In the South since nothing could be done legally to stop blacks from voting, secret terrorist organizations such as the **Ku Klux Klan** were set up to intimidate them. There was no major land reform. Radical schemes to take land from planters and give it to former slaves did not pass, and only poor-quality land was reserved for the former slaves under the Homestead Act.

Northern enthusiasm for Reconstruction began to fade in the 1870s. There were new controversies over the tariff and over the paper "greenbacks" that Lincoln had issued to finance war. General Grant was a disastrous President. The Democrats took power in most southern states. In 1876, the Democrats won the Presidential election but were cheated by Republican electoral fraud in Florida, Louisiana, and South Carolina. The Republicans offered the **Compromise of 1877**: the southern states would accept the election theft if the military occupation ended and states were allowed to manage their internal affairs.

This of course led to African-Americans losing their voting rights through poll taxes and phony literacy tests. The Supreme Court allowed this blatant violation of the Constitution. The most extreme measures also deprived poor white men of their vote, as in South Carolina where three-quarters of all voters lost their rights. The Supreme Court threw out laws forbidding segregation culminating in *Plessy vs. Ferguson* (1896) in which the Court approved segregation as long as there were "separate but equal" facilities provided. Lynchings accelerated, **"Jim Crow" Laws** enforced segregation everywhere. Thousands died violently as they tried to resist. Even northern magazines made blacks the butt of crude jokes and characterized them as intellectually inferior.

The French Third Republic

The War's End and the Commune

The Germans' triumphal march into Paris and their proclamation of Empire at Versailles humiliated Paris. It also feared the return of the monarchy after new elections gave the monarchists control of the National Assembly. On March 18, 1871, a revolt broke out when Thiers tried to get control over the cannon that commanded the heights over Paris. Leaders of the **Commune** wanted to complete the Great Revolution of 1789. Bismarck gave back the French prisoners of war so Thiers could deal with the revolt. The Communards made their last stand on May 28 and suffered very bloody reprisals. 25,000 died, and the commander ordered the shooting of all white-haired prisoners because they might have fought in the revolutions of 1848.

Thiers as President

Adolphe Thiers had hungered for power for forty years and was not about to give up that up to a restored king. His first task was to get rid of the debt and the German occupation. To Bismarck's vast surprise, the government sold bonds to the public, raised the money, and paid off the Germans. Now the French began to plot their revenge against the Germans. The monarchist Assembly was suspicious of Theirs and replaced him with a general, **Patrick MacMahon** (President 1873–79), who it was sure would bring back a king.

But there were three claimants to the monarchy: Napoleon III's son, the grandson of Charles X (Bourbon), and the Count of Paris, who was the grandson of Louis Philippe (Orléans). Bourbon was promised the first crack because he had no heirs. Then the crown would go to the Count of Paris. Bourbon blew his opportunity when he demanded the Bourbon flag instead of the tricolor. The Assembly reluctantly approved a "temporary" constitution, which lasted into the 1940s. Universal manhood suffrage would elect a Chamber of Deputies that would run policy. In the December 1875 elections, the republicans won a big majority over the divided monarchists. MacMahon, after a year and a half of fighting the Chamber, forced the Cabinet to resign and fought election battles against the Republicans led by **Léon Gambetta** (1838–82). Gambetta brought a new campaign style as he traveled by train across France and gave speeches to the towns and villages calling for a republic. About 80 percent of all registered voters and perhaps 25 percent of all the people in France voted in this election, and the republicans returned in force. MacMahon resigned in January 1879 and a republican became president.

Problems of the Third Republic

Gambetta's stumping and victory established French democracy. Division and anger still ran deep in France. The country still ached from the defeat in the war to Germany and the subsequent loss of Alsace and Lorraine. This combination of nationalist injury with mass politics could be toxic as it had been in the American South. In the late 1880s, a general named **Georges Boulanger** toyed with the idea of a military coup, but when the government charged him with conspiracy, he lost his nerve and fled the country. The movement had risen and collapsed quickly, but it was disturbing to see the monarchists teaming up with conservative and military interests against the constitution. A French company tried and failed to build a canal across Panama and had only secured government funding with massive bribes to members of Parliament. This revealed the growing power of corporations in the corruption of democracy. Even more distressing was that radical right-wing interests tried to portray this as a "Jewish conspiracy" although the company was not Jewish and there were few Jews involved in the "Panama Scandal." In 1894, the army accused and convicted a French Jewish Captain, Alfred Dreyfus, of selling secrets to the Germans, despite evidence to the contrary. Leftists in France defended Dreyfus while rightists attacked him. When the Right tried to use this **Dreyfus Affair** to bring down the Republic, the socialists abandoned their neutral stand and entered government to strengthen the regime. The public courts did not clear Dreyfus until 1906, and the French military did not vacate the court-martial conviction until 1995.

Bismarckian and Wilhelmine Germany

The Constitutional Structure

Germany had a federal structure that vested much power in the states, but only the Emperor could bring about constitutional change since he controlled a bloc of Prussian votes in the Federal Council. The Reichstag had some powers, but it was deeply divided with six major parties. Bismarck mastered control of the Reichstag parties, and this gave him a measure of security.

Attack on the German Catholics

In the 1870s, Bismarck worked with the National Liberal Party to complete unification. They passed measures against the Catholic Church in reaction to Pius IX's attacks on liberalism and the proclamation of papal infallibility at the Vatican I council in 1870. They called their broad attack on Church the *Kulturkampf* (Battle for Civilization). This did not work out well. The Catholic Center political party actually increased its seats as Catholics felt that they had to stick together. By 1877, Bismarck faced a growing problem with his National Liberal allies. They wanted a share of political power. Pope Pius IX died in 1878, and Bismarck tried to make up to German Catholics. His call for a protective trade tariff split the National Liberals and Bismarck forged a new working group in the Reichstag with conservatives and Catholics.

Attack on the German Socialists

The socialists replaced the Catholic Church as Bismarck's chief demon. The Social Democratic Party (SPD) had been founded in 1875 and had done well in its first election. The Reichstag passed an Anti-Socialist law in 1878 although it did not ban the SPD. In 1881 Bismarck introduced the first **social insurance legislation** in the world. He proposed accident insurance, then sickness insurance, and finally in 1889 the first old age pensions and disability, similar to the later American Social Security system. Despite this, the Social Democrats kept increasing their vote until they gained 20 percent of the vote in 1890, more than any other party.

The Dismissal of Bismarck

Bismarck's close ally William I died in 1888. His son Frederick had been the hope of liberals for thirty years because he was married to the daughter of the British Queen Victoria. When he became Emperor, he already had inoperable cancer and died within three months. His son succeeded as **William II** (ruled 1888–1918). William was a brash youth who sought popularity and changes in domestic and foreign policy. The socialist breakthrough of 1890 upset Bismarck. The Chancellor had not foreseen this when he put out the Constitution in 1867, and now he considered ripping it up. William II was appalled to hear Bismarck talk like this: did the Chancellor want a revolution? Bismarck was now seventy-five years old and perhaps too old for the job. He certainly saw things differently from the thirty-year-old Emperor. On March 18, 1890, William II dismissed

Bismarck as Chancellor. The Constitution had given the Emperor full power and Bismarck had no recourse. The people had not elected him and had little sympathy. The Reichstag had never forgotten how he had broken the laws and disregarded the Prussian Parliament. In 1895, a deputy proposed that the Reichstag send best wishes to Bismarck on his eightieth birthday. The Reichstag did not approve the proposal.

Wilhelmine Germany

With rich mineral deposits, high literacy, and good transportation, Germany emerged swiftly as a great economic power and passed Britain after 1900. It had huge electrical, chemical and banking cartels, and was also a center of scientific and intellectual achievement. William II had been born with a withered left arm, and some feel that William had an inferiority complex and was always trying to compensate with bombast and arrogance. Certainly, his mouth constantly ran ahead of his brain and he irritated many with his thoughtless statements. He wanted to bring in a broader program of social legislation to stop the Social Democratic rise, but after some legislation William became dissatisfied.

A chief fault in Germany was not just the Kaiser but his abysmal advisers. His chancellors could not restrain the Emperor or the bureaucracy filled with schemers such as Friedrich von Holstein (in the Foreign Office) and Alfred von Schlieffen (head of the army). The Reichstag did nothing to stop this. Its demands were not consistent, the parties squabbled, and many were strong supporters of imperialism and the build-up of the navy. The people were quiet: most were satisfied with things. The result was that after 1908, the army gained more and more power. The **Schlieffen Plan** for war envisaged a two-front war with Germany invading Belgium to get at France and knocking it out, then turning its full attention on Russia. It was never approved by the Cabinet or the Reichstag, and the people knew nothing of it.

Great Britain at Its Zenith

Party Politics

The modern Conservative (Tory) party was born under **Benjamin Disraeli** (1804–81) while the Liberal Party evolved out of the Whigs, led by free trader radical John Bright and **William Gladstone** (1809–98). As the population moved into the cities, Gladstone sought wider voting rights in 1866, but the Tories and defecting Liberals defeated it. Upon gaining office the Tories switched and passed the **Reform Act of 1867** (also known as the Second Reform Act). It added almost a million voters to the rolls. The electorate increased from 4 percent to 8 percent of the British population. The Liberal John Stuart Mill proposed that women have the same voting rights, but only seventy-three members of the 658-member House of Commons voted for this.

Disraeli hoped that the voters would reward the Tories, but the Liberals swept to victory in 1868 and Gladstone became Prime Minister. His Liberal government enacted a secret ballot for elections, and reformed the civil service so applicants had to pass an exam before joining. The Church of England lost its privileged religious position in Catholic Ireland. Britain finally followed the lead of most other nations and passed an Education Act in 1870 that provided free public elementary education.

By 1880, France and Germany had allowed all men to vote. The British system remained out of kilter despite the 1867 reform: Liberals won the popular vote in 1874 elections, but because the countryside still had greater weight, the Conservatives won more seats in the House of Commons. Disraeli as Prime Minister brought in significant health and housing legislation as part of Tory democracy; Conservatives consistently got one-third of the working-class vote.

The election of 1880 got started early in November 1879 when the seventy-year-old Gladstone ran in the **Midlothian Campaign** and stumped the country attacking Disraeli's policies in Bosnia and Bulgaria. Gladstone used the tactics of Gambetta to travel and speak. The seventy-five-year old Disraeli was too old and sick to respond and looked ineffective next to the vigorous Gladstone. This was the first mass campaign in Britain, and the Liberals swept back into power. About 10 percent of all people in Great Britain and nearly all eligible voters participated. The **Third Reform Act and Redistribution Act** (1884–85) gave the vote to about three-quarters of all British men (and about 16 percent of all Britons) and finally made the districts mostly equal. As had happened in the American Jackson era, party organization became much tighter and three parties dominated the Commons: Liberals, Conservatives, and Irish Nationalists.

The Irish Question

Gladstone's Land Act of 1870 protected the Irish from arbitrary eviction. Irish representatives supported the Liberals but became more nationalistic after 1870s under the leadership of **Charles Stuart Parnell** (1846–91). Gladstone tried to pass a Home Rule Bill for Ireland in 1886. **Joseph Chamberlain** protested, split the party, and took Liberal Unionists over to the Conservatives. At this time industrialists, once liberal, became more conservative. In 1893, another Liberal government passed a Home Rule Bill, but the House of Lords voted it down, breaking with long tradition that it followed the Commons. The Conservatives dominated politics led by **Lord Salisbury**, the Prime Minister, and Chamberlain, who served as Colonial Secretary. In 1906, Chamberlain precipitated a split in the Tories when he moved against free trade and the Liberals won a landslide.

A Labour Party

Socialism grew very slowly in Britain. It rejected Marxism in favor of the moderate views of middle-class intellectuals such as Sidney and Beatrice Webb of the **Fabian Society**. The Independent Labour Party was a very moderate, non-Marxist movement. It did not run candidates for the House of Commons until 1900 and worked with the Liberals up to the war in 1914. Twenty-nine Labour representatives won election in 1906. Although many Tories in the Commons supported labor unions, the House of Lords was completely opposed to unionism. The unions demanded a weakening of the power of the undemocratic House of Lords.

The Liberals and the Lords

After 1908, the main leaders were **H. Henry Asquith** (Prime Minister 1908–16) and **David Lloyd George** (Chancellor of Exchequer 1908–16; Prime Minister 1916–22). Their government put in military reforms and labor relief, but the Lords became increasingly aggressive and vetoed bill after bill. In 1909, Lloyd George proposed the "**People's Budget**" that funded spending increases with progressive income and inheritance taxes. When the Lords vetoed the People's Budget, the Commons and Liberals declared war on them because this was contrary to two hundred years of custom. After a couple of years of fighting the Lords and the Crown, the Liberals passed the **Parliament Bill of 1911** that reduced the length of the Parliament from seven to five years and gave the Commons the right to override the Lords' veto.

Asquith and Lloyd George put through a National Insurance Act of 1911 that was similar to American Social Security but still not as extensive as Germany's insurance programs. The Liberals also pushed for a new Home Rule Bill in Ireland. Lords and conservatives encouraged the Protestant North to resist all attempts at Home Rule, up to and including buying German guns to spread violence and terror.

The Italian Monarchy

Despite Italian unity, many divisions remained: north against south, believers in democratic government, doctrinaire liberals, and those devoted to the Pope and Church. Only 2 percent of the population was allowed to vote, and fewer than

50 percent of eligible voters bothered. Parliament controlled domestic affairs, but the king and military dominated foreign affairs. The royally-appointed Senate still had veto power.

The Italian constitution became more democratic in 1882 when 7 percent gained voting rights. That year saw the first socialist elected to the Italian parliament. Many Italians were landless or on marginal land and deeply impoverished. Many emigrated. Italian industrialization was slow. Railroads expanded tenfold from 1861 to 1891, and the rural population fell. In 1899 the first FIAT Auto plant opened. 48 percent were still illiterate in 1901. **Giovanni Giolitti** oversaw a series of liberal reforms that made disability and old age pensions secure, guaranteed a day of rest for workers, regulated the work of women and children, and made taxes fairer for the poor. In 1912, electoral reform gave the vote to all literate men over 21, all who had served in the military, and all over age 30. This doubled the electorate: 24 percent were now eligible and 60 percent of those voted in the 1912 elections. The big winners in the new mass politics were the extreme Left and the Catholic party. Unlike Britain and France, democracy had not taken root.

Alexander II Modernizes Russia

The loss of the Crimean War had deeply humiliated Russia and Emperor Alexander II (ruled 1855–81) understood that Russia had to change to reach the level of the other Great Powers. Firstly, Russia stayed out of European affairs until the middle 1870s. Secondly, Russia expanded its empire in Asia at the expense of China, Persia, and the Ottomans. Thirdly, Russia reformed its farm system. Alexander saw a backward and incredibly inefficient agricultural system. He freed all of the 22 million serfs in 1861, two years before Lincoln's emancipation of the American slaves. The serfs had to pay compensation, and the best land remained with the nobles. Peasant conditions were still wretched, and many landlords also lived in poverty because of inefficiency. Russian farm production grew gradually, and Russia became a major exporter of wheat. Alexander granted legal equality for all and reduced the twenty-five-year military term of service to six years. Russia's relations with Britain worsened. The two powers skirmished over Afghanistan. In 1867, Alexander sold Alaska to the U.S. as a way of making trouble for the British in Canada. The British were concerned that Russia might strike south to India.

The Progressive Era in the United States

Wealth and Labor

American corporations such as the oil and steel businesses grew to enormous size and power. Many feared the influence of Morgan and Rockefeller. The high rates charged by monopolistic railroads to haul grain hurt farmers. By 1890, the richest 9 percent of Americans owned 71 percent of all wealth. The Supreme Court gutted the first attempt at antitrust legislation breaking up the giant corporations. The workers' movements grew. By the 1880s, the workday was beginning to shorten: only one-quarter worked over ten hours. Radicals started to talk of an eight-hour day. In 1886, the **American Federation of Labor** used a strike to win concessions.

Populism and Progressivism

Farm and worker discontent merged in the Populist and Progressive movements. The price of wheat price had fallen from $1.50 per bushel to 60 cents. Cotton fell to 20 percent of its 1870 price. Poor education and religious fundamentalism left rural areas in the dust. In 1892, the People's Party was founded: it called for a graduated income tax (that means that the rich pay a higher percentage of their income), national ownership of railroads, telegraphs, and telephone systems, government loans to farmers to store crops in time of abundance, an increase of money supply by unlimited minting of silver coins (to raise farm prices), an initiative and referendum process to go around the corrupt politicians, and direct election of U.S. Senators. Voting participation rose to 19 percent of the total population. The People's Party had a hard time breaking into the Democratic/Republican system, but it improved its share in the 1894 Congressional elections.

The Presidential Election of 1896

The movement reached its crest in the American Presidential election of 1896. The Democrats nominated the pro-silver **William Jennings Bryan** (d.1925). At age thirty-six Bryan was the youngest major presidential candidate ever in the U.S. The People's Party also nominated him. The conservative Democrats stuck to the gold standard and nominated their own candidate. Most newspapers endorsed the Republican **William McKinley** (President 1897–1901). The *New York Times* called Bryan "insane." Bryan responded by taking to the stump and giving his famous "Cross of Gold" speech across the nation. McKinley stayed at home but spent $3.5 million, more than seven times Bryan's amount. The corporations poured money into the Republican campaign. Bryan won more states, and turnout was at a record 20 percent of population. Some historians allege that the election was stolen, but the official results at least gave McKinley the densely populated industrial states.

Progressivism at Its Peak

An anarchist assassinated McKinley in 1901, and **Theodore Roosevelt** became President (1901–9). He brought a series of suits against the trusts including Rockefeller's Standard Oil. Congress passed a Pure Food and Drug Act in 1906 and put land under preserve. Progressivism now came to the fore, out of the fights to reform the civil service, regulate big business, and the populist movement. It was neither socialist nor terribly sympathetic to blacks' civil rights. It won the right to initiative and referendum in eleven states. It stripped the Speaker of his dictatorial control over the House of Representatives. The Sixteenth Amendment to the Constitution allowed an income tax, which had been thrown out by the reactionary Supreme Court. The Seventeenth Amendment (1913) provided for the direct election of U.S. Senators by the people. Most cities took over public utility gas and water companies. The Supreme Court struck down a federal law to outlaw child labor. By 1916, almost three-quarters of the states had accident insurance laws (workmen's compensation).

In the election of 1912, Roosevelt, trying a comeback, lost in the Republican convention to his successor President Taft. Roosevelt ran as a Progressive, but both lost to the Democrat **Woodrow Wilson** (President 1913–21). The Socialist Party also hit a high point in this election. Wilson was an admirer of Gladstone and was the first President to address Congress since John Adams. He installed a telephone line directly between the White House and the Capitol. Wilson presided over a major reduction of tariffs, a graduated income tax, and the creation of the Federal Reserve as a central bank. The Federal Trade Commission and Clayton Antitrust Act toughened business regulation. However, Wilson, born in Virginia, did nothing to help blacks and refused even to study the issue.

The Suffragist Movement

The French Revolution had inspired Mary Wollstonecraft to pen her *Vindication of the Rights of Women* (1792), but there was little echo for fifty years. Humanitarians tended to focus on extending rights and votes to men or freeing slaves or ending the slave trade. Very few radicals considered full rights for women. Most girls received limited education. The spread of the Industrial Revolution, urbanization, and the fall of living standards, along with the rhetoric of the time, began to inspire women. Many favored abolition of slavery but ran up against prejudice that women should not speak publicly. The alcoholism and violence against women that hit their high point in the 1840s also motivated women to seek equal legal rights, the vote, and limits on the sale of alcohol. The Americans **Elizabeth Cady Stanton** (1815–1902) and **Lucretia Mott** (1793–1880) convened the **Seneca Falls Conference** in 1848 where they drafted a Declaration of Principles modeled on the Declaration of Independence. Stanton and **Susan B. Anthony** (1820–1906) led a movement for equal rights, equal pay, votes for women, and temperance.

The trend of liberalism was to focus on individual rights, not the family as a unit. John Stuart Mill sponsored an amendment in 1867 to give the vote to women under terms of Second Reform Act and wrote the *Subjugation of Women* in 1869 that argued powerfully for equal rights. The Municipal Corporations Act of 1869 under Gladstone gave single women the vote in local elections. European socialists, especially in Germany, made common cause with women's rights. In 1895, the German Socialists sponsored a bill to give all women the right to vote.

New careers opened up to women as stenographers and secretaries. There were 90,000 so employed in England by 1901. In 1893, the Bank of England (a bastion of conservatism) employed women as clerks. From the beginning women played important roles in the telephone industry. There were growing numbers of women in factories and retail shops. Many women, however, withdrew from salaried work or were fired after they became pregnant. The University of Zurich opened its doors to women in 1867, followed by the University of Paris. Many others followed although Oxford and Cambridge held out. The legal bar admitted women in France in 1900 and Britain 1903. By 1906, 40 percent of French women worked for wages.

The voting rights for women movement grew. In 1902, women gained the right to vote in federal elections in Australia. Thirteen American states, mostly in the West, allowed women the vote by 1914. Norway, Finland, and Sweden pioneered giving women votes in Europe. In Britain, no party backed votes for women and **Emmeline Pankhurst** (1858–1928) founded the Women's Social and Political Union in 1903; members heckled speakers and made street demonstrations; when imprisoned, they would go on hunger strike. The women turned to violence, burning politician's houses and smashing store windows.

The Balance of Democracy

Democracy comes from the Greek "government by the people." What does this actually mean? Is it the granting of voting rights? Should we distinguish between men and women getting the vote? What about clear cases of voter suppression as in the United States? Can majority rule itself become a tyranny, as Rousseau had warned? What if we consider how voting can be subverted by the rich as Montesquieu had warned?

The first thing is that the granting of the vote is only vaguely related to democracy as we would understand it. The granting of the vote to all men swept Europe after 1871: Switzerland (1874), Spain (1890), Belgium (1893), the Netherlands (1896), Finland (1906), Norway (1907), the Austrian part of Austria-Hungary (1907), and Sweden (1909). Norway and Finland granted women the vote at the same time all men got it. Other countries followed the lead of Britain and Italy and gave the vote to most men. This clearly opened an era of "mass politics." Political groups and parties organized people and held mass rallies. There was voting, debate in parliaments, and reporting on these debates in the newspapers.

But this does not add up to democracy. Although absolutism was fading away, kings and nobles still had considerable power. Most countries allowing most or all men to vote followed the example of Germany by putting up a facade behind which the traditional authorities still ruled. The people understood this and stayed away from the polls. Why bother to cast a meaningless vote? Of the powers of western civilization, I would say that democracy had only taken root in Britain, France, and the United States. The voters felt connected to their government, felt that they had a decisive voice in influencing the government, and that their votes mattered. Even though one-quarter of all men still lacked the legal right to vote in Britain, and even though there had been disenfranchisement, bribery, and vote-fixing in the U.S., people still had faith in the system. Those countries that had developed mass politics but not a rooted democracy were susceptible to fascist appeals. No fascist government has ever grown directly from an absolutist one. There has always been a stage of mass mobilization. The fall of absolutism and the rise of mass politics set the stage for the great confrontation between fascism and democracy.

THE RISE OF MASS CULTURE

By the 1880s, almost all of the great powers provided for compulsory elementary education. Britain had been one of the last in 1870. Despite the Jim Crow laws, the American illiteracy rate fell from 20 percent in 1870 to 11 percent by 1900. Nearly all of the states outside the South had compulsory education laws by 1900. The number of U.S. colleges grew from 350 to 500 in the period from 1878 to 1898. There were more public and group libraries. As literacy rose, so did the reading pool for books and newspapers. Britain, France, Belgium, the Netherlands, the Scandinavian countries, and Germany all had at least 85 percent literacy.

Before 1826, the hand-driven press could only print 200 sheets an hour. The steam-powered rotary press of the 1830s churned out 4,000 sheets an hour. This productivity breakthrough greatly reduced the costs, and newspaper owners began to appeal to working-class readers. In 1833, the *New York Sun* became the first cheap newspaper, selling 30,000 copies a day at the cost of one penny. The web press of 1871 printed on both sides of paper simultaneously. Advertising revenue offset expenses.

By the 1890s **Joseph Pulitzer** (1847–1911) had built the circulation of the *New York World* to over a million daily, using comic strips and scandal. Pulitzer's newspaper raised the money for the Statue of Liberty, which was installed in New York harbor in 1886. Newspapers reached their peak in 1910 in the U.S. with 1.36 papers per household. People often read both a morning and an evening paper. Pulitzer and **William Randolph Hearst** (1863–1951) owned chains of newspaper and countless others copied them, giving countries fairly homogeneous views. Newspapers were good at mobilizing popular outrage and focusing attention on certain issues or candidates. Very few were "objective" or neutral. There were many journals and magazines as well. In Europe, newspapers were centered in the capital cities and could be sent out by railroad in time for the morning job commute.

Building on the 1887 discovery of radio waves, the Italian inventor **Guglielmo Marconi** devised the radio and sent the first message across the Atlantic in 1901. However, radio could not be commercially successful until radio stations were built, and a large number of people owned radio receivers. After 1920, radio developed as a mass medium. In most European countries, nationally-controlled broadcast companies helped break down regional cultural barriers. In the U.S. privately-run radio networks were established on the model of the newspaper chains. After 1945, television became commercially viable and followed the radio broadcasting pattern.

The Grand Illusion

For the growing middle class in the thirty years before the World War I in Europe, this was a golden age. Cities became cleaner and brightened by gas light, then electricity with Edison's incandescent bulb. Working hours decreased and created new possibilities for leisure and entertainment. Democracy and education were more widespread, social legislation was expanding. Everything seemed to be getting better.

The bicycle was perfected around 1865, and the "penny-farthing" bicycle with a large front wheel became common: it allowed people more mobility at a faster speed than a horse. Women and short men used tricycles. In 1885, the pneumatic tire was invented and then in 1888, the safety bicycle. Thousands flocked to the public parks to go bike riding in the 1880s and 1890s. Racing champions were the first sports stars. In 1869, the Bon Marché department store in Paris moved to a much bigger building. These stores advertised to the masses and some established mail-order catalogs. By the 1880s, the department store had introduced credit payments for the working class.

By 1850, the sixty-hour workweek was common in England: five-and-a-half days with Saturday afternoon off. Social reformers did not want the extra time going into traditional male leisure activities such as drinking and wife-beating. Team sports such as baseball, cricket, football, soccer, rugby, and basketball (invented in 1891) became more popular: they took up time and energy. Leagues of teams representing schools, churches, workplaces, and neighborhoods were created. Finally there were professional national leagues for these sports. The English Football Association organized itself in 1863 and the baseball National Association in 1871. Sports encouraged movement along streetcar lines. In 1896, the modern Olympic games were revived. People flocked to music halls to see performances of broad comedy and music, went to dance halls, and attended the theater and opera. The first music hall for lower-class Londoners opened in 1849 and appealed to men who drank and smoked while watching various entertainments but later the music halls became more open to women and children. In 1895 and 1896, music halls showed the first movies. Museums opened to the public and education was understood as including teaching ordinary people what was beautiful and admirable in music and the arts.

TIMELINE

1833	*Royal William* makes first steamship trip across Atlantic
1844	Morse sends telegraph message
1848	Seneca Falls Conference
1857–60	Pasteur's experiments with yeast and fermentation
1859	Oil well in Pennsylvania
1863	London subway opens
1866	Trans-Atlantic cable laid
1869	Expanded Bon Marché department store in Paris
1876	Bell invents telephone
1877	Compromise in U.S. opens Jim Crow era
1877–78	Gambetta election in France
1879–80	Gladstone campaign in Britain
1885	Daimler-Benz automobile
1883–89	Bismarck introduces German social insurance
1890	Bismarck dismissed as Chancellor by William II
1895	Music halls show first movies
1896	Participation hits new high in U.S. Presidential Election
1901	U.S. Steel first billion-dollar corporation
1903	Wright brothers fly at Kitty Hawk, North Carolina

KEY TERMS

Louis Pasteur
Demographic Transition
John D. Rockefeller
J.P. Morgan
Eduard Bernstein
Compromise of 1877
Léon Gambetta
German Social Insurance
William Gladstone
The "People's Budget"
William Jennings Bryan
William Randolph Hearst

PRIMARY SOURCE DOCUMENTS

Louis Pasteur, http://www.fordham.edu/halsall/mod/1878pasteur-germ.html
Eduard Bernstein, http://www.fordham.edu/halsall/mod/bernstein-revsoc.html
Willie X, http://web.archive.org/web/19981203161408/www.signature.pair.com/
  letters/archive/argentina.html
William Jennings Bryan, http://projects.vassar.edu/1896/crossofgold.html
Listen: http://www.youtube.com/watch?v=HeTkT5-w5RA

Chapter 9

THE CLIMAX OF IMPERIALISM

Why a Second Wave of Imperialism?

Imperialism means the formation of an empire over other peoples. Either they are excluded from rule or they feel they do not belong in the ruling group. **Informal imperialism** refers to the imperial power limiting another country's scope of action by military, financial, or other threat. Europe's first wave of imperialism in the Americas had ended badly with widespread rebellions in North and South America. For a time, the Europeans avoided imperialism and colonialism. With mercantilism discredited, that reason for holding colonies was gone.

There has been strong debate over why another wave of imperialism developed in the late 1800s. Marxists such as Lenin said it was simply capitalists making money off colonies by sucking up raw materials while selling manufactured goods in a continuation of mercantilist traditions. But colonies, like war, are losing propositions in the modern world. It costs enormous amounts of money to defeat resistance and then build the necessary infrastructure of roads, railroads, ports, and mines to exploit a colony. It is doubtful that even King Leopold of Belgium, who ran Congo on the cheap with horrifying exploitation, made big profits. Private companies could not profit without enormous direct and indirect subsidies from governments. Few Europeans or Americans settled in overseas colonies. Some religious leaders of Christian missionary movements had supported imperialism to aid conversion, but again the religious results were soon disappointing. The French colonies accounted for only 12 percent of

French trade. The British colonies were better at 33 percent, but most of that was with Canada and Australia. If these were the motives, one might imagine that the Europeans would have abandoned imperialism quickly, but they held their colonies for eighty years or more until they ran out of money or the resistance drove them out.

The main motive was political. Imperialism was related to the rise of mass politics. It stirred national pride for the British or the French to see a large part of the globe bearing their national colors, never mind that much of that land was worthless desert. With democracy emerging over liberalism, appeals to popular opinion increased, and little was more popular then imperialist expansion. France and Britain mindlessly engaged in a race for the Nile. Germany and Italy felt compelled to join in. Voters in the United States actively supported removal and (if it came to that) extermination of the Indians. The anti-imperialists were lonely marginal figures who were ridiculed. Even socialists praised imperialism because, in Karl Marx's scheme, these areas had to be brought to the capitalist stage before they would be ready for socialism. Bismarck hoped that France might forget Alsace and Lorraine if it gained in Africa. Italy could ally with Germany and Austria and forget about the remaining bits of Italian territory under Austrian control.

The Consolidation of British Control over India

India (including modern Pakistan and Bangladesh) had never been united in its history. From ports it acquired in the first wave of imperialism, the British gradually moved inland. By 1818, the British controlled most of central and southern India as well as the Ganges delta and river valley. The British were surprised that the population did not rebel, but the residents were pleasantly surprised that once taxes were paid to British or their native allies at the same levels or slightly lower, they were left in peace for the year, not beleaguered by bandits, wars, or additional requests. The British trained native troops who they called "**Sepoys.**" By 1824, the British had an army of 200,000 with 170 Sepoy regiments and only sixteen European regiments. There was terrible suffering in the Ganges Delta as the import of cheap British-made goods destroyed the Indian cloth industry. Muslims knew they could not take on the British directly but declared holy wars against Hindus in Bengal and the Sikhs in the Punjab. In 1845, the British intervened in the Punjab and conquered it by 1848. However an attempt to conquer Afghanistan in 1842 led to the Afghans slaughtering the entire British force. The first railroad in India opened in 1853, followed by the first telegraph in 1854.

The steady British advance and lack of respect to the natives led to the **Sepoy Mutiny** (1857–8). There were bitter atrocities on both sides, and the war cost a full year's revenue from India. Britain took full control of India and completely reorganized the army and civil service. The opening of the **Suez Canal** in 1869 made trade to India much easier by cutting the distance to London by 5,000 miles. The **India Act** (1858) set up a Secretary of State for India in London advised by a fifteen-member Council of India. A British Viceroy ruled in the name of the queen. Over 560 enclaves of princely rule remained. A small civil service of some 3,500 politically-connected British officials ruled 300 million in the subcontinent. A regular British army kept control with those peoples who had been loyal in the Mutiny, notably the Sikhs and Gurkhas. The British introduced a modern system of primary and secondary education. They put in irrigation projects and built the third largest railroad network in the world. India produced tea and jute, but also revived as a major clothes manufacturer even though the British arranged for favoritism for British-made goods by setting heavy tariffs against Indian-made goods while removing Indian import taxes.

In 1885, some from the educated elite of India met in the **Indian National Congress** to demand equal rights and more self-government. Various leaders founded newspapers. From 1895 to 1905, economic depression, famine, and bubonic plague caused a decline in India's population. By 1907, some radicals were calling for complete independence.

Manifest Destiny and American Imperialism

In the 1840s, promoters of war had claimed that it was the "Manifest Destiny" of the United States to stretch from the Atlantic to the Pacific Ocean. The victory in the Mexican War had brought Americans to the coast but Indians still dominated almost half of the area. After the 1849 gold rush to California, the American government systematically stripped Indians of their land. The government pushed Indians out of Kansas and Nebraska after 1854 to build a railroad. During the Civil War, most of the quarter-million Indians living in the Great Plains rose up against the whites, and federal troops retaliated bloodily. Guerrilla wars raged throughout the American west. The staggering corruption of the Interior Department undermined any agreements that were reached. After the Civil War, the government settled on a policy of confining the Indians to two large reservations in Oklahoma and the Dakota Black Hills. This led to more fighting. The 1870s saw many Civil War veterans wage systematic war upon Indians. The large number of battle-hardened troops gradually wore the Indians down. The destruction of about three-quarters of the buffalo herds in the early 1870s also robbed the Indians of their livelihood. The government gave Indian land to gold and silver prospectors, plains farmers, ranchers, and the railroads. This was a form of "internal" imperialism and colonialism that nevertheless had some resemblance to later cases.

THE SCRAMBLE FOR AFRICA

The Growth of Influence on the African Coast

Before 1870, Europeans clustered in coastal depots and in certain provinces such as Egypt. Central African diseases kept them back. Also European weapons were not sophisticated enough to overcome large numbers of Africans. After 1870, better-bored rifles and repeating guns and better medicine began to come in, making the conquest of the interior possible. The British army adopted the **Maxim gun** in 1889 that could shoot 500 rounds a minute. The British reestablished the Gold Coast (1874) and Lagos (1861) colonies as a move against the illegal slave trade on the West African coast. The Niger delta provided a palm oil supply that was as profitable as slaving. An 1854 expedition up the Niger River proved to the British that **quinine** from cinchona bark of the Andes Mountains was effective against malaria. Nevertheless, a parliamentary committee in 1865 recommended a withdrawal from West Africa except for the repatriation center at Sierra Leone for former slaves.

In the 1870s, Disraeli took steps in South Africa and Egypt. Egypt had run up heavy debts to the Europeans in the 1860s. The British suppressed anti-European riots in 1882 and took over as the effective governors. A shift in West African coastal power came in 1868 when the British, who favored the coastal enemies of the Ashanti, and the Dutch, allies of the Ashanti, switched forts along the coast for administrative convenience. A **Fante Confederation** formed to deal with the Ashanti. The Dutch withdrew rather than protect their allies. British broke up the Confederation as a conspiracy. When the Ashanti invaded in 1873, Disraeli decided on major military action and Britain defeated the Ashanti in the **Ashanti War** (1873–4).

In southern Africa, diamonds were found in the soil of the Orange River in 1867, then the giant "Star of South Africa." This was in the land of the **Boers**, descendants of Dutch settlers from the 1700s, who had moved away from the Cape of Good Hope after the British took over during the Napoleonic Wars. The Boers established two republics: the Transvaal and the Orange Free State. Nearby were a number of African groups, the most powerful being the Zulus.

In 1879, the British, trying to improve relations with the Transvaal Republic, began the **Zulu War**. The Zulus gained some early victories, but then the British brought modern weaponry to bear and defeated them. The British annexed Zulu land in 1897.

The Ambitions of King Leopold

King **Leopold II** (ruled 1865–1909) of Belgium, seeking glory outside his own limited role in a tiny country, financed explorations of central Africa by the journalist/adventurer **Henry M. Stanley** (1841–1904), who had fought on both sides of the American Civil War. In one adventure that thrilled newspaper readers of the *New York Herald*, Stanley set out to locate the missing missionary David Livingstone in 1871. Stanley explored the Congo River and traveled to the sea, but this failed to interest the British. Then Leopold authorized Stanley to sign over 500 treaties from 1879 to 1884 with African leaders and establish trading stations. Leopold used these treaties to claim the huge Congo River basin. The French made their own claims in the Congo and began to expand across the empty Sahara Desert. Both Britain and France had interests in the Sudan and the risk of war grew.

The Berlin Conference

The German Chancellor Otto von Bismarck presided over the **Berlin Conference** (1884–5) to sort out the African claims and guarantee free trade and navigation along the Congo River. The Europeans divided up Africa and later decided some disputed areas by force. Neither the British nor the French got everything they had wanted. The Conference recognized Leopold's hold over the neutral Congo. It agreed to work against slavery and the slave trade. Meanwhile, a Muslim uprising rocked Sudan. It was led by Muhammad Ahmed, who called himself **The Mahdi** (The Expected One). The Mahdi had built an army, and when the British sent a force up the Nile, he lured it out into the desert, defeated it, and took its repeating guns and cannon. In 1885, the Mahdi took Khartoum, the capital of Sudan that dominates the Nile. In doing so he slaughtered a British garrison. Although the Mahdi died not long thereafter, his forces controlled Sudan until 1898, when the British sent a much larger and better-equipped force. At the **Battle of Omdurman**, the British slaughtered perhaps ten thousand Mahdist soldiers while losing only twenty-eight of their own. The Mahdi remains a symbol of Muslim resistance to western imperialism to this day. The British continued up the Nile in their bid to gain a solid strip to build a Cape to Cairo railroad. But the French were driving east to the Nile. This culminated in a confrontation at **Fashoda** in September 1898. The French had an inferior force and had to withdraw.

The Rush is On

Many Africans welcomed the European help in their tribal rivalries. Some such as the Ashanti fought hard and were not annexed until 1901. The French pushed south from Algeria, north from Brazza's Congo, and east from Senegal towards Lake Chad. The British pushed out from their own enclaves in western and southern Africa. They made sure the Germans could not link up with the Boers by "protecting" Bechuanaland (Botswana). Leopold consolidated his hold over Congo with steamships going along the river and completed a railroad link in 1898. He took the Katanga copper region by force in 1891. Leopold's Congo became the example of the worst of European imperialism. The agreements claimed the land as Leopold's private land, not subject to the government of Belgium. Leopold claimed he made a profit, but had to borrow money from the government of Belgium, which took over the Congo right before Leopold's death.

The Italian Defeat at Adowa

Menelik II (ruled 1889–1913) was determined to maintain Ethiopian independence. He secured modern arms and built an army of close to 100,000 men in this East African territory. An Italian force of 20,000 set out from Massawa in Somaliland. The Ethiopians slaughtered 6,000 Italians in March 1896 at the **Battle of Adowa**. Menelik then gained European support in modernizing Ethiopia. They funded a railroad to link the new capital of Addis Ababa to French Djibouti. When Menelik died, Europe was busy with the crises that would lead to the World War, so it left Ethiopia alone.

The Boer War (1899–1902)

In 1884, gold was discovered in Transvaal. Prospectors flooded in. **Cecil Rhodes** (1853–1902), a British businessman got control of many of the gold mines, then the diamond mines. Rhodes also sent agents north of the Limpopo River, conquered the Ndebele nation, and established a protectorate. This colony was named Rhodesia. The Transvaal President **Paul Kruger** (1883–1902) tried to keep outsiders, especially the British, away. German Emperor William II was sympathetic to Kruger, which made the British angrier at Germany. Rhodes became Prime Minister of the Cape colony and sponsored a raid in 1895 to conquer the Boers. British Colonial Secretary Joseph Chamberlain disavowed this raid after it failed miserably. War broke out in October 1899. The Boers were tough guerrilla fighters and the British used brutal tactics to break the Boer resistance. 75,000 Boers died, including 25,000 women and children in British concentration camps. When the war ended, the British recognized the Boers' rights but incorporated Transvaal and Orange Free State into the Union of South Africa. This Union gained dominion status in 1910.

JAPAN AND CHINA

China's Decay

China and Japan followed different paths in the nineteenth century. The contrast deepened as their relations with the western world became more complicated. China was largely rural with a population around 300 million in 1800. It had few animals, tools, or storage facilities. In a reverse of the conditions that created capitalism in western Europe, China had lots of labor and few resources. Labor-intensive farm handicrafts produced tea and silk, the major exports. There was little credit and only limited currency in copper coin and silver bullion. There was no institutionalized science and invention. Since the middle ages, China had run a trade surplus with the West. Europeans had wanted Chinese porcelain, tea, and silk, but they had sold few products to the Chinese. In part this was because there was a huge gap between rich and poor in China, and a domestic market was virtually non-existent. China has struggled to this day to develop its domestic market. The ruling class in China only accepted European gold and silver for their goods. Around 1800, the Europeans succeeded in selling opium, a highly addictive drug, to the mass market in China. Despite Chinese attempts to ban opium, the trade balance reversed and now money flowed from China to the West. China fought and lost wars to the opium-trading British. The Chinese economy and political system collapsed into a bloody civil war in the 1850s as millions died. The European found that a divided and blood-soaked China was bad for business, and by the 1860s, European accounting and military experts supported the imperial government of China with loans, weapons, and organizational skills.

The Isolation and Opening of Japan

Since 1603, a hereditary **shogun** (military leader) of the Tokugawa family had ruled Japan with the Emperor remaining as a figurehead. The shoguns had traded with only one European country, the Netherlands, through only one port, Nagasaki. The shoguns also taxed the nobles and peasants very heavily. This had the effect over time of limiting population while piling up money resources. Without planning it, Japan had recreated the conditions for capitalism. A money economy slowly replaced the rice economy as warlords had to grow money-producing goods in order to maintain two residences locally and at Edo (modern Tokyo), the shogun's capital. Japan became a united market and urbanization grew as the population of Edo approached a million. Farm productivity grew slowly. Japan was largely at peace for 250 years. There was a clear rise in living standards during the shogunate, even for peasants; this helped create a domestic market, unlike China.

In 1853 and again in 1854, **Commodore Matthew Perry** sailed into Edo harbor with one-quarter of the entire fleet of the United States Navy. Perry demanded that Japan open trade with the U.S. This led to a crisis and increasing violence. On the one hand, there was an antiforeign reaction that led to an armed battle between Japanese warlords and Europeans in 1862. On the other hand, some warlords promoted violence to force the shogun out of power. The last shogun resigned in 1867. Reformers, chiefly young **samurai** (warriors) from the outlying provinces, declared that the Emperor was restored to "full authority." In 1868 the fourteen-year-old Emperor **Mutsuhito** took over. His reign from 1868 to 1912 became known as the *Meiji* (Enlightened) era and marked the birth of modern Japan. The Emperor swore that the public would rule, and that he would call an assembly, have public discussion of the issues, allow people to have the job of their choice, and base laws on the just laws of Nature.

Japan Becomes a World Power

The government took the leading role in organizing and encouraging business, especially mining. It took a foreign loan in 1869 to finance railroad construction. Railroads were critical to Japanese development because the country's rugged coastline made water trade difficult. The rickshaw was invented in Japan in 1869; it combined western technology with cheap labor and spread throughout Asia. The government founded a central Bank of Japan in 1882. The Japanese reclaimed much farmland and made all the land more productive with a 21 percent growth in productivity just in the 1880s. The constitution of 1889 gave 1 percent of the people voting rights. Japanese production first concentrated on comparative advantage by making sake, miso, and soy sauce that were immune from foreign imitation. By 1913, one-quarter of the world's cotton yarn exports came from Japan. As a late industrializer, Japan skipped over much of the steam stage and went directly to electricity.

Conflict

China was so massive in size and so firm in tradition that a Japan-style transformation was almost impossible. Conservatives reasserted themselves after 1860. China did not have the capital reserve of Japan. The government discarded plans to build a modern navy in 1889 in favor of building another big palace. There was little change in the traditional culture, and the government superimposed new institutions on the older pattern. Tension between the two powers of east Asia grew in the 1880s over influence in Korea. This broke into a full **Sino-Japanese War** in 1894. Despite China's much bigger size, the modern Japanese army and navy made quick work of the outdated Chinese forces. To its displeasure, Japan found that it had to share influence in Korea with Russia.

The Balance is Broken

The Chinese defeat in 1895 upset the balance of power in eastern Asia. China asked Russia for help and granted concessions to Russia to build its Trans-Siberian railroad. European fleets descended on China and tried to grab ports in "ninety-nine-year" leases. In 1897, the Germans took Tsingtao and the Russians took Port Arthur. In 1898, the French took Kwangchow, and the British made a ninety-nine-year lease of Hong Kong. Establishment of "spheres of influence" was the first step to partition. The American Secretary of State promoted an **"Open Door"** policy to preserve equality of trade in China and keep the treaty ports open to all nations.

The Boxer Rebellion

Secret societies rose in China, including the "**Boxers**" (the translation is actually closer to the "League of Righteous and Harmonious Fists.") Many of these societies advocated Japan-style modernization. The Boxer Rebellion shook China in 1900 when nationalists took over the area in Beijing around the embassies. Seventy-six foreigners died defending the legations, including the German ambassador. After the rebellion, the Russians took part of Manchuria, angering both Britain and Japan. In 1902, Britain and Japan made an alliance. This marked the end of Britain's diplomatic isolation.

THE GROWTH OF U.S. IMPERIALISM

American imperialism was related to the rise of democracy. After the U.S. seized the lands of the Plains Indians, it moved into the Pacific. In 1875, the Kingdom of Hawaii gave the United States the right to build a naval base at Pearl Harbor in exchange for the right to sell sugar in the U.S. free of any tariff. The U.S. undermined the monarchy of Hawaii and finally took full control of those islands in 1898.

Riots erupted in Spain's colony of Cuba in 1895 after a raise in the U.S. sugar tariff compounded general unhappiness. Spain responded brutally by putting people into concentration camps to cut the rebels off from food and help. McKinley tried to stay out, but Pulitzer's *New York World* and Hearst's *New York Journal* pushed for intervention. Riots swept Havana in 1898 and McKinley sent the battleship *Maine*. It blew up mysteriously in Havana harbor, and 260 died. The newspapers now goaded Congress and McKinley into the **Spanish-American War**. Spain lost Cuba, Puerto Rico, Guam, and the Philippines to the U.S. Since the war was fought for Cuban independence, the U.S. could not readily seize control of Cuba, but it did put through a law (the **Platt Amendment**) that the U.S. could intervene in Cuba whenever it chose. The anti-Spanish rebellion in Philippines now became anti-American when the U.S. did not grant independence to these islands. The U.S. had to send 70,000 soldiers and killed up to 200,000 Filipinos.

In 1903, the Dominican Republic defaulted on European bonds. Europe wanted to intervene, but President Theodore Roosevelt issued the **Roosevelt Corollary** (1904) to the Monroe Doctrine: the U.S. would exercise international police power and run finances in Latin America until the nation stabilized. The Roosevelt Corollary and the Platt Amendment signaled the intention of the United States to control Latin America, and nationalist anger against the U.S.

grew in Latin America. There had long been a desire to build a canal across Central America. When the French Panama project failed because of Yellow Fever, the U.S. took up their role. The Colombian senate refused to grant a ninety-nine-year lease and the U.S. promoted a revolution backed by American gunboats in 1903. The U.S. leased that Canal Zone in perpetuity, but did give it back in 1999. Engineers completed the Canal in 1914. In 1921, the U.S. paid Colombia $25 million in compensation.

THE RUSSO-JAPANESE WAR

Russia expanded its influence in Korea after China's defeat and claimed the coast of Manchuria through its railroad lines. On February 8, 1904, Japanese torpedo boats attacked the Russian fleet at Port Arthur. Port Arthur fell in January 1905. The British would not allow the Russians to bring their Black Sea fleet out through the Straits nor would they let the Russian Baltic Fleet use the Suez Canal. The Russian fleet had to go all the way around, but the Japanese annihilated it at the **Battle of the Straits of Tsushima** (May 27, 1905). The **Treaty of Portsmouth** (1905), mediated by Roosevelt, recognized Japan's control of Korea, restored in theory China's administration over Manchuria, and gave Japan Russia's lease on the Kwantung Peninsula, the South Manchurian Railroad, and the southern half of Sakhalin Island. In 1910 Japan formally annexed Korea.

TIMELINE

1857–8	Sepoy Mutiny
1868	*Meiji* "restoration" in Japan
1869	Suez Canal opens
1884–5	Berlin Conference
1885	The Mahdi takes Khartoum
1894–5	Sino-Japanese War
1898	British defeat Mahdists
	British confront French at Fashoda
	U.S. annexes Hawaii
1898–1900	Spanish-American War
1899–1902	British-Boer War
1900	Boxer Rebellion
1904	Roosevelt Corollary to the Monroe Doctrine
1904–5	Russo-Japanese War
1914	Panama Canal opens

KEY TERMS

Sepoy Mutiny
Suez Canal
Leopold II
Berlin Conference
Battle of Adowa
Spanish-American War
The Boxer Rebellion
Russo-Japanese War
Boer War
Cecil Rhodes
Fashoda
The Mahdi

PRIMARY SOURCE DOCUMENTS

Annexation of the Hawaiian Islands, http://www.fordham.edu/halsall/
mod/1898hawaii1.html
Rudyard Kipling, http://www.fordham.edu/halsall/mod/Kipling.html
Elisa Greathed, http://www.fordham.edu/halsall/mod/1857greathed.html
Fei Ch'i-hao, http://www.fordham.edu/halsall/mod/1900Fei-boxers.html
Alfred Hake, http://www.fordham.edu/halsall/islam/1885khartoum1.html
Matthew Perry, http://www.fordham.edu/halsall/mod/1854Perry-japan1.html
Tadayoshi Sakurai, http://www.fordham.edu/halsall/mod/1905portarthur.html

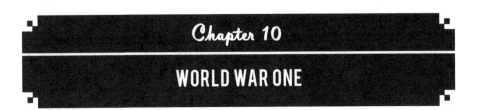

Chapter 10

WORLD WAR ONE

BISMARCK'S EUROPEAN ORDER

The Situation

The unification of Germany had imperiled the entire balance of power by creating a powerful German state located in central Europe near all the trouble spots. Otto von Bismarck created a security system that had two foundations. First, it isolated France diplomatically. France could not beat Germany unless it had another great power as ally. Second, it refused any territorial gains for Germany, acted as an "honest broker" for all the other powers, and tried to allay fears about any further German expansion. If the other powers trusted Germany, they would have no interest in breaking Germany back into the states of 1870.

The New Security Problem

Aside from the declining Ottoman Empire, which had been the main threat to peace in Metternich's Concert of Europe, there was now a declining Austria-Hungary. After Prussia defeated it in 1866 and ousted it from German affairs, it turned its full attention to southeastern Europe. This brought conflict with Russia, which shared Orthodox Christianity with several of the nations and still dreamed about controlling the Straits. Could Austria-Hungary decline gracefully without dragging down the rest of Europe? Could Bismarck keep both Austria and Russia as allies? These were complicating factors for his European order.

The War Scare of 1875

To Bismarck's great surprise, the French paid off the indemnity by the middle of 1873 and made no secret of their desire to reverse the verdict of 1870. Germans began to think that preventive war was the best strategy, and Bismarck suggested that Germany might attack France and cause so much damage that France would drop out of the ranks of the great powers. This bullying deeply worried the other great powers. British officials and the Russian Emperor Alexander II visited Berlin to let Bismarck know that this was not acceptable and that he would face a general war if Germany attacked France. Bismarck now shifted to a policy of war prevention.

Balkan Revolts

Serbia encouraged revolts against Turkey across the Balkans. The Turkish army crushed Serbia, which now appealed for help. Russia intervened in June 1877. Disraeli, the British Prime Minister, wanted to support Turkey, as Britain had in the Crimean War, but his great enemy, Gladstone, had written a piece detailing the Turkish atrocities in Bosnia and Bulgaria, and British public opinion was very anti-Turk. All the British could do was block the Straits with their own ships. The Turks were no match, and Russia imposed the **Peace of San Stefano** in March 1878. Russia claimed large gains in the Balkans and a dominance in southeastern Europe while only throwing some small bones to the Austrians.

The Congress of Berlin

Fearing a war among the great powers, Bismarck called them to meet in June and July of 1878. Romania, Serbia and Montenegro become fully independent. Bulgaria became autonomous. Austria-Hungary occupied Bosnia and Herzegovina, much to the unhappiness of Serbia, which wanted those provinces. Russia got a little of Romania and some of Turkey's Asian lands but was angry at Bismarck for what it saw as a sellout. The British occupied the island of

Cyprus. The Congress gave France a green light to occupy Tunisia, which it did in 1881.

Bismarck's Treaty System

Bismarck made his first peacetime treaty, the **Dual Alliance**, with Austria-Hungary, in 1879. Concerned, the Russians renewed the **Three Emperors' League** in 1881 with Germany and Austria-Hungary: the partners would be neutral in case of war with a fourth power. The treaty provided for mutual consultation in Balkan affairs. A clause allowed Austria-Hungary to annex Bosnia when it wished. The only partners left for the French were the British or Italians. The **Triple Alliance** of 1882 tied Italy to Austria-Hungary and Germany: they would help Italy if France attacked; Italy would help if two or more powers attacked Germany and Austria-Hungary or if France attacked Germany.

The Bulgarian Crisis

After the Congress of Berlin, Russia thought it could install a puppet ruler in Bulgaria, but **Alexander of Battenberg** would not take orders. Bulgaria annexed some Turkish lands and beat off a Serb attack. In August 1886, Russia pulled out its military support, and Alexander's government collapsed. The Three Emperors' League expired. Bismarck feared that Russia and France would team up if he denied the Czar's ambition to dominate southeastern Europe. The **Mediterranean Agreement** of March 1887 brought Britain in to help against Russian expansion. Under the **Reinsurance Treaty** (June 1887) Russia and Germany would stay neutral when the other was at war unless it had been caused by a Russian attack on Austria-Hungary or a German attack on France.

The Dual Monarchy of Austria-Hungary

After 1867, the Austrian half of Austria-Hungary set up a parliament but the Emperor continued to appoint the ministers. From 1867 to 1879, the Liberals dominated Austria backed by the rapidly growing German-speaking middle class. They improved the judiciary, liberalized the press laws, moved toward modernization and free trade, and abolished anti-Semitic laws. In 1879 the Austrian Emperor Francis Joseph turned to **Count Edward Taaffe**

(Prime Minister 1879–93). Taaffe's coalition was made of conservatives, Slavs, and Poles, and made concessions to each nationality. Taaffe's concessions led to violent reaction among Germans, especially in Bohemia, which saw the formation of the proto-Fascist German Workers Party. In 1907, Austria allowed all men to vote and, as in Germany, the Social Democrats began to rise in power. In Hungary, the Hungarian minority exerted a stranglehold over all other minorities. The parliament was ineffective, and there was no serious move to democracy. Francis Joseph symbolized the old-fashioned nature of the monarchy as he continued to use oil lamps long after electrification became widespread in his empire.

THE COLLAPSE OF BISMARCK'S EUROPEAN ORDER

The Franco-Russian Alliance

William II found Bismarck's European Order too complicated and saw a contradiction between the Austrian and Russian policies. How could Germany have agreements with both countries when they hated each other? From a strictly legal point of view, Bismarck pointed out, there was no conflict. If Russia attacked Austria-Hungary, the loophole in the Reinsurance Treaty allowed Germany to defend Austria-Hungary. Both of these treaties were strictly secret, but Bismarck had shown the Russians the text of the Dual Alliance so they knew exactly how Germany was bound to Austria-Hungary.

One of William II's first acts after he dismissed Bismarck was to tell Russia that he would not renew the Reinsurance Treaty of 1887. William hoped to make an alliance with Britain, which was clashing in Central Asia with Russia. Baron Holstein of the Foreign Office disliked the Russians. He and William wanted to show their independence from Bismarck. Britain in 1890 did not want any alliances and turned the Germans down. After a hundred years of unique British interruption, Europe was returning to its traditional core of power: the Low Countries, North Italy, and a hundred miles of land on either side of the Rhine. This made William overconfident in Germany's power.

Bismarck's worst fear soon came to pass in January 1894 when France and Russia announced an alliance. This ended France's diplomatic isolation, and destroyed one of the pillars of Bismarck's European Order. Yet Europe did not go to war in 1894. There was a reservoir of faith in Germany and a belief that it was a force for stability and peace.

The End of British Isolation

The Boer War was a deep shock for Britain. It discovered that the rest of the world disliked it, and that it had no friends. In 1900 Prime Minister Salisbury and Joseph Chamberlain sought a German alliance. This time the Germans refused. Holstein believed that Britain was a declining power, based on its poor showing against the Boers. Germany was already handcuffed to one declining power, Austria-Hungary. The British had reasons of their own to be angry at Germany. The German **Admiral Alfred von Tirpitz** had begun a great warship-building program. He said it was for self-defense, but the British saw a threat. Germany already had the most powerful army in the world. If it could challenge Britain on the seas, then what? Germany also began to flex its new economic muscles and reduce Britain's business with Turkey. Britain and France had begun to move toward each other after their confrontation at Fashoda in 1898. No issue divided them. **Théophile Delcassé**, French Foreign Minister from 1898 to 1905, looked for allies against the Germans. In 1898, he had gotten the Italians to modify their position in the Triple Alliance. The **Entente Cordiale** of 1904 between Britain and France settled a number of colonial disputes. France recognized Egypt as a British sphere of influence, and the British recognized Morocco as a French sphere of influence. This did not bind Britain to an alliance, but it was a treaty of friendship that tilted Britain against Germany.

The First Moroccan Crisis

In 1905, William II landed in Morocco, hailed the ruler there as independent, and asked that Britain and France set aside the Entente Cordiale. General Schlieffen, the head of the army, wanted war in 1905 since Russia had just lost a war in the Far East. Holstein thought if France was scared enough, it might agree to friendship with Germany. Chancellor Bernhard von Bülow saw an opportunity to break the Entente. France backed down, and Delcassé resigned. But the Germans pushed too far and demanded an international conference. Then power shifted in Britain as the Conservatives who were favorable to Germany were defeated by the Liberals, and Sir Edward Grey became Foreign Secretary. He was more suspicious of the Germans, and the Germans had to back down as Schlieffen and Holstein resigned.

The Triple Entente

Its loss to Japan curbed Russia's ambitions, and it needed more French and British capital to support industrialization and rebuild its armed forces. In 1907, Russia signed a treaty of friendship recognizing Afghanistan as part of the British sphere of influence and dividing Iran between Russian and British spheres of influence. Russia turned back to the Balkans. The **Triple Entente** of Britain, France, and Russia was complete and Germany faced the great danger Bismarck had feared as nothing remained of his security system.

THE ROAD TO SARAJEVO

Three Dangerous Tendencies

1. There was much more reliance on allies. Countries feared becoming isolated, so allies could be dragged into a war against their will.

2. There was a big increase in armaments, especially naval weapons. From 1904 to 1913, French and Russian military spending grew 80 percent, Germany 120 percent, Austria-Hungary 50 percent, and Italy 100 percent.

3. The military's influence on policy-making increased. Admiral Tirpitz beat back all attempts to make a naval pact with the British. In 1912, British War Minister Lord Haldane visited Berlin to try to smooth things out and again offered an arms limitation treaty. Again, Admiral Tirpitz refused to sacrifice the naval program. Britain moved closer to France, Germany closer to Austria-Hungary. Mobilization plans became tyrannical and crowded out all room for negotiation. Because most treaties and plans were secret, people were largely unaware of the dangers and powerless to change them. The Allies combined had about 2 million soldiers ready, Germany and Austria-Hungary had 1.3 million. The German Schlieffen Plan was designed to offset this by making use of Germany's good interior lines and the time lag for Russian mobilization. The German army was supposed to defeat France while huge and underdeveloped Russia was still mobilizing its army.

The Bosnian Crisis

The formation of the Triple Entente raised the danger that Britain and Russia might work together to carve up Turkey. In 1908, junior army officers known as the "Young Turks" staged a revolution in the Ottoman Empire, forced liberal changes, and called for modernization. The great powers, especially Russia and Austria-Hungary, feared that a newly assertive and effective Turkey might reverse the trends of the previous hundred years and even reclaim some lost territory. Austria was especially worried about the province of Bosnia. Technically, it was still Turkish land, but Austria-Hungary had run it and occupied it since the Congress of Berlin. The Foreign Ministers of Austria-Hungary and Russia met. They agreed to let Austria-Hungary annex Bosnia in exchange for letting Russian warships through the Straits. Austria-Hungary's unilateral announcement of annexation infuriated the Russian Foreign Minister, who found the Straits action blocked. He said he had been double-crossed by the Austrians and that Russia would have attacked except Germany stood by Austria and forced Russia to back down. The crisis heated things up in the Balkans and made Russia more determined not to back down the next time.

The Second Moroccan Crisis

The new German Foreign Minister Alfred von Kiderlen-Wächter decided to show his own brand of foreign policy in 1911 once again in Morocco. He protested a French dispatch of troops and sent the warship *Panther* to enforce his protest. He then demanded French Congo for a German withdrawal. Everyone was puzzled: what was Germany up to? All had agreed to French action in 1906. After long negotiations, French got a free hand in Morocco, and Germany got some wasteland in Africa.

Tripoli and the Balkan Wars

The Turkish empire was crumbling. Italy seized Tripoli in 1911 before France could take it. The Balkan countries (Serbia, Bulgaria, Greece and Montenegro) allied and declared war on Turkey in October 1912. They won easily. The division of the land was difficult, and the Balkans allies created an independent Albania. A second war immediately broke out when Bulgaria attacked Serbia and was beaten back. The Austrian-Russian rivalry was at its peak, and Serbia was determined to get Bosnia and other lands. While the Serb government often was moderate, its army and public wanted Serbia to unite the southern Slavs into a larger nation (Yugoslavia) as Prussia had for Germany and Sardinia had for Italy. This meant that Serbia must not only take Bosnia, but also Croatia and Slovenia from Austria-Hungary.

THE GREAT WAR

Murder in Sarajevo

No great power, not even Russia, was willing to do for Serbia what France had done for Sardinia in 1859. The Serbian army resorted to terrorism in Bosnia. There were five assassination attempts against Habsburg officials. Bosnian students tried three times to kill the Hungarian governor of Croatia. In 1913, Germany and Austria-Hungary tried rewarding Serbia by giving it more land in Albania then punishing it when it tried to take even more. While the Serbian government backed down, it made no attempt to control the army.

June 28, 1914, archduke **Franz Ferdinand**, the heir to the Austrian throne, was assassinated in the capital of Bosnia, Sarajevo. The assassins were tools of the head of Serbian military intelligence, Colonel **Dragutin Dimitrijevic**, known as Apis ("the Bee"). For a month, Europe held its breath, but the crisis seemed to be subsiding. William II went off for his summer holidays sailing in the North Sea after a meeting with his officials where they agreed to back up Austria. The would become known as "the blank check." On July 23, Austria sent a harsh ultimatum to Serbia demanding full authority for an investigation into the assassination. The Serbs knew the investigation would turn up Apis and his ties to the terrorists. When they delayed, Austria declared war. Only now did William II and the German Chancellor Bethmann Hollweg try to restrain Austria, even as the head of the German army encouraged the Austrians to make war. The German army feared that Russia would only get stronger in the years to come and wanted to cripple France and Russia before this happened.

Under the Schlieffen Plan, Germany had to begin mobilization before Russia finished, or it would not have the troops ready to face the Russian mass. When Russia refused a partial mobilization, Germany went ahead. Russian Emperor Nicholas II swore not to make peace as long as an enemy stood on Russia soil, even though no enemy occupied any part of Russian soil until he made war. The Schlieffen Plan called for a massive attack on France and, in order to expand the war front, Belgium. Germany and all other European powers had signed a treaty in 1839 to respect Belgium's neutrality and to fight any country that violated that neutrality. The head of the German army rebuffed William II's last-minute attempt to scrap the Schlieffen Plan. The military leaders had become the real masters of Germany. Britain's position was unclear. It seemed for a time that it might not honor the Belgian neutrality treaty. But when Germany invaded Belgium on August 3, the British Cabinet decided on war.

European War to World War, 1914–16

The Schlieffen Plan called for soldiers to move twenty to twenty-five miles a day in weeks of blazing summer weather, taking no account of resistance. The Germans at first advanced rapidly but gradually fell behind the demanding timetable and got stuck outside of Paris. They then fell back to higher and more defensible positions, dug in, and sent some troops east to deal with Russia. The head of German General Staff apparently saw the fatal flaws in the Schlieffen Plan and how war would bog down and suffered a nervous breakdown. General **Erich von Falkenhayn** replaced him. The Russians had invaded East Prussia virtually unopposed but General **Paul von Hindenburg** and his main assistant **Erich Ludendorff** drove them back at Tannenburg and the Masurian Lakes in 1914. The Germans had left the Austrians alone to deal with the first Russian blow, and it destroyed the best of the Austrian army. The Austrians also found it slow going to conquer Serbia. By 1916, the Austrian army was recruiting men over age fifty. In the many crises of the Austrian empire, the army had always been the one institution that held things together. Now it was made of raw recruits and inexperienced and incompetent officers and the doom of the empire was near.

The **Allies** (Britain, France, Russia) had advantages but they could not be brought to bear on the war. The German colonies were insignificant, but the Allied colonies were underdeveloped and could largely only supply manpower. The war in Europe killed or injured more than 80,000 Africans who fought on the Allied side. The German industries devoted to export production were retooled to war, so a blockade did not shut them down. There was little war at sea so Britain's huge naval superiority did not count for much and Britain still could not attack Germany from the sea. Once the front stabilized into trenches, both sides set up to four miles' depth of defenses, and no army could make a big push and break through all the defenses. Germany had gained an advantage with its 1914 offensive and its fallback to the high ridges. That gave it a natural advantage even when the British and French attacked with greater numbers. With good communication and transportation, Germany could shuttle troops between Eastern and Western Fronts when needed. The German tried to spread war around the world using their U-boats (submarines) to attack supply ships and stirring up resistance in British colonies from Ireland to Afghanistan.

In 1915, the Germans finally did things the right way: they kept a defensive line in the West while trying to smash the Russians. Working with the battered Austrian army, they drove Russia out of Poland, Lithuania, and Galicia. The Austrians overran Serbia. The Allies looked for ways around the bloc of the **Central Powers** (Germany, Austria-Hungary, Turkey). The Turks repulsed Allied landing attempts at **Gallipoli**. This simply diverted Allied forces and resources from the main fighting in France. Italy had at one time been an ally of Germany, but the terms of the Triple Alliance said Italy only had to intervene if Germany was attacked. Since Germany and Austria-Hungary had launched the first attacks, Italy had declared neutrality. The Allies persuaded Italy to join them by promising large amounts of Austro-Hungarian land. The war between Italy and Austria-Hungary along their mountainous border was bitter and bloody.

Despite Germany's success in 1915, Falkenhayn reversed policy and tried to bleed the French by luring their soldiers into the areas around the fortress of **Verdun** and then cutting them to ribbons. This backfired and nearly as many Germans died in the months-long battle. The Russians got a chance to launch a counter-offensive and won back most of the areas they lost in 1915. Hindenburg replaced Falkenhayn as supreme commander in August 1916.

Effect on Domestic Policies in Europe

The war affected every government. None of them made it all the way through the war. Emperor Francis Joseph of Austria-Hungary died in 1916 after a sixty-eight-year reign. The Russian Revolution of March 1917 overthrew Nicholas II as we will discuss in more detail in the next chapter.

Britain

David Lloyd George continued to gain power in the cabinet. He was Minister of Munitions, then Minister for War. In May 1915, Prime Minister Asquith widened his government to include Conservatives and Labour Party leader Arthur Henderson in minor posts. Asquith lost authority and could not make effective decisions. The Conservatives and some newspaper owners conspired with some of Asquith's own Liberals. Lloyd George forced out Asquith in December 1916. Lloyd George created a small war cabinet of five members to make rapid decisions. In 1916, Britain imposed the military draft for the first time in its history. Asquith and his group of Liberals remained angry at Lloyd George for what they regarded as a betrayal.

France

The war had taken a terrible toll in land, blood, and treasure. Many French politicians wanted peace and there were several mutinies in 1917. The Prime Minister resigned as head of government. After much debate on the war in November 1917, the fierce militarist **Georges Clemençeau** became Prime Minister to see the war to the end.

Germany

The German government lied that France had attacked first. This helped convince the Social Democrats, who comprised one-quarter of the Reichstag, to vote for war credits. The Reichstag also gave sweeping legal powers to the government. As the war bogged down, eighteen Social Democrats broke away. Germans started to avoid buying war bonds, forcing the government to pay for the war with printed money. In July 1917, the Reichstag passed an empty **Peace Resolution**, but Hindenburg and Ludendorff forced the resignation of Bethmann Hollweg and put in a puppet. From this point on, they, not William II or the Reichstag, ruled Germany.

The Allied Victory

The Communist Revolution of November 1917 forced Russia out of the War, but the United States had entered in April 1917 because of submarine warfare against its ships and German intrigues in Mexico. Although the U.S. could not bring troops and heavy equipment to the Front for over a year after the declaration, its economic might and small arms were fully brought to bear. The U.S. was bankrolling the Allies with loans, just as Britain had bankrolled the anti-Napoleon alliance.

Germany forced a harsh peace on Soviet Russia in early 1918. This allowed the Germans to shift their eastern forces to the Western Front for one final offensive before the American troops could make their presence felt. However, they had to leave a large number of troops to police their gains and puppet states in the east. The last offensive began in March 1918 and crawled to a halt in front of Paris in July. Germany's allies collapsed, and the German troops retreated. The Allies at last conquered the trenches as the German forces disintegrated. On September 29, 1918, Ludendorff called for a ceasefire and a new German government on a popular base. He effectively turned the government back over to William II and the new Chancellor **Prince Max of Baden**. The Emperor and Chancellor put in long-needed democratic reforms and begged the U.S. for a peace conference. At the end of October, a renegade group of German admirals tried to launch a suicide attack on the British blockade. The sailors refused and sparked a revolution that swept over Germany in a matter of days. William II fled into exile. On November 11, 1918, the temporary German government and the Allies agreed to an Armistice (ceasefire) on terms very unfavorable to the Germans. The War was over.

Social and Economic Effects of the War

Total War

This was the first conflict that fully involved civilians. Their governments taxed them heavily, drafted more soldiers than ever, put in ever more strict rationing, and the enemy could bomb them or shell them. Starting in blockaded Germany, there were strict limits on consumption. The United States banned the use of scarce materials for making alcoholic beverages and then, in part because German-Americans owned many breweries and partly in response to the temperance movement, passed a constitutional amendment prohibiting all alcoholic beverages. The military draft tended to hit farmhands more than skilled industrial workers who were needed to make guns and bombs. This left crops to rot in the fields. The German grain harvest of 1917 was only half what it had been in 1913. Other countries soon imitated Germany.

Central Economic Planning

After socialists had called for government-run economic plans in vain for decades, the war proved the need for big economic and financial plans. The total costs of World War I were about $100 trillion in 2011 dollars. Nations had to eliminate inefficiency. The government lavishly funded crash research for substitutes for unavailable materials. By December 1916 Germany made employment compulsory for all men aged seventeen to sixty. Millions of women came into the salaried workforce for the first time. By 1917, women were 43 percent of the Russian workforce. Women became about one-third of the German industrial workforce. Sunday rest was disregarded, and the working day was often extended beyond ten hours. "Merchants of death" enjoyed big profits and were hardly taxed. Even conservative governments reached out to labor unions for help. Unions became a vital and accepted part of the economy, and some governments included socialists. In the democracies of Britain and

France, there was a growing feeling that labor unions and their workers were being unfairly exploited.

Censorship and Propaganda

All countries enacted strict laws against treason. In the United States, the Sedition Act passed in seeming violation of the Constitution. The government used it to imprison many leftists, including the head of the American Socialist Party. All countries rigorously censored newspapers. The French even executed the editor of an antiwar newspaper. For the first time, governments set up propaganda offices to mold public opinion and manipulate the truth.

A World Lost

Liberalism in economics and politics declined. The needs of the state were more important than personal freedoms. The state controlled the movement of people across borders. The trade system shriveled. Britain lost 25 percent of its foreign holdings, France 33 percent, and Germany 100 percent. The governments never gave up much of the authority they claimed during the war. Industrialists liked having a close relationship with government and guaranteed contracts. There had been a leftist surge in union membership and socialist voting in Britain, France, Germany, and the United States. War profits had fattened the big corporations, and now they struck back. After the war, the U.S. launched a **Red Scare** to imprison, drive out, or silence many on the left and prevented the formation of a mass socialist party as had happened in other countries. This spilled over to even more violence against African-Americans as the Ku Klux Klan spread beyond the old Confederate states.

Millions had died, and millions more suffered serious wounds. The war had killed up to 13 million soldiers and 10 million civilians. Then a terrible influenza epidemic had killed 40 million worldwide in 1918 and 1919. Millions of Americans, Germans, and French saw the big cities for the first time and preferred to settle there. Villages were devastated, and many were disillusioned. Almost everyone had seen friends killed or severely wounded. What had sustained them was that the war was so terrible that there could never be war again, thus the World War would be "the war to end all wars." They soon discovered that the war had not ushered in a period of peace and friendship.

THE PARIS PEACE CONFERENCE

President **Woodrow Wilson** became the first U.S. President to come to an international peace conference, and he seemed to be in the driver's seat. The other prominent leaders were Lloyd George of Britain, whose coalition of Liberals and Conservatives had just won a huge election victory in the glow of victory; Clemençeau of France, eager for revenge; and Foreign Minister Vittorio Orlando of Italy, hoping for big gains. The Allies did not allow the Germans to participate in the negotiations and did not recognize the Communist government of Russia as legitimate.

The Terms of the Peace

The Conference was held in and around Paris. There were treaties signed separately with each of the defeated Central Powers (Germany, Austria, Hungary, Bulgaria, Turkey).

The German Settlement

The Allies disarmed Germany after the armistice even as they kept up the blockade. In the harsh winter of 1918–19, Germany suffered more than most from starvation and the influenza epidemic. The Allies compelled the Germans to sign the **Treaty of Versailles** in the same Hall of Mirrors where the Germans had proclaimed their empire back in 1871 and humiliated the French. The Allies stripped Germany of all of its colonies, business patents, and foreign investments. The Treaty gave over much land with Germans to the new nations of Poland and Czechoslovakia. France regained Alsace-Lorraine. France took the industrial Saarland for fifteen years and hoped to have it permanently. The Treaty demilitarized the Rhineland (the area of Germany west or thirty miles east of the Rhine River) and sharply restricted the German army. Germany could not have an air force or submarines. A later settlement demanded $37 billion in reparations payments for the damage done during the war. The Germans found this harsh, but the Treaty did not reverse Bismarck's accomplishment and split Germany into independent states.

The Settlement in Eastern Europe

The **Treaties of Saint-German and Trianon** dismantled the Austro-Hungarian Empire into the separate nations of Austria, Hungary, Czechoslovakia, and Poland. Serbia gained Bosnia and Herzegovina as well as Croatia and Slovenia.

It formed a new country, Yugoslavia. The treaty forbade Austria from merging with Germany because this might be seen as a reward for Germany.

There were two main problems. The first was economic: areas that had been integrated into the German, Austro-Hungarian, and Russian empires were torn apart and cobbled together into very different nations. The countries were too small and not equipped to deal with the resulting economic instability. The second problem was political: east-central Europe consisted of small ethnic groups that had been dominated by the two large groups: the Germans and the Russians. For the first time in three hundred years, both of the big groups had been weak at the same time and so by a historical freak accident, the small nations of east-central Europe had won their independence. But as soon as the Germans and Russians recovered their strength, they would try to regain their position. This is what happened in the 1930s and 1940s.

Mandate for Revision

The Allies understood that the Peace of Paris was not perfect. At the conference, they established a **League of Nations** that was supposed to be the forum to make adjustments and keep the peace. But the League was weak from the start because the Allies did not invite Soviet Russia to join in its founding and the United States rejected membership.

The Emergence of the United States

By 1890, the United States had passed China to become the largest economy in the world and passed Britain to become the richest nation. Since the end of the Civil War in 1865, the U.S. had taken advantage of vast resources in farmland, raw materials, and transportation technology, especially railroads. Paul Kennedy has noted that its consumption of modern fuels equaled the five great powers combined. With all this power and prestige, the U.S. abdicated its responsibility to uphold the world system as the Republican-dominated Senate rejected both the Treaty of Versailles and the League of Nations. This would create a fundamental flaw in the global security system throughout the period between wars. France, the U.S., and Britain signed a defensive alliance that would keep some American presence in Europe and assure France, but the treaty collapsed with the Senate's refusal.

TIMELINE

1879	Dual Alliance between Germany and Austria-Hungary
1887	Reinsurance Treaty between Germany and Russia
1890	Reinsurance Treaty lapses
	Bismarck forced out as Chancellor
1894	France and Russia sign defensive alliance
1898	Germany begins naval program
1904	*Entente Cordiale* between Britain and France
1905	First Moroccan Crisis
1907	Britain and Russia sign treaty of friendship
1908	Bosnian Crisis
1911	Second Moroccan Crisis
1912–13	Balkan Wars
1914–18	World War I
1919	Peace of Paris

KEY TERMS

Congress of Berlin
Dual Alliance
Reinsurance Treaty
Alfred von Tirpitz
Entente Cordiale
First Moroccan Crisis
Schlieffen Plan
Treaty of Versailles

PRIMARY SOURCE DOCUMENTS

World War I poetry, http://www.fordham.edu/halsall/mod/1914warpoets.html
Vera Brittain, http://www.wise.virginia.edu/history/wciv2/vera.html
Ernst Maria Remarque,
http://web.archive.org/web/19980116133459/http://pluto.clinch.edu/history/wciv2/
    civ2ref/aqwf.htm
United States Espionage Act, http://www.fordham.edu/halsall/
    mod/1916espionageact.html
Treaty of Versailles, http://www.fordham.edu/halsall/mod/1919versailles.html

Chapter 11

RUSSIAN REVOLUTIONS

THE REVOLUTION OF 1905

Revolutions are not always the result of miserable and oppressive conditions but can happen when things are getting better. Rising expectations can lead to a revolution. You can also have a revolution when the modernization of society lags behind economic modernization. After 1866, Alexander II had turned increasingly reactionary and wiped out academic freedom. In 1881, a terrorist bomb killed Alexander II. His son **Alexander III** (ruled 1881–1894) was harshly reactionary. He cut down on the very limited voting rights his father had granted and increased the religious oppression of Russia's Jews, including organized murder. Russian industrialization began in his reign. The size of the Russian economy grew fourfold in the twenty-eight years before World War I. This is why German generals worried about the Russian giant and felt there should be war sooner rather than later. Newly-industrialized areas had awful conditions in the early 1900s similar to those of England in the 1820s and France in the 1840s. The government had outlawed labor unions so there was no peaceful outlet to express grievances as there was in other nations.

Against the reactionary regimes of Alexander III and his son **Nicholas II** (ruled 1894–1917) rebels rose including liberals based on the small but growing middle class, Social Democrats based on the even smaller class of industrial workers, and Socialist Revolutionaries, who drew support from the peasants. Nicholas' reign began badly with the traditional distribution of coronation presents in 1894. The desperate crowd stampeded and around 1,300 died.

When the crops failed in 1901, the peasants plundered around ninety noble houses. In that year, Socialist Revolutionaries shot and killed the Education Minister. In 1902, they killed the Interior Minister. In 1904, they killed another Interior Minister, while the governor of Finland died violently in a separate incident. In 1905, the Socialist Revolutionaries killed the Grand Duke Sergei, military governor of the Moscow region. Opposition groups called for universal manhood suffrage, a legislative assembly, and civil liberties in a constitution, which would come from the crown.

As Russia's war against Japan turned disastrous, liberals started holding banquets for reform in imitation of French liberals in 1848. Port Arthur surrendered to the Japanese in December 1904, shocking many. A group of workers marched to the Winter Palace in St. Petersburg on January 22, 1905, to ask the emperor for help. The police opened fire and killed (officially) 130 persons. Nicholas II convened a "consultative assembly" and allowed religious tolerance, but the liberals called for a constituent assembly to be elected by universal male suffrage in a direct, secret, and equal vote. Peasant revolts in the countryside plundered more than two thousand manors. On June 14, the battleship *Potemkin* in the Black Sea mutinied. In August 1905 Nicholas agreed to call an elected Duma that would advise him. That did not satisfy the rebels. A general strike in October 1905 rocked Russia. The emperor finally issued the **October Manifesto**. There would be a legislative assembly called the **Duma** elected by a large number of voters. It would control ministers of government. He guaranteed civil liberties including freedom from arrest, freedom of opinion, assembly, and association, and a free press. The revolutionary sentiment ebbed.

Constitutional Government

The idea of a constitutional government was particularly hard for Russia because it had an illiterate population, no existing political parties, and ethnic conflict. The October Manifesto might have worked as a constitutional regime had its principles been applied in good faith by men of good will in an atmosphere of patience. None of that existed. Nicholas began to go back on his word by ruling some subjects out of bounds and decreeing that an undemocratic upper house had to approve all laws. Parties began to form in the Duma: the conservative "Union of the Russian People," the liberals split between the contented Octobrists and "Cadets" (Constitutional Democrats) who wanted more liberalism. The Socialist Revolutionaries continued to plot, while the Social Democrats split between the moderate Mensheviks and the small revolutionary group that called itself **Bolshevik**.

Peter Stolypin (Prime Minister 1905–1911) tried to reform agriculture and modernize Russia. Peasant life remained miserable; peasants spent 60 to 70 percent of their budget on food and most of the rest on clothing and lodgings. Peasants lived in eighteen-by-twenty-one foot cottages, many with earth floors, animals for warmth, and holes rather than chimneys. They covered the walls with dung in winter to patch the holes. When the Socialist Revolutionaries moderated their views, the radicals split off and accelerated their violence; there were perhaps 1,400 political deaths in 1906 and 3,000 in 1907. There were 17,000 assassinations by terrorists from 1905 to 1914. Russian politics was marked by more violence than any other European country. Stolypin cracked down hard. He brought suspected terrorists before military courts martial and executed over a thousand suspects. He sent agents to infiltrate terrorist organization, but these double agents often demanded outrageous acts and riled up nonviolent people. A police agent associated with a revolutionary group assassinated Stolypin in 1911. While some thought Stolypin was Russia's last hope, the truth was that the Emperor was about to dismiss him anyway.

Russia during World War I

Russia was completely unprepared for a modern war. The army had bad leadership, the lower ranks of officers lost many casualties, and an influx of recruits diluted the quality even further. Soldiers fought well at times, but lacked the stamina and stubbornness to shake off bad leaders. The first commander-in-chief was the Emperor's uncle. The Emperor took personal command in 1915 despite a lack of competence. For a time, one-quarter of all Russian soldiers went to the front unarmed; their commanders told them to pick up weapons from the dead. Britain and France provided little direct aid because Turkey blocked the Straits. Nicholas refused to make peace with the progressives of the Duma or make serious concessions to the Poles. He relied more on his wife Alexandra's advice, and she in turn was increasingly influenced by the monk **Gregory Rasputin** (d. 1916), who was able apparently to control the hemophilia of Nicholas' son Alexis. When Nicholas took personal command of the forces, he left Alexandra and Rasputin in control of St. Petersburg. By the end of 1916, the government was supplying the army properly, but diverted nearly everything for military purposes. Russian farmers were producing 8.8 bushels of grain per acre at a time when British farmers produced thirty-five bushels. Food prices increased to double or quadruple the prewar level.

THE FEBRUARY REVOLUTION, 1917

The parties in the Duma became more radical. They demanded the participation of the Duma in the government, removal of the most odious ministers, the participation of non-bureaucratic agencies in army supply, and "a government enjoying the confidence of the nation." Alexandra plotted to send the moderate leaders to prison in Siberia. A group of conspirators including the Emperor's nephew murdered Rasputin in December 1916. From March 8 to 11, 1917, a series of strikes and riots shook Petrograd (St. Petersburg) with the Duma in session and Nicholas away at army headquarters. Some 1,500 were killed and injured. The Duma formed a provisional government made up of the progressive bloc plus **Alexander Kerensky**, a Socialist Revolutionary who headed the labor bloc. On March 12, a *Soviet* (council) of workers and soldiers in St. Petersburg formed. Nicholas abdicated on March 15. These events are often called the "February Revolution" because the Russian Orthodox church had not adopted the Gregorian (Catholic) calendar and was twelve days behind. Thus the "February Revolution" occurred on March 12, and the "October Revolution" occurred on November 7.

Provisional Government

The Provisional Government shifted to the left, and Kerensky emerged as the main figure. The government abolished the death penalty, declared all legally equal regardless of race, religion, or class status. The Petrograd Soviet had loose rules, no jurisdiction, and a fluid membership. The Mensheviks and Kerensky led the Soviet. Kerensky remained very popular: he received over 800 votes when the Congress of Soviets met in May and elected an Executive Committee; Lenin, by contrast, got only twenty votes.

Kerensky made three key mistakes. Firstly, he stayed in the War and launched a new offensive in July 1917; the Russian people wanted peace. Secondly, he delayed convening an assembly to write a new Russian constitution. The process was cumbersome and Russia was in chaos, but the delay until December was fatal. If he had convened the Assembly in July before the Bolsheviks could muster strength, things might have been different. Thirdly, he did not endorse breaking up the big estates into land for the peasants. Kerensky came from a peasant movement and supported land reform, but he was in coalition with more conservative elements and did not want to endorse the peasants taking things into their own hands. Kerensky wanted an elected assembly to put through a legal land reform. Kerensky's refusal to acknowledge the growing pillaging of the estates raised the suspicion that the government would eventually support the nobles and restore the estates to them. While his political base in the peasantry never turned against Kerensky, they were cool and suspicious enough that it opened the door to a more radical movement.

LENIN AND LENINISM / THE OCTOBER REVOLUTION

Lenin's Background

Vladimir Ilyich Ulyanov (1870–1924) had become a revolutionary early in life when the government hanged his older brother in an alleged plot against Emperor Alexander III. He took the revolutionary name Lenin. The authorities arrested him in December 1895 and sentenced him to five years in Siberia. George Plekhanov (1857–1918) was one of the leading Russian Marxists. He believed that Russia was in what Marx had termed the feudal stage. Russia would have to pass through the capitalist stage before socialism. At the 1903 Congress of Social Democrats, Lenin broke with Plekhanov and the Mensheviks and led the more radical Bolsheviks out of the party. **Bolshevik** means "majority" even though it was not a majority of the Social Democratic party. They had no more than eight thousand members in 1905. When the Bolsheviks took the position that they would not work with the government in the War, the government arrested all five of their Duma deputies in November 1914 and deported them to Siberia. Lenin went from one place of exile to another. He lived in Switzerland through most of World War I. When he heard about the February Revolution, he was desperate to return to Russia.

Marxism-Leninism

Lenin had to modify Marxist thought considerably because Plekhanov and the Mensheviks had faithfully described Marx's ideas.

1. Lenin believed that Marx's predictions had not happened because of imperialism, something Marx could not have foreseen. Lenin saw it as "The Highest Stage of Capitalism" (the title of his 1916 book). An increasing concentration of capital in fewer hands marked this stage. The exchange of goods gives way to a massive export of capital. This was not particularly accurate. As we have seen, the United States and Russia were the prime beneficiaries of this export of capital, and they were not colonies. But Lenin

needed to draw three conclusions. First, as the imperialists divided the world, eventually there would be no more free land and the powers would fight among themselves, thus World War I was an imperialistic conflict. Second, even backward agricultural countries such as Russia could have a proletarian revolution because the entire world was enmeshed in the capitalistic system. Third, capitalists were buying off workers in industrialized countries such as England and Germany with the money from imperialistic exploitation of areas of world. Again, as we have seen, colonialism was not particularly profitable and businesses that made a profit required massive direct or indirect subsidies from governments. Lenin scorned labor unions as an elite that did not represent the worker's true interest. This is why there had not been a workers' revolution in the industrialized countries as Marx had predicted.

2. A new type of party. Rather than the mass movements that Marx had worked for in his lifetime, Lenin wanted a very small elite vanguard that would lead the revolution. He took this straight from the anarchist Bakunin (an enemy of Marx) and the Russian terrorist organizations. **Democratic Centralism** would govern the Communist Party. The lower levels of the Party would elect higher ranks. Once decisions are made, everyone must abide by them or leave the party. This was a good way to avoid traitors. Decision-making under Lenin extended to the Communist Party Congress of about 900 which met annually. His successors restricted the decisions to smaller bodies.

3. Lenin elevated Marx's phrase of the "Dictatorship of the Proletariat." In the transition period after the revolution, there would still be some capitalists around trying to overthrow the regime. A dictatorship would be necessary for a while to suppress the capitalists before classes and the government withered away.

Lenin was looking to get back from his Swiss exile to Russia, and the German high command accommodated him in its quest to send revolutionaries to enemy countries. It put Lenin and his associates into a "sealed train" so Lenin would not look like a German agent. When Lenin returned, he forced the Bolsheviks to drop any cooperation with the temporary government. Plekhanov denounced Lenin with the work *On the Theses of Lenin, or Why Delirium Is Sometimes Interesting.*

The October Revolution

Kerensky claimed for years that he had been betrayed not only by Lenin and the Left, but also by the right, especially when military commander Lavr Kornilov (1870–1918) (described as having the "heart of a lion, brains of a sheep") revolted in August and marched on Petrograd. Kerensky released the Bolshevik prisoners to help organize the defense of Petrograd. When Kornilov backed down, the prestige of the Bolsheviks rose, and they gained control of the Soviets in Petrograd and Moscow. For their part, the Rightists always claimed that Kerensky was too much of a leftist and excluded them from power when they could have helped him against Lenin. Kornilov only disobeyed orders when he believed Kerensky to be a puppet of the Petrograd Soviet.

Against others' judgment, Lenin persuaded the Bolsheviks that the time had come for revolution before the elections for the Constituent Assembly. The Bolsheviks would certainly win few votes in these elections. **Leon Trotsky** (1879–1940), who had only joined the Bolsheviks at the end of July 1917 and been elected chairman of the Petrograd Soviet on September 23, organized the actual revolution. Trotsky used the Red Guards of the Petrograd Soviet on the night of November 6–7 to seize key points and surround the Winter Palace while Lenin snuck around the city in disguise to see how things were going. The Bolsheviks dominated the All-Russian Congress of Soviets that met on November 7. It declared Kerensky's government deposed and elected Lenin as Chair of the "Council of People's Commissars," with Trotsky as Foreign Minister, and Joseph Stalin as Minister for Nationalities. Finland took the opportunity to break away from Russia.

Lenin interfered in the elections and banned the Cadet party. However, Kerensky's Socialist Revolutionaries were the big winners with 370 out of 707 seats. The Bolsheviks, with all the vote-rigging, got only got 170 seats. The Assembly met for one day and elected Kerensky's associate Chernov as President. The Red Guards then dissolved the Assembly. This would be the last popular assembly to meet formally in Russia until the Congress of People's Deputies in 1989.

First Decrees

Lenin dissolved all centers of opposition, demobilized the army, and ousted imperial officers. He recognized the ongoing land reform. Poland, Lithuania, Latvia, and Estonia declared their independence from Russia. Nationalist movements appeared in Ukraine, Belarus, Azerbaijan, Georgia, Armenia,

Russian Asia, and the far north. Lenin announced that he was canceling all debts owed to foreign powers. The Communists signed the controversial Treaty of Brest-Litovsk ending the war with Germany at great cost to Russia. The Party Congress only ratified the Treaty because Lenin made a great speech. Lenin assured the delegates that the terms did not matter because Communism would soon sweep Germany and all national borders would dissolve. Lenin set up a secret (or political) police called the **Cheka**. In the next several years, the Cheka would kill up to 50,000 in the "Red Terror."

The Civil War

Brest-Litovsk and the canceling of debts angered the Allies and the British landed a force of 40,000 to prevent ammunition from falling into German hands. Japan landed 72,000 troops in the east to seize key areas. The United States sent a small force of 8,000 to assist the Japanese. The Communists had used the traditional red flag of revolution and were known for short as "Reds." The Allies formed and supplied anti-communist "White" forces made up of those opposing Lenin's regime. These forces varied in their politics from those who wanted to restore the Emperor to Kerensky and his Socialist Revolutionaries. There was also considerable geographic disunity. Kornilov and then General Anthony Denikin commanded around the Black and Caspian Seas. In south central Russia, a Czech legion seized points along the railroad and made their way home to Czechoslovakia while fighting the Communists. Admiral Alexander Kolchak, supported by the Socialist Revolutionaries, was centered at Omsk in Western Siberia. General Alexander Yudenich commanded yet another army in Estonia.

In March 1918 Lenin appointed Trotsky as War Commissar. Trotsky had to build up a Red Army from nothing. He restored some imperial officers who he trusted. Reliable political commissars supervised the military at all levels. The Communists were concentrated in the center around Moscow and were able to shuttle troops and supplies about as they needed them. The "Whites" quarreled among themselves. Some would not accept land reform and that cost them peasant support. The various armies would not coordinate their attacks, so the Reds could fight them one by one. In February 1920, the Communists captured and executed Kolchak. After they gained a ceasefire with Poland in the middle of 1920, the Reds crushed the southern force. By the end of 1920, the war was pretty much over, although the last foreign troops did not leave until 1922. Up to 7 million died in the civil war and the ensuing famine. Another

3 million left the country. The Communists were unable to regain the western end of the Russian empire.

Lenin brought economic control to a new level by ordering "War Communism" to deal with the war. The government nationalized industries and made labor compulsory. It imposed general rationing and nationalized land. It forced peasants to give up food so that cities would not face the kind of bread shortages that had sparked the revolutions in the first place. After the Civil War, Lenin had to consider how to repair a land shattered by two terrible wars. The government also had to make concession to non-Russian nationalities. The Communists put out a constitution that divided the land into a number of "Soviet Socialist Republics." These republics had come together as a Union of Soviet Socialist Republics, and although the Russians dominated this Union, the nation would be called the U.S.S.R. or Soviet Union.

Early Soviet Foreign Policy

The Communists believed that their seizure of power was the first step in a worldwide revolution. They thought Germany would be next, and the turmoil that swept Germany after the armistice seemed to prove them right, but then the government rallied and crushed the communists' uprising. Lenin founded a Communist International (**Comintern** for short) in March 1919 to promote revolution. For a while, that was the only Soviet foreign policy; it had no ambassadors. How could you have relations with a government you were trying to overthrow?

In 1922 the Soviets sent the Foreign Commissar Georgei Chicherin to Genoa to meet the Allies at a European economic summit. Still angry about the canceled debts, the Allies gave Chicherin a cold shoulder. He reached out to the other outcast nation and signed the **Treaty of Rapallo** with Germany. As a sign of friendship, the Soviet Union sent grain to a hungry Germany in 1923. In 1924, the Soviets established normal relations with some countries. However, the Comintern clashed with the Foreign Ministry and continued to work for revolution and alienated many countries with intrigues and terrorist acts. By 1927, the Soviet Union was isolated.

The New Economic Policy

In 1921 Lenin and Nicolai Bukharin came up with the New Economic Policy (N.E.P.). This marked a partial return to capitalism. It allowed some private industry for firms with fewer than twenty employees, and a class known as NEPmen rose, especially in the retail trade. The Communist Party kept control of the "commanding heights" of finance, large and medium industry, modern transport, foreign trade, and wholesale commerce. The N.E.P. allowed peasants to produce privately and trade for profit. The **Kulaks** (fists) denoted prosperous peasants. By 1927, the Soviet economy was returning to 1913 levels. Trade unions regained some independence. There was not enough of an urban labor force to build industrial power. Citydwellers were trying to return to the land and the sources of food while the government had to force peasants into the cities to work.

THE EARLY STALIN REGIME

Joseph Dzhugashvili (1879–1953) was the son of a shoemaker. Unlike most other Bolshevik leaders, Stalin had never lived abroad. In 1922, Lenin suffered two strokes and never recovered. The maneuvers for succession began with two leading figures: Trotsky, the builder of the Red Army, and Stalin, who had gained control of the Communist Party machinery as General Secretary and had been carefully building loyalty. Trotsky was far the more flamboyant and charismatic figure. Other Communists were jealous and feared him. Also Trotsky was of Jewish heritage, and he declined Lenin's offer of appointment as a successor because he believed that Russia would never allow a Jew to lead it. In his political testament, Lenin warned the Communists against Stalin, who he considered rude and rigid. But other leaders believed that Stalin was dull and that they could easily manipulate him.

Stalin Comes to Power

After Lenin died in 1924, Stalin ruled as part of the "Troika" with Grigory Zinoviev, the head of the Comintern, and Lev Kamenev, the leader of the Leningrad (St. Petersburg) party organization. They removed Trotsky from his army position. By 1927, Stalin allied with Bukharin to get rid of Zinoviev and Kamenev. The Party Congress condemned "all deviations from the general Party line." In 1929, Stalin ousted Bukharin from the leadership, exiled Trotsky, and stood alone as leader. Stalinism contained three major changes to Marxism-Leninism: 1) **Socialism in one country**. In sharp contrast to Trotsky's idea of continuing world revolution, Stalin wanted to take care of the Soviet Union first and then worry about the rest of the world. 2) **Revolution from above:**

the Communist Party would clearly lead with the "support" of the proletariat. 3) **The fostering of Russian patriotism and nationalism** to fight the Nazis in World War II.

The Building of the Totalitarian State

The 1936 Constitution set up eleven republics: the Russian Federation, Ukraine, Belarus, Azerbaijan, Armenia, Georgia, Turkmenistan, Uzbekistan, Tajikistan, Kazakhstan, and Kyrgyzstan. Each republic had a foreign border to ensure that "if they wanted to they could secede." In practice, there were three centers of power: the Communist Party, the army, and the secret police. Stalin, although essentially ruling alone, maintained and refined the machinery set up by Lenin. The Party remained an elite group although most wanted to join because of privileges. The party in 1929 had 1.5 million members, of whom one-quarter were functionally illiterate, and only 8,000 had been members in 1917. The Communist Party Congress met far less frequently than in Lenin's day. It did not meet at all from 1939 to 1952. It elected the Central Committee, which in turn chose the Secretariat (which determined Party membership), the Organization Bureau (Orgburo), and the Political Bureau (Politburo). The Communists were obsessed with the history of the French Revolution and especially feared the rise of a Napoleon-like figure out of the army. The Party's officers indoctrinated new recruits in communist ideology to prevent this.

The Constitution guaranteed all basic human and civil rights and gave all people over 18 the right to vote. Communists boasted that it was the freest constitution in the world. However, the "rights had to conform to the interests of the workers." There was no separation of powers among the executive, legislative, and judicial branches because the Supreme Soviet (Congress) would name all members. The Politburo was renamed the Presidium but only Stalin had real power.

Collectivization and the "War against the People"

End of the N.E.P.

By 1928, Russian industry had recovered to its pre-war level, and there was a growing middle class, especially among the peasants. Stalin believed that a war was coming against the capitalist world that would not allow the Communists to succeed. World War I had proved that a nation had to be industrialized to win a modern war. As a Marxist, he was also appalled that history seemed to be running backward: the Soviet Union was de-industrializing and becoming less urban. During the Civil War, half of all the people had left Moscow and two-thirds had left St. Petersburg. Western Europe had financed the first stage of Russian industrialization, but it would not provide new loans as long as the Communists refused to honor the old debts. The U.S.S.R. would have to rely on its own resources to buy western technology and expertise, and that meant squeezing the peasants and shipping raw materials such as coal and oil abroad. As world food prices dropped after 1929, Stalin needed to export more and more crops to finance industrialization. Stalin's government created new branches of industry from nothing: chemical, auto, agricultural machinery, aviation, machine tool, and electrical. There were over 1,500 new factories, including massive complexes in the Ural Mountains and Western Siberia. By 1935, the Soviets were self-sufficient in coal and oil. Stalin outlawed abortion so he would have "healthy Soviet heroes" for his army.

The War against the People

Private plots had been producing 20 percent of all the food in the Soviet Union. Stalin confiscated the private plots and ordered **collectivization** of farm land into giant farms worked by the peasants with what limited machinery there was. The Communists transformed 26 million farms into 250,000 collectives. Stalin first announced that he was reducing the price that the government paid for crops. The peasants retaliated by withholding crops. This caused a food shortage in the cities and a shortfall in exports. When Stalin announced that he was taking away private plots, the Kulaks reacted by slaughtering animals and withholding food. Half of all the horses and cattle in the U.S.S.R. died from 1929 to 1933, two-thirds of sheep and goats, and 42 percent of hogs. The secret police arrested many peasants and sent them to Siberian labor camps (**GULAGS**). The government shot others. Without enough food, starvation and disease ran riot. Worst hit were the richest farm areas. There were 10 to 15 million unnatural deaths in the 1930s from the famine that swept the U.S.S.R. 10 percent of all Ukrainians disappeared; 1 million out of 4 million Kazakhs vanished. As a result, there was little increase in grain production from 1928 to 1938.

"The Great Terror"

Stalin was demanding and often unreasonable. He slept most of the day, worked through the night, and called aides at all hours. He was crude and not very bright but had a peasant cunning. He devoted all of his time to running the country. Discontent grew with his policies: in 1932, two Politburo members drafted a 200-page statement denouncing Stalin and calling him an "evil genius." Stalin asked the secret police chief **Yagoda** to shoot them. Yagoda had no problem shooting peasants or even party members, but to kill two leaders he wanted specific authorization from the Politburo. In 1933, a new law allowed "traitors" to be shot. Under the Law of Co-Responsibility, all associates and family members could be charged with the same crime as an accused person. Stalin set up a special section to deal with the purge under **Nicolai Yezhov.** The leader of the Leningrad party and possible Stalin successor Sergei Kirov was assassinated in 1934, perhaps on Stalin's orders. Stalin removed 200,000 unreliable members from the Communist Party.

In August 1936, there was a public "Trial of the 16" including Zinoviev and Kamenev. They were charged with crimes they could not possibly have committed. The government convicted and executed them. In September 1936, Yezhov replaced Yagoda as secret police chief. There were more public trials in 1937 and 1938, including Bukharin. In 1937, Stalin began to purge the army. This was encouraged by the German Nazi SS, which fanned Stalin's paranoia by giving him forged documents showing military treachery. The Soviet army purged three of its five Marshals, thirteen of the fifteen army commanders, thirty-eight of the fifty-eight corps commanders, 110 of the 195 division commanders, 220 of the 400 brigadier generals, and seventy-five of the eighty members of the supreme military council. This left the Soviet military much weaker, just as the Germans intended.

The Grim Total

Soviet mathematicians trying to estimate demographics came up with the following figures: from 1929 to 1935 15 million died unnaturally; from 1936 to 1939 3.5 million; from 1941 to 1945 28 million (including those killed by Germans); and from 1946 to 1950 4 million. There was a total of 50 million unnatural deaths. In February 1990, the Soviet secret police reported that 3,778,234 were sentenced for "counterrevolutionary activity" in the Stalin years and of those 786,098 were executed. Others estimate up to 8 million taken by secret police. The Soviet population slipped down to 165 million.

TIMELINE

1905	Revolution forces Nicholas II to grant a constitution
1905–14	Political violence sweeps Russia
1917	February Revolution forces Emperor out
	October Revolution brings Communists to power
1918–20	Civil War
1921–29	New Economic Policy
1924	Lenin dies
1929	Stalin becomes unquestioned leader
1929–35	Millions die as Stalin institutes crash modernization
1935–37	Stalin purges Communist Party
1937–38	Stalin purges army

KEY TERMS

Alexander Kerensky
Vladimir Lenin
Leon Trotsky
Cheka
New Economic Policy
Joseph Stalin

PRIMARY SOURCE DOCUMENTS

V.I. Lenin, http://history.hanover.edu/courses/excerpts/111lenin.html
Lenin, http://www.fordham.edu/halsall/mod/lenin-staterev.html
Joseph Stalin, http://www.fordham.edu/halsall/mod/1928stalin.html

Chapter 12

THE RISE OF FASCISM

WHAT IS FASCISM?

The Italian dictator **Benito Mussolini** coined the term fascism to identify Italian nationalism with the glory of the ancient Roman Empire. The *fasces* were cylindrical bundles of rods from which an ax protruded. They were carried by lictors who guarded the praetors, consuls, dictators and emperors. *Fasces* symbolized power and unity. Mussolini used the term to define his movement before ever trying to define exactly what fascism is. It was not until 1932 that he wrote *The Doctrine of Fascism*. The definition of fascism has always been elastic in part because Mussolini seized power before he wrote the theory. Already by 1932 there were "fascist" movements of various stripes all around Europe and overseas.

Some give fascism a broad definition: almost any right-wing regime of the era between the world wars. Others offer a very narrow definition and try to separate a traditional right and a radical right from the fascists; thus the only fascist regimes were Mussolini's and Hitler's. Mussolini himself wrote of thirteen fundamental ideas of Fascism. Among these ideas were fascism as a spiritual movement opposed to materialism and a religious movement where the individual binds himself to a larger will and law. Fascism was for the state and against the individual because "outside the State there can be neither individuals nor groups." "Fascism is opposed to socialism, which confines the movement of history within the class struggle and ignores the unity of classes established in one economic and moral reality in the State." "Fascism is opposed to democracy, which equates the nation to the majority."

Ernst Nolte suggested that fascism consists of antimarxism, antiliberalism, anticonservativism, the leadership principle, a party army, and the aim of totalitarianism. It was anticonservative because the fascists were proud revolutionaries and in their speeches, they tended to attack the main conservative institutions: big business and big landowners. When they got into power, fascists tended to ignore their speeches and favor these groups above others. There was always a leader at the top who the fascists saw as superior to all other men. Violence was an important part of Fascism and not an accident. Every fascist movement had an organized group of violent bullies that might go by the name of "combat squad" or "storm troopers" or "protective staff." This was the party army. Finally, the fascists aimed at total control not only of power, but also the economy, society and cultural life. Their dreams of power were therefore much greater than the old absolutists and with the modern transportation and communication technologies of the twentieth century, they had a greater ability to realize this dream.

There were significant differences between fascists and the communist movement that Lenin had started in Russia. First, communism was an international movement. Although Russia had the first communist revolution and was always the guiding force, there was always the idea from Marx that economic class mattered much more than language and that when the revolution triumphed, national boundaries would melt away. Communists always had a blind spot when it came to nationalism, and in the end it was a major factor in bringing down communism. Fascism glorified the nation-state and held it supreme to all else. The people of one nation were to dominate all other nations. This attitude made it difficult to win friends and allies and tended to push the nations to war. Combined with their antiliberal economic policy and an impossible desire for self-sufficiency, it almost ensured that fascist nations would destroy themselves while communist countries lasted decades despite doubtful economic ideas. Communism also was more aggressive in bringing down wealthy people than fascism. As long as they made certain sacrifices, the fascists would allow the rich to keep most of their property.

Louis-Napoleon Bonaparte had subverted democracy in France. When he staged a coup against the Republic and established an Empire, he put it to an up-or-down vote, showing that a cleverly-worded plebiscite without educated debate will endorse anything the ruler desires. Otto von Bismarck of Prussia had used the democratic ideal against liberals trying to enforce the Prussian constitution by going over their heads to the people. Fascists took the next step.

The Cult of the State

Classical liberalism had generally championed the individual against the state and in the name of a free market tended to shy away from government regulation of business. In the last quarter of the nineteenth century, liberalism lost ground to socialism as the Western economies went through violent booms and busts, leaving businessmen ruined, workers unemployed, and families suffering. After 1900, there were some small moves toward regulation, anti-trust measures, and social insurance spending by liberal parties.

Conservatives and Marxist socialists both believed in a strong state and both drew their intellectual beliefs from Hegel. In his *Philosophy of Law* (1821), Hegel wrote that the State has the right to protect itself against those who indulge in "subjective feeling and particular conviction" which leads to "the ruin of public order and the law of the land." The authoritarian kingdom of Prussia that Hegel served seemed to be the realization of political rationality. Hegel glorified militarism by conceiving that "in duty the individual finds his liberation" and "self-sacrifice...is...the real existence of one's freedom." It was not too far a jump from there to the fascist idea that the purpose of a man's life is to die in the service of a fighting state. Hegel promoted self-sacrifice, duty, and discipline opposed to Jefferson's Enlightenment ideals of life, liberty, and the pursuit of happiness. In his *Philosophy of History* (1837), Hegel saw the State as the "realization of Freedom." "All the worth which the human being possesses—all spiritual reality—he possesses only through the State." "The State is the Divine idea as it exists on Earth." Hegel rejected the democratic ideal that the people are the state as a "perversity" and a "ruse." While promoting order in internal politics, Hegel was an enthusiastic supporter of international anarchy. Men and states stagnate in peace and corruption grows. War purges this and promotes national unity. "As a result of war, nations are strengthened, but peoples involved in civil strife also acquire peace at home through making war abroad."

Roots of Fascism

Fascism could only grow out of a mass system that had politically mobilized the masses but not rooted them to democracy. Both Mussolini and Hitler took power in democratic regimes. Frustrated nationalism also a played role. The American South after the Civil War had some fascistic tendencies. France in the 1870s had experienced mass politics and a national wound from its loss to Prussia in the war of 1870. The radically nationalistic League of Patriots combined both left and right in a popular French nationalism, although it collapsed after the Boulanger Affair of 1888. The Bohemian part of the Austro-Hungarian empire also saw a proto-fascist movement grow. When Chancellor Taaffe in the 1890s tried to give more rights to the Czechs, this caused a reaction in the German-speaking part of Bohemia known as the **Sudetenland**. They formed a German Workers Party (DAP) in 1904 to promote national rights.

THE ITALIAN VARIANT

Italian Nationalism

As we have seen before, the rise of democracy was closely linked with imperialism. As Italy became more democratic, it became more expansionist. It invaded and occupied Libya and the Dodecanese Islands of the southern Aegean Sea in 1911 and 1912. It came into the First World War because of the Allied promise of Austrian and Turkish land and colonies. The Italian government had also made big promises to the people when it entered war: land reform would give land to poor, and there would be special benefits for industrial workers. The military mobilization fell disproportionately on the southern peasantry. More than 600,000 Italians died, and the economy was a shambles. Many felt that the Allies had cheated Italy at the Paris Peace Treaties. Italy gained the land up to Brenner Pass (including 200,000 German-speakers) and the city of Trieste from Austria, but had wanted Fiume as well.

Mussolini's Background

Mussolini (1883–1945) was the son of a blacksmith in Romagna. Before the war, he had been the editor of the Socialist party newspaper *Avanti*. Sorel and Nietzsche deeply influenced Mussolini, and he believed in the idea of a revolutionary vanguard and elite. Most Italian socialists opposed the war, but Mussolini supported it and was expelled. He joined *Il Popolo d'Italia* (The People of Italy), a newspaper financed by prointerventionist business interests. He set up a "fascist movement" which claimed it had pressured parliament into obeying "the will of the people" and declaring war. Mussolini joined the army and served seventeen months until he was injured in a training accident.

Political Discontent

To encourage mass politics, the Italian constitution in 1919 added proportional representation to the 1913 male vote. This encouraged many small parties and led to unstable coalitions and short-lived governments. The Catholic Popular and Socialist parties were the biggest mass parties, but they would not cooperate because of religious differences over the position of the Pope, who still refused to recognize the unification of Italy and the loss of his lands. The Liberal party opposed major economic reforms. The unions responded by leading strikes in industry and on land. Peasants attempted to force land reform in the Fall of 1919. The elections of that year gave the socialists about one-third of the seats in parliament.

A number of groups were disillusioned with the government: wealthy landowners and industrialists were upset with constant strikes and unrest and looked for a strong leader. Nationalists wanted greater Italian gains than Paris had given Italy and cheered when the poet and one-eyed war hero Gabriele d'Annunzio led an expedition against Yugoslavia in September 1919. His followers wore black shirts following the dress of Italian commandos from the war: black for death. Finally, veterans came home from the war to find little work and less appreciation. Like most governments, Italy had given many factory workers draft deferments to keep up industrial production, but the veterans regarded them as shirkers.

The Fascist Movement Begins

Mussolini formed the first *Fasci Italiani di Combattimento* (Fighting Squad) in March 1919. Mussolini combined a jumble of Marxist and nationalistic ideas but started off as mainly socialist and democratic. Taking from Marx and Lenin, Mussolini stated that the class struggle was on the world stage with "bourgeois" nations such as France and Britain and Germany allied against "proletarian" nations such as Italy. The Fascists gained support in the countryside where big landlords and allied industries funded the fascist agrarian league to attack socialist peasant leagues and beat up strikers.

Deals with the Devil

The Fascists won only a single seat in the elections of 1919. Even in their home area of Milan, only 2 percent voted for them. The Milanese socialists carried a coffin past Mussolini's apartment to mock his failure. Mussolini began to develop ceremonies for meetings including flags, uniforms (black shirts from D'Annunzio's venture), and the wearing of daggers. In the wave of violent strikes, the government did nothing and only Fascists seemed willing to take on the problem. They drew support from war veterans, the middle class, and some college students. The government forced big business and landowners to make concessions on unions, conditions, hours, and pay. It legalized the peasant land seizures, and the number of landowners in Italy doubled from 1.1 million to 2.3 million in the ten years from 1911 to 1921. Many peasants lost interest in any further reforms. By the end of 1920, the Fascists had declared war on the Socialists: they sent squads of thirty to fifty men to sack Socialist headquarters, beat up Socialists, and force them to swallow foul-tasting cod liver oil. 207 died for political reasons in the spring of 1921, most of them Socialists. In this three-month period the Fascist Party grew 20,000 to 188,000 members. One-quarter of the members were under the voting age of twenty-one, and half were army veterans.

Liberal leader Giolitti made an appeal for Fascist votes in May 1921 and guaranteed Mussolini some seats as part of a deal. The Fascists received thirty-eight seats, and Mussolini won 200,000 votes in Milan. Mussolini defined the Party as a "revolutionary militia placed at the service of the nation. It follows three principles: order, discipline, hierarchy." When the Socialists declared a protest strike in August 1922 against violence, the Fascists declared war on them and threw them out of their own offices. When the government took no action, the Fascists took over some town councils in the north. By October 1922, only Turin and Parma still had strong Socialist parties. For many groups, Fascists were very useful against the Left. There were Fascist sympathizers in the Church, the royal family, and even the Cabinet. Mussolini recognized that the Fascists were at the height of their power and that it was a matter of time until Giolitti put together a Liberal/Catholic coalition. At that point, the Fascists would be a nuisance and the government would crush them. In October 1922, 26,000 Black Shirts marched on Rome. There was no real danger of a fascist coup. The government asked King Victor Emmanuel III to declare a state of emergency and arrest the Fascist leaders, but instead the king appointed Mussolini as Prime Minister with one-year emergency powers to restore order and introduce reforms.

Full Power

Mussolini's Cabinet of 1922 had four Fascists, four Liberals, two Catholic Popular party members, one Nationalist, and two military leaders. He cracked down hard on d'Annunzio's Nationalists (too much competition) and the Communists, who had split from the Socialists and wanted a Soviet-style government. He forced the Nationalists into the Fascist Party. Mussolini set up a new organization called the **Fascist Grand Council** to provide a governing executive.

The center-right coalition voted for the **Acerbo Electoral Law** in 1923. It not only did away with proportional representation (that is, the party that gets one-third of the vote will get one-third of the seats) but went to the other extreme. The party that received the most votes and at least 25 percent of the vote would get two-thirds of the seats. Each party hoped it would be the beneficiary. The Fascists had a big victory in the elections of April 1924: they won one-third of the vote but three-fourths of the seats. Three months later, the Fascists murdered the Italian Socialist leader. The opposition pulled out of Parliament as a protest. This was a big mistake as Mussolini ousted the non-Fascists from the government in 1925. He imposed strict censorship, destroyed independent labor unions, forbade workers from striking, and abolished the other political parties in 1926.

Fascist Government

Mussolini had the right to initiate all legislation and rule by decree when he chose. He was responsible only to the king. He controlled all government appointments. He expanded the large police and militia forces. In 1929, he signed the **Lateran Pacts** with the Pope. The Pope recognized the government of Italy and received political control over the small area of Rome around his Vatican palace. Liberal governments had offered this same deal for nearly sixty years, but the Pope only accepted it from a fascist dictatorship. The Pacts helped cement Catholic loyalty to Mussolini.

Corporatism is a political theory that conceives of modern government in a different way from democracy or dictatorship. Instead of direct votes for a congress, parliament, assembly, or council, representatives of the government, business, and labor will make policies. Examples of true corporatist government are very rare; perhaps the government of New York City from 1975 to 1990 would qualify where the big business interests and labor unions rescued the financially-strapped city and put in tax and land policies for business and landlords while preserving union jobs.

Fascist Italy was the more typical result. The government dissolved independent labor unions in favor of puppet "labor fronts." These puppets would sit down with government and business officials to work out a consensus. Labor courts would deal with disputes. This system pleased landlords and industrialists but not too many other people. In 1928 a corporative chamber of 400 representatives picked indirectly by public and private groups, agencies, and professions replaced the Chamber of Deputies. In 1938, this was converted into the Chamber of Fasces and Corporations selected by the government. The Fascist Party's Grand Council was supposed to be the chief coordinator of policy. By the 1930s, the corporatist fiction was that the economy was organized into twenty-two "corporations" where representatives of Fascist-organized labor groups, employers, and the State set working conditions, wages, prices, and industrial policies. The reality was that the Italian administration continued almost undisturbed. Mussolini supposedly "headed" eight agencies personally, but in fact he governed none.

The fascist government reduced unemployment by starting huge public works and transportation programs and extended social insurance programs. The massive budget deficits weakened the financial structure. The fascist attempt to make Italy self-sufficient in grain simply distorted trade and made bread more expensive. Mussolini wanted a strong currency, but his increasing of the lira's value devastated exports by making Italian goods too expensive on the world market. By 1930, Italy had the lowest standard of living in Western Europe. Mussolini did not touch structural problems such as the social and political backwardness of the south, banditry, the Mafia, malaria, and income maldistribution. Mussolini banned abortion in 1930. After 1930, Mussolini's foreign policy became more adventurous as he tried to distract people from the economic woes.

Totalitarian State?

Mussolini used the word totalitarian to refer to the structure and goals of the new state, but it was far from the truth. He hardly changed social and economic institutions. The regime only censored directly anti-government material. Most political cases ended in absolution and the Italian secret police founded in 1930 was not as gruesome as the German or Russian versions. In the Fascist era from 1922 to 1943, there were 5,000 political prison sentences. The government sent 10,000 into internal exile, and executed ten formally, although unofficial political violence continued. Unlike Germany, there was no major propaganda ministry until 1937. Even in politics, King Victor Emmanuel III remained the Head of State with power to dismiss *Il Duce* ("the leader") if he wanted. The military retained considerable autonomy. State officials, not Fascist party leaders, ran the police force.

THE GERMAN VARIANT

The Founding of the Weimar Republic

The German Revolution

When Ludendorff and Hindenburg told William II that the war could no longer continue, William saw that he had to make major changes. The Chancellor added members of the Catholic Center, Progressive and Social Democratic Parties to the Cabinet. When renegade admirals ordered sailors on a suicide mission against the British blockade, they revolted and revolution swept Germany. The Social Democrats were willing to accept some kind of monarchy, but William II and his sons had to go. When Hindenburg denied William the use of the army to crush the revolution, William had to abdicate. The Social Democratic leader **Frederick Ebert** became Chancellor. Ebert called for an elected national assembly to meet as soon as possible. He had seen what happened in Russia the year before and would not become the German Kerensky. The left-wing Independent Socialists demanded that power be put into workers and soldiers' councils instead of an assembly. For a time, Ebert seemed to bow, but the Progressives and Catholic Center as well as the army backed Ebert. All men and women above the age of 20 gained the right to vote. Ebert's Socialists dominated a Congress of Workers and Soldiers' Councils that met in December. It agreed to have elections for an assembly that would write a new constitution for Germany the next month. The **Spartacist League**, a fringe leftist group of Independent Socialists, constituted itself as the Communist Party of Germany at end of December and called for non-participation in elections. In January, right before the elections, the Spartacists tried to seize Berlin. Ebert called in the army and the **Free Corps**, bands of veterans. They murdered the Spartacist leaders and crushed the revolt ruthlessly. There would be no Russian-style revolution in Germany.

The National Assembly

The parties committed to a democratic republic won about three-quarters of the seats. The assembly met in the small city of Weimar because Berlin was still in turmoil, so the republic would be known as the "Weimar Republic." The Assembly elected Ebert as President and the Social Democrat Philipp Scheidemann would handle the day-to-day government as Chancellor. The Constitution created proportional representation in the Reichstag to give the smaller parties a voice. Unfortunately, this led to unstable coalitions and short-lived governments. The Constitution tried to give ordinary citizens the right of law-making through the initiative and referendum process, but this would be abused. The President and Chancellor could, in times of emergency, invoke **Article 48** of the Constitution and put in decrees, subject to the veto of the Reichstag.

Antirepublican Forces

Extremists on the far right and left hated the Republic. Many judges and army officers remained right-wingers. In March 1920 the Free Corps joined a right-wing politician named Wolfgang Kapp and tried to overthrow the Republic. When President Ebert asked the army to fight this **Kapp Putsch**, it refused. The Socialists called for a general strike of workers, and that brought down Kapp. The government did not punish the army for its disloyalty because it wanted a force to put down a new communist revolt.

The Inflation

There had been moderate inflation around the world since the gold discoveries in Alaska and elsewhere in the 1890s. The Germans largely paid for the war with borrowed money. The German national debt rose from 5 billion to 150 billion marks. During the War, the German money supply increased 1,000 percent. The Governments had imposed wage and price controls to keep inflation from getting out of control. After the War, the price controls came off, and prices rose. Germany was hard hit as the mark lost a lot of its value against the U.S. dollar. The mark continued to tumble from 1920 to 1922 as the Kapp Putsch typified a period of violence, especially right-wing violence against prominent center and left politicians. The murder of Foreign Minister Walther Rathenau sent the mark into a tailspin, and German prices rose in reaction.

The Allies demanded reparations payments in kind (for example coal and timber) so that Germany would not pay in devalued paper money. France and Belgium felt that Germany was deliberately falling behind in its payments. They invaded the Ruhr valley, Germany's industrial heartland, in 1923. Britain refused to endorse this. The German government called for "passive resistance." It subsidized groups resisting the French and paid the salaries of striking workers. These massive payments sent the budget deficit and inflation spiraling out of control. The German economy collapsed: people needed wheelbarrows full of money to buy a loaf of bread. Some groups benefited, but the middle classes lost their savings, and the resistance and inflation wiped out the labor unions' money reserves.

The invasion of the Ruhr and inflation brought violence to a fever pitch. The French tried to create a puppet regime in the Rhineland. Communists entered the government in the states of Saxony and Thuringia, and Ebert invoked Article 48 to suppress these governments. Finally, on November 9, 1923, an ex-corporal named **Adolf Hitler**, along with Ludendorff, tried to overthrow the government of Bavaria in Munich in what was called **the Beer Hall Putsch**. The government arrested Hitler, but a judge gave him a very light sentence in a country-club prison, and Hitler served only a few months. The elections of May 1924 increased number of extremists: Nazis, Communists, and Nationalists.

The Golden Age, 1923–1929

Gustav Stresemann and the Dawes Plan

The conservative **Gustav Stresemann** (Foreign Minister 1923–29) now came into his own as leader. He headed the small People's Party that had succeeded the National Liberals. Stresemann was briefly Chancellor in 1923, but became best known as Foreign Minister for promoting cooperation between Germany and other countries. Stresemann's government ended the passive resistance. His Finance Minister **Hans Luther** introduced a new currency to stabilize prices, and the government's decrees ensured an orderly budget.

Once Germany had taken the first step, the United States pressed for stabilization. American banker and former government budget head Charles Dawes led a group to arrange reparations payments, stabilize the German economy, and provide prosperity for Europe (**the Dawes Plan**). Foreigners gained some control over German banks and railroads in exchange for huge American loans to Germany. Germany could now pay the reparations on a reduced schedule, and the Allies then paid back part of their massive war debts to the United States. After the Reichstag passed the Dawes Plan, the French and Belgians pulled out of the Ruhr. The right-wing Nationalist party had given the Dawes Plan some support and would be more moderate for the next several years and enter two Cabinets.

Storm Clouds on the Horizon

Stresemann and Luther hoped to speed the French withdrawal from the rest of Germany. They were willing to recognize permanent borders with France and Belgium, including Alsace-Lorraine. This led to the **Treaties of Locarno** in

1925. The League of Nations admitted Germany the following year. Internal pressures began to build. President Ebert had died in 1925. The victor in the elections was none other than General Hindenburg, the losing commander in World War I. The worldwide fall in crop prices hurt German farmers, and they took out their anger on the Nationalist Party in 1928. That party responded by lurching to the right and opposing Stresemann's foreign policy. The Foreign Minister had negotiated a favorable modification called the **Young Plan** in 1929 but had to fight a bitter campaign. The voters approved the Young Plan, but Stresemann died shortly thereafter at the age of fifty-one. The Nationalist Party was not the only one to the move to the right in the twenties. The Catholic Center became more conservative while the Protestant centrist parties dwindled to almost nothing. Fascism began to grow on the right.

The Nazis

Hitler's Background

Hitler was born in 1889 as the son of an elderly Austrian customs official. He was a bad student and did not complete the equivalent of high school. He was ill-disciplined and lazy and resistant to all authority. He applied to the Vienna Academy of Fine Arts in October 1907 and was rejected; it deemed his second application in October 1908 so poor that it would not admit him to the entrance test. The School of Architecture would not admit him because he had not received a school-leaving certificate. In 1909, he went to Vienna anyway. He took occasional odd jobs and sold postcard paintings but generally lived the life of a bum, surviving in flop-houses with other men of the street. He would read bits and pieces of various books and histories, many of which had a mystical or religious bent, and these seemed to increase his sense of being in a fantasy world. He constantly talked of the people he hated: the Jews, the priests, the Social Democrats, the Habsburgs.

Hitler's Ideology

Hitler claimed that his virulent hatred of Jews began in Vienna. It might have started earlier, but there is no proving this. Hitler fell under the racist spell of Adolf Lanz, who preached on the glory of a blond-haired Aryan race. In 1906, Lanz had hoisted the swastika above his castle headquarters as the symbol of the Aryan movement. Lanz used a very debased form of the philosophy of Nietzsche to argue that Aryans were racial supermen. Races should never mix, and Lanz's solutions to "inferior races" included sterilization, forced labor, and mass murder.

THE RISE OF FASCISM

During his Vienna years, Hitler was particularly impressed by three movements: the Christian Social Movement, which had been led by Vienna Mayor Karl Lueger, the Pan-German (All Germans together), and the Social Democrats. Hitler hated the Austro-Hungarian Empire, especially the non-German peoples who constituted the majority. From Lueger, he saw a popular movement that appealed to the masses. Hitler felt Lueger was inconsistent on racial views, because Lueger's anti-Semitism was based only on religious and economic grounds, not racial. After his campaigns, Lueger had not only tolerated Jews, but appointed some to city office. To Hitler, Christian Socialism was not nationalist enough. On the other hand, the Pan-Germans were not concerned enough with the common folk. They were too elitist and too narrow for a popular political movement. They needed to combine in a new idea, as Hitler would outline in his book *Mein Kampf*. The Social Democrats' propaganda, press, and hold over the workers impressed Hitler, although he despised that program and party and believed that it was a Jewish conspiracy. He believed that the Social Democrats' radicalism and refusal to compromise gave them strength in the eyes of masses.

When the Austrian government called him for military service, Hitler dodged the draft and hid out in Bavaria in 1913. He claimed that he wanted to leave the decadent empire, but it caught up with him and he returned in January 1914. However, the draft board rejected him as physically unfit. Hitler's career plans were no firmer than when he had lived in Vienna. The war rescued him.

Hitler during the War Years

Hitler volunteered for the Bavarian army, which was desperate for men. According to Hitler, five-sixths of his regiment was killed or wounded during the battle of Ypres in 1915. Hitler's job was very dangerous as he ran messages among the trenches as the bullets flew and the shells rained down. Hitler was wounded in the leg in 1916, recovered, and returned to duty. During this time, he visited Munich and was appalled to see low morale, draft dodgers, and the black market. The army promoted him to corporal, and he ended the war in a hospital as the result of a gas attack. He received the uncommon decoration of Iron Cross, First Class. Germany's surrender shocked him because all had seemed well on the front when he was gassed in the summer of 1918.

Early Nazism

Right-wing terrorists and Free Corps members flocked to Munich as a haven. The government of the state of Bavaria turned a blind eye. Hitler joined the Political Department of the Munich District Command. The army had him speak to soldiers against socialism and communism, then told him to spy upon the meeting of a small radical group, the German Workers Party, in September 1919. This group had been founded by a Munich locksmith named Anton Drexler. At this meeting of fewer than thirty persons, Hitler was infuriated by the talk of Bavaria separating from the rest of Germany. Drexler invited Hitler to join the executive committee. Within two months, Hitler had attracted two hundred people with his speeches. Drexler put Hitler in charge of party propaganda. On April 1, 1920, Hitler resigned from the army. Hitler changed the party name to the National Socialist German Workers Party, adding "Socialist" to fool the people that the Nazis supported the lower classes. "Nazi" is a German shortening of National. Major Ernst Röhm secured police and army protection for the Nazis.

Hitler "steeled" his speeches; he kept them to a few constantly repeated messages. In *Mein Kampf*, he urged speakers to tell big lies; a gross lie, even if refuted, leaves an imprint. He used verbal violence by constantly including words such as "smash" and "force." He held mass meetings and demonstrations to show the movement's power. Violence attracted as many people as it repelled, and so he formed a "defense force" early on. In October 1921, the Nazis named this the *Sturmabteilung* (Storm Section) under Röhm's command. By that time, Hitler had pushed Drexler out as Party leader.

Nazism in the Wilderness

After the Beer-Hall Putsch, Hitler dictated *Mein Kampf*. He decided to take power legally, as Mussolini had in Italy. Other Nazi leaders included Gregor and Otto Strasser in the northern, more industrial areas. As the Storm Troopers got out of the control, the Nazis established a second party army, the SS (*Schutzstaffel* or Protective Staff). There was the Hitler Youth and groups for Nazi schoolchildren, students, women, teachers, lawyers, and doctors. In 1928, the Nazis named **Joseph Goebbels** to head their propaganda campaign. In the campaign against the Young Plan, the much larger Nationalist papers printed Hitler's speeches and brought them to millions.

THE GREAT DEPRESSION

Economic Origins of the Great Depression

The inflation of the wartime and postwar period did more than income taxes or inheritance taxes to wipe out the wealthy classes. Only the richest could keep up the elaborate households. The financial crash of the late 1920s wiped out many other fortunes. A few rich people were able to increase their wealth by manipulating currencies and buying assets at artificially low prices.

The stabilization of the 1924 Dawes Plan brought an end to the postwar inflation, but other economic problems developed. Most nations returned to a form of gold standard, but tried to pretend that World War I had not changed the balance of economic power as gold had shifted to the United States and other neutral countries. Winston Churchill, the British Chancellor of the Exchequer in 1925, foolishly returned to the pre-war gold standard and exchange rate with the dollar despite vast changes. This meant artificially low interest rates in Britain, and capital gushed out of that country because investors did not get a satisfactory return. In 1927, the Federal Reserve tried to lower American rates to compensate, but this just made borrowing money for stock speculation easier. When the Berlin market crashed in 1927, it made New York look very attractive. Then in 1929, the Fed tightened up on credit and investors got caught in a borrowing spiral trying to meet stock purchases. Many had borrowed **on margin**: under the rules of the time, they could buy stock with just 10 percent of the money but if there was a margin call that they must put up the other 90 percent or sell the stock.

The return to gold tended to put downward pressure on raw material prices because it limited the money supply. Many farmers across the western world had borrowed money to buy the new farm equipment running on internal combustion engines. Many had mortgaged their farms. As the prices fell, farmers increased production just to earn the same amount of money. Increased crop production caused the prices to fall even more. By the beginning of 1929, many countries had entered a depression.

In the leading world economy, the United States, there was growing inequality. The Republicans in 1921 had passed a massive tax giveaway to the rich. By 1929, 27,000 families with the highest annual incomes had as much money as the 11 million families at the bottom. The two hundred largest American corporations controlled half of the nation's corporate assets. The top 1 percent of all financial institutions controlled 46 percent of the nation's banking business. This inequality blighted the American consumer market. As dark clouds gathered, the one bright spot seemed to be the New York Stock Exchange, which continued rising in 1929. On "Black Tuesday," October 29, 1929, the market crashed and would continue to fall for four years. It did not recover its value until 1954. Financial companies were especially hard hit with the Shenandoah Corporation, for example, losing 99 percent of its value. In one week, the price of U.S. Steel stock went from $262 to $22 per share.

Hoover and The Depression in the United States

Maldistribution of wealth became a crucial problem. Unemployed workers could not buy goods, thus leading to more layoffs. The U.S. lost 38 percent of its GDP from 1929 to 1932. Unemployment rose to 13 million. Treasury Secretary Mellon, the chief adviser on the economy, urged that nothing be done. President **Herbert Hoover** gradually decided that government-business action should be taken and provided some federal action such as buying up crops and putting in public works. They were drops in the ocean, and Hoover would not unbalance the budget. He cheerfully signed the **Hawley-Smoot Tariff** in 1930 that put high tariffs on most manufactured goods. This ignited a worldwide trade war that hurt everyone's economy. World trade dropped by one-third.

Hoover would not allow federal funds to be used for individual relief. Three years into the crisis, he agreed to the Reconstruction Finance Corporation that gave loans to big businesses: banks, railroads, and insurance companies. Banks desperately scrambled for capital to stay solvent; they cut the credit lines to Europe, bankrupting European firms. Governments devalued their currencies and abandoned the gold standard. Hoover issued a "moratorium" (delay) on payment of debts and reparations in 1931. This delay would become permanent.

Heinrich Brüning and the Depression

The Great Depression hit Germany full blast in 1930 as American bankers would not extend any more short-term loans. Germany had already been slipping since 1927. From 1929 to 1932, unemployment rose from 1.3 million to 5.1 million. Chancellor **Heinrich Brüning** now brought the same austerity used by Hoover. He raised taxes, cut spending, and exalted a balanced budget above everything else. He thought he could rally support by calling early elections in September. This was a disastrous decision as the Nazis became the second-biggest party in the Reichstag. Brüning and Hindenburg used Article 48 to force through the austerity budget. The failure of Brüning's program discredited the government and led to more extremism as people suffered. In 1931, Brüning ignited a banking crisis with another austerity decree and a threat to default on reparations. The Stalin program in the Soviet Union destroyed a major German export market.

Hitler Comes to Power

In 1932, Hitler challenged Hindenburg's re-election as president. Brüning campaigned hard for Hindenburg, and his government banned the SA and SS. The Nazis lost, but they had canvassed every village looking for votes. In their campaign, they used films, records, and posters. Hindenburg was now eight-four years old. Maybe he was senile, maybe just confused. He certainly was under the influence of his son and General **Kurt von Schleicher.** Schleicher persuaded Hindenburg to dismiss Brüning. Hindenburg chose **Franz von Papen**, the leader of no party, as the next Chancellor. Papen lifted the ban against the SA and SS and smashed the Social Democratic government in the state of Prussia. Because Prussia still dominated Germany with population and land area, as long as its government remained democratic, Germany could resist authoritarianism. The Social Democrats could not rely on strikes as they had in the Kapp Putsch because of the Depression and high unemployment.

Papen called new elections because he thought he could assemble a non-partisan majority. This was an even greater disaster than in 1930. The Nazis emerged as the largest party, and the Communists were the third largest. Between them the extreme right and left had more than half of the seats in the Reichstag, making parliamentary government impossible. Businessmen now took Hitler seriously and contributed to his party. In many towns and villages, the only parties left were the Nazis and the Socialists. Business and political leaders had demonized socialism since the days of Bismarck so many people would never dream of voting for them. Schleicher and Papen tried to bring Hitler into their government but were shocked to hear him call for mass murder and a dictatorship. A new set of elections in November 1932 suggested that maybe the Nazi movement was peaking. Papen considered a pure dictatorship, but Schleicher asked for a chance at being Chancellor. He put in some public works projects to reinflate the economy. There is some evidence that the economy was recovering at the end of 1932. Schleicher also tried to split the Nazis and win over Gregor Strasser, but Hitler kept control over the Party and expelled Strasser. Schleicher fell from power. Papen persuaded Hindenburg to appoint Hitler as Chancellor with Papen as Vice-Chancellor to keep Hitler in line. On January 30, 1933, a frightful new chapter opened for Germany and the world.

TIMELINE

1922	Fascists march on Rome and take over Italy
1923	French invasion of Ruhr leads to German hyperinflation
	Hitler attempts "Beer Hall Putsch"
1924	Dawes Plan stabilizes Germany
1925	Mussolini completes Italian dictatorship
	Treaties of Locarno
1926	Germany joins League of Nations
1929	Lateran Pacts
	Great Depression begins
1933	Hitler becomes Chancellor

KEY TERMS

Benito Mussolini
Acerbo Electoral Law
Lateran Pacts
Gustav Stresemann
Dawes Plan
Hawley-Smoot Tariff

PRIMARY SOURCE DOCUMENTS

Benito Mussolini, http://www.fordham.edu/halsall/mod/mussolini-fascism.html
Adolf Hitler, http://history.hanover.edu/courses/excerpts/111hit1.html
Anna W., http://www.library.yale.edu/testimonies/excerpts/annaw.html

Chapter 13

DEMOCRACY VERSUS FASCISM

"THE DECLINE OF THE WEST?"

At the end of World War I, the German Oswald Spengler published *The Decline of the West* and suggested that western civilization was about to go under, ending a cycle of development. The 1920s and 1930s were gloomy ones in the democracies, and not just because of the economic catastrophe. There was a cultural disillusionment and intellectual disorientation as reflected in the great English-speaking poets of the time. **T.S. Eliot** penned the brilliant poem "The Waste Land" in 1922. The Irish poet **William Butler Yeats** was a believer in historical cycles and had written about the Easter 1916 rebellion in Dublin. In 1920, he published "The Second Coming," a poem suggesting that extremism and doom were rising. There were new styles of painting, more jarring than ever. The invention of photography had ended the goal of painters and sculptors to be as realistic as possible. Now the visual arts tried to express other things such as motion and emotion. Many people, both common and elite, rejected modern art.

The nineteenth century had carried on the Enlightenment's confidence in science and technology and the ability of reason to discover all. But the early twentieth century saw this confidence fading. Although few non-scientists understood all the details, **Albert Einstein**'s Theory of Relativity challenged many assumptions when he published it in 1905. This German physicist showed that: 1) The natures of time and space are not always subject to absolute measurement. Time slows down when it approaches light speed. 2) Mass and energy are interchangeable $e=mc^2$ where c is equal to the speed of light. Thus the destruction of a small mass can release enormous amounts of energy. This would eventually be applied to make the atomic bomb and nuclear reactors. 3) Space is curved: objects in motion create their own gravitational field.

Another troubling thinker who shook the comfortable world was the Austrian psychologist **Sigmund Freud**. Freud published his major work *The Interpretation of Dreams* in 1900, but his theories did not achieve mass publicity until after World War I. Freud showed that irrational feelings and sexual impulses governed much human behavior. It was not as rational as the Enlightenment writers had thought. He suggested that there was a three-part division of the mind: the id contained basic desires, especially sexual desires; the superego was the conscience that repressed impulses and imposed standards; the ego mediated between the two. Repressed desires could bubble up from the unconscious so people could not explain their actions. Freud had a sensational tour of the United States in the 1920s and was a big hit. Among certain classes there was a miniature version of the sexual revolution as Freud argued that repressing impulses can lead to trouble.

The war had directly dealt psychological blows. The supreme achievement of science seemed to be killing machines that could slaughter people at a distance. Many families and social groups were shattered by the millions killed and wounded. Many came home with Post-Traumatic Stress that was called "shell shock." One might think that the War would have led people to distrust authority, but it had the opposite effect. The "experience of the Front" seemed to be that all you had in life was your unit and your commander and that you should pay any price. This was the air in which fascism thrived, and even in the democracies there was a search for such a commander. The War had created stronger states that were more tightly organized and demanded more of the people even in peacetime.

There was also political disillusionment. Prior to the war, many had believed to some degree that democracy was the highest form of political development and that every country was on that road. The communist takeover of Russia was the first great blow to the idea that everything was becoming more democratic and progressive. Dictators took over in Italy and Turkey in 1922, in Poland after 1926, in Yugoslavia after 1929, and in many European countries in the 1930s. These dictators were not the comical remains of absolutist government but leaders who proved that dictators could also appeal to the masses and set up strong regimes.

Finally, there was disappointment over the peace treaties. It had been called the "war to end all wars." After 1930, it was clear that World War I had solved almost none of the problems of the world. War raged in Asia, the nations of east-central Europe squabbled, Russia remained a prisonhouse of nations, Germany and others forced a scrapping of the peace treaties, world trade broke down, the gold standard died, and the League of Nations stood by helplessly. Another major war seemed certain. All those millions had died for nothing.

Britain after the War

Although the loss of life was been proportionately less than in Germany or France, the War devastated the British economy. It lost one-quarter of its foreign investments. National debt had increased ten-fold. Britain had lost much of its trade share in many markets. In Latin America, for example, the British lost their dominance in trade to the United States. Japan was expanding its trade in Asia, often at British expense. Since it had been the first nation to industrialize, by the 1920s Britain had the oldest industrial plant. Workers felt that they had been underpaid during the war and now demanded wage hikes in a series of strikes. The government enacted the eight-hour day and boosted wages. The unemployment rate remained above 10 percent of the workforce through the 1920s and then doubled when the Depression hit in 1930. Britain retreated from the free trade position held through most of the nineteenth century. It also abandoned the gold standard and devalued its currency by over 25 percent. These economic problems boosted the position of the British Labour Party, which replaced the Liberals as the main alternative to the Conservatives. The Parliament expanded British democracy in 1918 by giving the vote to women.

Ireland

The year before the German High Command sent Lenin into Russia to spark a communist revolution, it had sent Roger Casement to Ireland. The Home Rule law had been passed by the Liberals before the war, but the Conservatives had sparked Protestant riots in the north and encouraged the northern Protestants to form an armed force equipped with rifles from Germany. The War suspended the move toward Irish Home Rule.

British colonies such as Ireland, Canada, Australia, and New Zealand felt that their volunteer soldiers were always being put in the most dangerous places of battles by the British commanders. The **Easter Rebellion** in Dublin shook Ireland in 1916 as revolutionaries held the General Post Office for six days before the British captured the office with great bloodshed. Sixty-four rebels, 132 soldiers and police, and 318 civilians died. In the spring of 1918, the British tried to impose the draft on Ireland. After the war, the Sinn Fein ("ourselves alone") Party won most of the Irish seats in the British Parliament. Sinn Fein boycotted that parliament and set up its own Irish Parliament. It formed the

Irish Republican Army (IRA), led by **Michael Collins**, and launched a guerrilla war in the cities.

Lloyd George, a Liberal presiding over a mostly Conservative government, opposed this and sent in brutal war veterans known as the **Black and Tans** from the color of their uniforms. The battle was a bloody stalemate and Lloyd George pushed through a Government of Ireland Act that gave freedom to only twenty-six of Ireland's thirty-two counties. In the controversial elections that followed in 1921, Sinn Fein (which was completely opposed to the division) swept the southern counties. Four northern counties were seen as supporting the pact. Two northern counties were declared in support, but opponents charged vote fraud. Collins agreed to the division of the island with the southern part becoming a dominion loosely associated with Britain. The extremists led by **Eamon de Valera** denounced this and launched a civil war. For a year and a half the extremists killed moderates such as Collins and attacked key buildings. The moderates won, but de Valera was elected President in 1932 and over the next five years broke most ties between Ireland and Great Britain. During World War II, the Irish government was sympathetic to the Nazis (de Valera as President gave condolences for Hitler's death at the German embassy in Dublin) but remained officially neutral.

Britain and India

Britain also had growing problems with India. It had angered Hindus when it partitioned Bengal in 1905 and angered Muslims when it rejoined the parts in 1911. India sent 1.2 million troops to aid the British in World War I, and 100,000 Indians died. The British had promised India a path toward dominion status. India lost 12 million dead in the terrible influenza epidemic of 1918–19. The Amritsar Massacre in 1919 increased the Indian Nationalist movement when British soldiers killed almost 400 and wounded 1,200 in an unarmed crowd. After 1921, **Mohandas Gandhi** (d.1948) was the leader of the all-India Congress. Gandhi united popular peasant groups and urban laborers with Muslims and made Congress into a mass party. He insisted on nonviolence and Indian reliance on their own industry and institutions. The British reform of 1921 extended voting rights to a few people for a consultative council. In 1930 Gandhi led a crowd to the sea to defy British law against Indians making salt. This law was a relic from the days of mercantilism. The British arrested Gandhi and provoked a wave of strikes. The **India Act of 1935** provided for a federation of all Indian provinces and gave it a constitution similar to other British dominions. Burma became a separate colony. The Congress Party won most provincial elections.

France in the 1920s

The French came out of World War I with great loss of life, heavy debt, and a devastated northeastern area. France rebuilt the industrial area with money from German reparations and foreign loans. In the 1920s, France had a balance among prosperous agriculture, a smaller industrial working class than Britain or Germany, and a large middle class. France devalued the franc by 80 percent and stabilized its budget. Like the United States, France became attractive to investment and gold. From 1928 to 1930, France put in social insurance laws similar to those of Britain and Germany. France resisted the Depression for the longest period of time and did not have an economic downturn until the winter of 1931/1932. Like Germany, France had proportional representation, many political parties, and unstable governments. A strong Communist party formed seeking a Russian-style revolution.

THE NAZIS IN POWER

The Consolidation of Nazi Power

After Hindenburg appointed Hitler as Chancellor, the Nazi leader called for a new set of elections, which he intended to fix. On February 27, 1933, a fire destroyed the Reichstag building. The Nazis arrested a Dutch Communist and convicted him. We will never know whether he was guilty or not. Hitler used the fire to suspend civil and individual liberties using Article 48 and enacted the death penalty. The elections occurred a week later. Despite bullying and rigging by the Nazis, they only won 44 percent of the vote and had to ally with the Nationalists to gain a majority. Hitler used a "Red Scare" to blame all Communists for the burning of the Reichstag and would not allow the elected Communist representatives to sit in the Parliament. The Nazis set up new institutions called "concentration camps" outside of major cities to imprison political opponents. Hitler then unveiled an **Enabling Act**, which gave the Cabinet all the powers of the Reichstag. It also gave Hitler decree powers for four years. Only the Social Democrats spoke against the bill as it passed 441 to 94. The other groups thought the Act would only be temporary because it would end as soon as the Nationalists left. They did not realize that Hitler would soon abolish all parties and that this Act had set up a dictatorship that would last for twelve years. Unlike Mussolini, Hitler did not bother with a quasi-parliamentary body such as the Grand Fascist Council. Even the Cabinet eventually stopped meeting formally.

The Nazis' priority was to put people to work. They used massive deficit spending on public works such as highways and the military. This helped pull Germany out of the Depression and boosted Hitler's popularity. Papen and Schleicher had started many of these plans. The Nazis smashed all independent centers of power in just a few months. They ended the long tradition of federalism in Germany by removing all rights from the states. They purged the civil service of most "non-Aryans and undesirables." Hitler appointed Goebbels to lead a ministry regulating all art and culture and putting out propaganda. The Nazis smashed labor unions and put many labor leaders into concentration camps. Then the government decreed that the Nazi Party was the only legal political party and all others were dissolved. Legally, this should have voided the Enabling Act and ended the dictatorship, but no one dared to offer a challenge. Hitler appointed his crony **Hermann Göring** to lead the Prussian state. By the end of 1933, there was full censorship of the press and the government had removed any potential opposition from the judiciary, civil service, and universities.

Crushing Opposition

There was some unrest within the Nazi party itself. The stormtroopers were a particular problem. Röhm wanted to replace the army with SA troops, much to the anger of the generals. There were more than two million stormtroopers, while the Treaty of Versailles limited the army to 100,000 troops. Hitler knew he would need the support of the generals to consolidate power when the aged President Hindenburg died. Apparently the generals demanded that Hitler suppress Röhm's plans. On April 1, 1934, Hitler named **Heinrich Himmler**, who was already the head of the SS and the Bavarian police, to be head of the Prussian Gestapo (Secret Police).

June 29/30, 1934 became known as the **Night of the Long Knives**. Himmler's SS murdered Röhm, other SA leaders, two aides to Vice-Chancellor von Papen who had plotted against Hitler, former Chancellor Schleicher, and Gregor Strasser. The Nazis killed at least four hundred people that night. On August 2, Hindenburg died, removing the last independent authority. The soldiers swore allegiance to Hitler personally. 90 percent of the voters approved the change combining Chancellor and President into the position of *Führer* (Leader). The first stage of consolidation was complete: the only non-Nazis left with authority were the old nobles and Prussians who dominated the army.

In March 1935, Hitler announced that he would not abide by the Versailles limits on armed forces. He ordered a military draft to expand the army to 550,000. This weakened the ties between units and officers and reduced the power of the general staff officers. By February 1938, Hitler felt strong enough to reorganize the army and put in a reliable commanding general. The moderate Foreign and Defense Ministers were replaced by the extreme Nazi **Joachim von Ribbentrop** and Hitler himself. By the middle of 1938, Hitler and the Nazis had total control.

Nazi Society

The Nazis dissolved all women's organizations and set up their own Women's Bureau. They promoted *Kinder, Kuche, Kirche* (children, church, kitchen). Women had made up to 35 percent of the workforce under Weimar; the Nazis pushed them out but when they restored the draft, women came back into the salaried workforce in greater numbers than ever. Long hours, low pay, and hard work led to a decline in productivity for all. The Nazis encouraged population growth by giving financial incentives, banning birth control clinics, and imposing harsh penalties for abortion. The Nazis also promoted proper sexual behavior and marriage and attacked "degenerates," especially homosexuals. After the murder of Röhm (the most prominent Nazi gay man), the government took a hard line: it threw gay men into concentration camps and forced them to wear a pink triangle. The Nazis believed that hard work would turn them into "men." Taking eugenic ideas to their logical conclusion, the Nazis sterilized over 300,000 persons against their will. From 1900 to 1930, the United States had forcibly sterilized 11,000. In 1938 and 1939, the Nazis killed almost 100,000 people because of disabilities that the Nazis tied to racial inferiority.

Anti-Semitic Laws and Actions

Sets of racist beliefs governed Hitler and therefore Nazism. They believed that there was a hierarchy of races with the pure Nordic Aryan at top and various "inferior" races, the worst of which were the "sub-human" Jews who were constantly scheming, in their view, to corrupt the "higher" races. In *Mein Kampf* (page 679) Hitler said:

If at the beginning of the war twelve or fifteen thousand of these Hebrew corrupters of the people had been held under poison gas, as happened to hundreds of thousands of our very best German workers in the field, the sacrifice of millions at the front would not have been in vain.

Hitler drew on long-standing European trends of religious anti-Semitism as well as intense German nationalism.

There were bursts of anti-Semitic activity in 1933, 1935 and 1938–9. The laws of 1933 excluded Jews from the civil service, the legal profession, medicine, teaching, cultural and entertainment enterprises, and the press. Under pressure from Hindenburg, the civil service laws excluded Jewish veterans of World War I. Nazi bully boys launched violent attacks on Jews and Jewish businesses, and the government did not punish them. 1935 saw a second burst. There were more acts of terror and boycotts of Jewish businesses. The government banned Jews from entering theaters, cinemas, and swimming pools. The **Nuremberg Laws** (September 1935) included: 1)The Reich Citizenship Law, which distinguished between citizens and subjects, depriving "subjects" of their full rights. The law defined Jews (whatever their present religion) as being descendants of three fully Jewish grandparents. 2) The Law for the Protection of German Blood and Honor forbade marriage and extra-marital relations between Germans and Jews. It banned Jews from flying the German flag or employing female Germans under the age of forty-five.

Germany toned down its antisemitism for the 1936 Olympic games in Berlin, and the International Olympic Committee obliged Hitler. The U.S. Olympic Committee, on its own, banned two Jewish champion runners from competing. Starting in July 1938, Jews had to carry special ID cards. Stormtrooper violence grew, and mass arrests began in May with Jews sent "temporarily" to concentration camps at Buchenwald, Dachau, and Sachsenhausen.

After the assassination of an embassy official in Paris by a Jewish teenager, the Nazis launched **Kristallnacht** (the Night of Shattered Glass) (November 9/10, 1938). They set synagogues on fire, violated cemeteries, destroyed buildings, and arrested 26,000 Jews. There was a new round of anti-Jewish laws that barred all Jewish children from the schools, imposed curfews on Jews, forbade them from entering public places, and excluded Jews from owning, managing or working in any retail or mail-order stores. Expulsion from Germany accelerated: a Reich Central Office for Jewish Emigration was established under **Reinhard Heydrich** (d.1942), head of the Security Service branch of the SS. Some in the SS drew up plans to ship German Jews to the East African coast, but they never implemented the plan. Jewish emigration increased greatly but was limited by the refusal of other countries to take more than a certain number of Jews. Jews who left also lost their property and could not transfer funds out of Germany, so many could not get out.

THE SPREAD OF AUTHORITARIANISM

The new or newly-expanded countries of east-central Europe had a number of problems in common: 1) they still had border disputes after the Peace of Paris; 2) these disputes often led to clashes and most needed a large army, either to defend themselves or attack someone else; 3) most had internal ethnic group problems: Romania was 76 percent Romanian, Poland was 69 percent Polish, Yugoslavia was 46 percent Serb, and so on; 4) there was a rapid population growth of 39 percent between the wars in East-Central and Southeastern Europe; 5) they had unstable political systems based on France's chaotic multiparty system; and 6) the Depression made everything worse.

The population of Poland included 14 percent Ukrainians, 10 percent Jews, and 5 percent Belarussians. In 1926, President **Joseph Pilsudski**, the former army leader, staged a coup against his own government and set up a dictatorship. After he died in 1935, the colonels ran the country. When the Austro-Hungarian Empire split up, one-third of all of Hungarians were not included in the new state. Admiral Nicholas Horthy headed a right-wing dictatorship for more than twenty years. There was also a strong fascist movement in Hungary. In 1941, Hungary helped Germany attack the Soviet Union. As the Soviet Army advanced in 1944, the Germans overthrew Horthy and installed a fully fascist government. While the new nation of Czechoslovakia had uneasily combined two groups, it did fairly well. It had strong leaders who were committed to democracy. The only real border dispute was with the weak Germany, so it did not need a big army. The country had a good industrial base and a literate and educated population. Czechs had been the backbone of the Austrian civil service. However, when the Depression hit, it was the industrial and coincidentally the German-speaking area of the Sudetenland that was hit hard by unemployment. This made the Sudeten Germans susceptible to the appeal of Hitler.

THE POPULAR FRONT IN FRANCE

Stalin and the Comintern had ordered the German Communists to attack the socialists as the main enemy and refuse all cooperation with the Weimar Republic. After the Nazis seized power and threw the Communist leaders into concentration camps, Stalin reconsidered. The Comintern called for a "Popular Front" with other leftists to combat Fascism. In France, Socialist leader **Léon Blum** formed a broad coalition with Communists and left Radicals. He won a big victory over the conservatives led by **Pierre Laval**. The Popular Front passed a social program, but the Parliament defeated the economic measures. It limited work to forty hours a week and tried to reflate the economy by giving public workers a 12 percent raise. Businesses and bankers tried to sabotage the Popular Front by sending their money abroad. When the Popular Front collapsed in 1937, the left blamed it on a right-wing conspiracy. There was growing extremism as many French rightists said "Better Hitler than Blum."

THE SCANDINAVIAN RESPONSE

The Great Depression hit Scandinavia hard. Unemployment reached 31.5% in Sweden, 42.5% in Norway, and 42.8% in Denmark. Class conflicts worsened as companies employed strikebreakers. Scandinavian Nazis founded parties in the 1930s. However, cooperative movements had long dominated agriculture and large-scale democratic Folk Schools had fostered a similar culture that brought classes together. In 1933, Social Democrats in Denmark and Sweden made alliances with the Agrarian parties to gain support in exchange for subsidies, lower farm taxes, and a currency devaluation to stimulate farm exports. Unlike Germany, where the farm groups and voters had backed the Nazis, these discontented voters supported the Social Democrats.

Governments passed laws against strikebreaking and enacted national paid holidays. Danish taxes rose 30 percent and Swedish taxes 50 percent to pay for an extensive program of social insurance, including unemployment insurance, old-age pensions, public works to put the unemployed to work, and payments to farmers and fishermen. The economy of Sweden and Norway grew by 50 percent in the 1930s, while the rest of the continent, except for Germany, was mired in Depression.

FRANKLIN D. ROOSEVELT AND THE NEW DEAL

By 1932, the American economy had hit a bottom. Cities were going bankrupt. Homeless families built "Hoovervilles" of boxes and rusty sheet metal. Thousands of tramps roamed the countryside. In July 1932, 20,000 unemployed veterans marched on Washington and demanded their promised war bonuses. When 2,000 refused to leave and built Hoovervilles, President Hoover sent in troops under General **Douglas MacArthur** to break them up.

The Democrats nominated New York Governor **Franklin D. Roosevelt** in 1932. FDR had sponsored relief measures in New York and had been Assistant Secretary of the Navy under Wilson and the Democrats' Vice-Presidential candidate in 1920 before polio struck him and left his legs paralyzed. His campaign was short on specifics and called for maintaining the balanced budget. Roosevelt called for a New Deal, which would consist of "bold, persistent experimentation." FDR won overwhelmingly, and the Democrats swept into control of Congress.

Between the November election and the March inauguration, the American banking system crumbled. By March 4, 80 percent of states had suspended banking operations. FDR called Congress into special session, declared a bank holiday, and forbade the export of gold. Congress gave the President the power to fix the price of gold by proclamation; FDR set it at $35 per ounce, 40 percent higher than the earlier level. It would remain at that price until 1971 (although the price of gold on the open market was usually higher). Congress passed an emergency bank law, reopened banks under Treasury Department licenses, and set up the Federal Deposit Insurance Corporation to guarantee deposits. The government set up the Home Owners Loan Corporation to refinance mortgages and prevent foreclosures. Congress established the Securities and Exchange Commission to force the full disclosure of all stock issues and regulated banks much more closely.

FDR and the Congress also dealt with unemployment: minimum wage and maximum hours legislation became law. Workers gained the right to bargain collectively. Business codes outlawed child labor. The government saved thousands of farmers by giving them agricultural subsidies while limiting production. Public works programs put people to work. The New Deal was enormously popular even if it did not end the Depression right away. Roosevelt moved to more aggressive actions in 1935, including old-age pensions (Social Security) and unemployment insurance funded by a payroll tax. The government raised taxes on the rich. The **Wagner Act** (1935) established a National Labor Relations Board to restrain employers from unfair labor practices. After a reactionary Supreme Court struck it down, the government reestablished the minimum wage at forty cents an hour.

FDR had campaigned on a balanced budget and was cautious about borrowing money. In 1937, the American economy had almost recovered its 1929 level, but then the government cut back New Deal spending and a "Roosevelt recession" resulted. FDR's advisers invited the British economist **John Maynard Keynes** (d.1946) to the White House. Keynes urged deficit spending to pull nations out of Depression. Not until 1938 did FDR call for a massive public works bill financed by deficits and loans. In 1939, the United States was finally out of the Depression, though its economy was still weak.

APPEASEMENT AND THE DIPLOMATIC CRISIS OF THE 1930S

At the peace conference in Paris, the Allies tried to construct a security system to keep the peace. They promoted the idea of **collective security**. If any nation broke the peace, all of the other nations would join together and overwhelm the aggressor. The mechanism for collective security wold be the League of Nations. Since the League had its headquarters in Geneva, Switzerland, the security arrangement was sometimes called the **Geneva System**. This system was fatally flawed from the beginning. The Allies did not invite the Soviet Union to join the League at its beginning, and the United States Senate rejected membership in the League. Britain and France were left as the main enforcers of the peace and they never had enough power to make collective security work. Whenever the first serious challenge appeared, the system would collapse.

The Roots of Appeasement

Appeasement was the policy of making concessions in order to head off a war. Most famously, it was used by Britain and France in the 1930s as an approach to the fascist governments in Germany and Italy. Britain and France used this policy for clear reasons, and the reasons changed over time.

The first reason for appeasement was the terrible damage done by World War I. Britain had gained very little and France had gotten back Alsace-Lorraine. The war had devastated their economies and killed and wounded millions of their citizens and torn much of their social fabric.

Secondly, many believed by the 1930s that the Treaty of Versailles had treated Germany unfairly. At the Paris Peace Conference, the Allies had heaped the blame on the Germans to justify a fine that would match their war debts to the United States. By the 1930s, most believed that the blame for the war fell on many countries. The continued separation of Austria from Germany violated the principle of self-determination that the Paris Peace Conference had promoted. In the United States, many believed that bankers and "merchants of death" had tricked the U.S. into the war in order to protect bank loans to Britain and France and promote weapons sales.

Thirdly was the position of Britain. Britain had undercut France when it refused to support France's invasion of the Ruhr in 1923. Since that time, France would not take the initiative to enforce the Treaty of Versailles unless it had British backing. Britain was slowly recovering from the Depression and by 1935 was starting to have its best prosperity since before the War. British leaders feared that a new war would destroy this fragile growth. In June 1935, a private firm polled 11.5 million Britons in what came to be called the **Peace Ballot**. 11 million favored League of Nations membership, 10.5 million favored economic non-military sanctions if the peace was broken, 6.5 million favored the use of force in such situations, and 2.5 million opposed any use of force. Personalities also shaped British appeasement. The Prime Minister, Stanley Baldwin of the Conservatives, was not very interested in foreign policy. British Foreign Secretary Samuel Hoare was a slippery character mainly concerned with domestic politics. His enemy Robert Vansittart was the senior civil servant in the Foreign Ministry. Vansittart had a deep distrust of the Germans but was sympathetic to Italian imperialism and hoped that Italy could be split off from Germany. He was in favor of appeasing Mussolini.

Fourthly, the Depression had caused most countries to turn inward. The skyrocketing of unemployment strained most budgets, money was scarce, and governments were reluctant to spend money on the military, much less send their armed forces far away for abstract notions of "world order," "balance of power," or "protecting small nations from big bullies."

Fifthly, conservative governments ruled Britain and France for most of the 1930s. They were far more concerned about communism than fascism. Their great hope was that Germany and the Soviet Union could get into a long war and beat themselves bloody while Britain and France sat back and watched. The conservative government in France signed a military alliance with the U.S.S.R., but the Chamber refused to ratify it.

Hitler's Foreign Policy

In *Mein Kampf*, Hitler had not written much about foreign policy, except to suggest that Germany must have strong allies, either Britain or Italy. In his second unpublished book he showed little regard for the United States. He called it a "mongrel" nation of inferior races that had not done much in World War I. Hitler had been out of the war in the last months when the Americans contributed to the crush of numbers that brought down the German army. Hitler had a "plan of stages:" 1) Get control of Germany; 2) Expand Germany's position in Central Europe; 3) Get control of important parts of Europe; 4) After a long period of racial purification, Germany could become the dominant power in the world. Hitler promised the generals that Germany would not fight a two-front war as it had in the First World War. Hitler did not have a rigid timetable. If he planned for a big war, he did not intend it until the early 1940s. He did not want to mobilize the full economy for war and risk his popularity by imposing civilian shortages. As a result, Germany did not reach peak war production until 1943.

Before 1934, France had the best air force, but the discovery of lighter materials and stronger engines made the entire French force obsolete. Suffering from the Depression, France did not want to spend vast new sums on building a new air force that might become obsolete. In March 1935, Hitler rejected all limits from Versailles. Germany could build an all-new **Luftwaffe** because Versailles had banned it from building an air force. Panzer tanks, the classic "World War II tank" with thicker armor and more powerful guns, did not appear until 1937 and 1938. German personnel were far superior to the Allies and used better tactics in the war.

The Failure of the League of Nations

The Japanese Offensive in Manchuria

In a practical sense, the War began before Hitler ever gained power. The first significant breach of the peace occurred in East Asia. The German defeat in World War I had discredited the German-model political system that Japan had used. In 1925, the government extended the vote to every man. The high point of Japanese democracy came from 1924 to 1932. The parliament passed labor legislation, including national health insurance and labor disputes mediation. The government cut the military's share of the budget from 42 percent in 1922 to 28 percent in 1927.

The Depression and trade war hurt Japanese exports terribly; Japan lost 50 percent of its export value, and wages fell 31 percent. The collapse in farm prices hurt rural Japan. Many blamed the government which seemed to work hand-in-hand with big corporations such as Mitsui or Mitsubishi. The end of German democracy made a big impression. In 1931, the government took Japan off the gold standard, and some recovery began.

In 1931, the Japanese army acted without authorization to attack Manchuria because of its fear that the Nationalists were revitalizing the Chinese government and would reclaim Manchuria. The Japanese Cabinet split on this action. The Prime Minister opposed the Manchurian war, but an ultranationalist assassinated him in 1932. After that came cabinets of "national unity" that included military officers. The League of Nations appointed the **Lytton Commission** to look into the Manchurian issue. It reported in 1932 what everyone knew: the Japanese had staged an unprovoked attack and should leave Manchuria. The only punishment was the League's recommendation that the nations should not recognize Japan's puppet state in Manchuria. Japan showed its contempt by withdrawing from the League. It continued to attack Chinese territory and demanded that China put itself under Japanese control.

Japanese Dictatorship Grows and Expands the War

In 1936, the ultranationalist elements of the Japanese army rebelled, and the military gained even more power. From 1932 to 1935, the government purged itself of all the leftists who had criticized the Emperor. The religious interpretation of the state that the Emperor was a living god became official. After 1936, Japan was a military dictatorship. Elections in 1937 showed that the Japanese people overwhelmingly opposed the dictatorship, but it changed nothing. Pro-military parties won only nineteen seats of 466. The dictators ignored the parties in the parliament, decreed laws against "dangerous thought," and spent much more on the military. In 1937, Japan opened a full war against China. It quickly moved down the coast, sacking cities with great brutality. Beijing fell to the Japanese. Most notorious was the "**Rape of Nanjing**" involving both rape and slaughter. But by 1939, Japan was bogged down as it tried to push into the vast Chinese interior.

The Stresa Front (1935)

Italy and Germany did not automatically become allies after the fascists took over in Germany. Independent Austria lay between the two states. Hitler wanted to take over the land of his birth, and Mussolini opposed this. In July 1934, Austrian Nazis murdered the Austrian Chancellor Engelbert Dollfuss. When it seemed that Hitler might try to come over the border and take over Austria. Italy moved its troops to the Brenner Pass to intervene in case Germany invaded. Hitler's repudiation of Versailles led Mussolini to believe that Germany's first target would be Austria. The Stresa Front was a treaty of friendship between France, Britain, and Italy. They all agreed to support the status quo in Europe which implicitly meant containing Germany while remaining mute on Italian designs in Africa.

Ethiopia

Mussolini had long wanted to avenge the Italian humiliation at Ethiopian hands at Adowa and he had ideas about turning Mediterranean into an "Italian lake." In late 1934, Italy began to threaten Ethiopia, and Britain commissioned a study that concluded that Britain had no vital interests in Ethiopia and should not object if Mussolini refused to pull out. This was a secret document and was distributed only to top-level officials. Unfortunately, one such official was its ambassador to Italy. An Italian spy stole the report from the embassy safe so Mussolini knew that Britain would do nothing.

In October 1935, Italy invaded Ethiopia. The battle lasted seven months. The Ethiopians put up a fiercer struggle than expected, but they could not match the poison gas, airplanes, and tanks used by Italy. Mussolini had to use the troops from the Austrian border, which meant he could no longer protect Austria against Hitler. The League of Nations voted sanctions against Italy including a ban on Italian goods, and on exporting arms to Italy or doing financial business. However, it did not cut off Italy's oil nor did it close the Suez Canal to Italian supplies of troops and arms. These might have gotten Mussolini's attention and brought Italy's war to a halt. British Foreign Secretary Hoare met with French Foreign Minister Laval, and they worked out the secret **Hoare-Laval Pact** (December 1935) which gave most of Ethiopia to Italy and made the rest into an Italian puppet. Baldwin had told Hoare to stay out of war, and Hoare had followed instructions but had to resign after the secret treaty was leaked and there was a firestorm of protest.

The Rhineland

Versailles had demilitarized this area, and Germany had agreed to respect the western borders at Locarno. Ignoring the advice of the conservative generals, Hitler marched troops across into the Rhineland and denounced Locarno. France was in the middle of a government crisis and was waiting for new elections. Britain was diverted by the situation of its new king Edward VIII trying to marry an American divorcée. Both France and Britain were indecisive. The militarization of the Rhineland showed that the security system had no teeth. Belgium refused to cooperate further with French defenses. This was critical because the French had spent enormous amounts of money on the **Maginot Line**, a complex of trenches, supply depots, and fortifications. Belgium was expected to defend the area north of the line with French help. France's alliances with eastern European countries weakened as Czechoslovakia, Poland, Yugoslavia, and Romania doubted that France would come to their aid if they were attacked.

The Spanish Civil War

Polarization of Politics

After decades of turmoil after the Revolutions of 1820, Spain in 1876 gained a limited democracy dominated by the rich and privileged. Anger grew after 1900, especially among industrial workers in Catalonia and landless peasants in Andalusia. The anarchist movement attracted many in these regions. Spain industrialized rapidly from 1915 to 1930 causing the usual dislocations and revolutionary upsurge. The military overthrew the democratic government in 1923. The onset of the Depression dashed the raised expectations. The Anarcho-Syndicalists formed a powerful trade union. Local elections in April 1931 swept various Anarchists, Syndicalists, Liberals, and Socialists into power. All they had in common was their support for a Spanish Republic and their dislike for the conservative Spanish Church. Beyond that, they were very divided. Violence between the Left and the Right grew as Spain was evenly divided. Catalonia tried to gain more rights.

The left-wing parties formed a Popular Front for the February 1936 elections. The Left won a narrow victory, but the Spanish voting system was similar to Mussolini's Italy: a party that won got the lion's share of the seats. The Right was angry, felt marginalized, and formed its own broad movement, the **Falange**, that combined conservative, radical right, and fascist movements. In July 1936, General Francisco Franco led a large part of the army to rebel against the Republic.

The Course of the War

The Spanish government tried to build a new leftist army to fight the regular army that was in revolt. Leftists around the world came to Spain to fight in the "International Brigades." They intended to fight fascism, but found the reality was quite complicated. The Soviet Union was the only power fully backing the Republic of Spain, but it pressured the government to allow Russian secret police units to operate. Many communists were more interested in killing anarchists, socialists, and followers of Trotsky than in fighting Franco. Italy sent regular troops to Spain to fight on Franco's side because Mussolini wanted a Mediterranean ally. Germany gave some air support. The German terror bombings appalled the world. For the first time, it saw what modern air power could do to a civilian population. France and Britain realized how far they had fallen behind Germany. Most of the West stayed neutral. The French Socialist Prime Minister Léon Blum declared an open border to allow supplies in, but the British forced it closed. Italy and Germany provided a naval blockade so foreign supplies could not get to the Republic. Spain had become a "proxy war" where fascists and communists fought without direct conflict between Germany and the Soviet Union.

Democracy Defeated

Franco conquered the last cities of the Republic in the spring of 1939 as his professional army was too strong for a "people's army." 700,000 died in combat with another 100,000 civilians perishing. Franco put over 100,000 people into concentration camps. The Republic was too divided, and the Church backed Franco strongly. Franco restored the Catholic Church to its full power and established a military dictatorship that ruled Spain until he died in 1975.

The Formation of the Axis

Much of the Italian economy collapsed because of the Depression. The state took over a number of the sectors out of necessity. Cynicism grew, and many who had been a part of government retired or died. The government forced workers to take cuts in pay from 1927 to 1935. From 1935 on, permanent war embroiled Italy in Ethiopia and then Spain, Albania in 1939, and then the full Second World War. The government increasingly favored heavy industry (steel, weapons) over light consumer industry. High tariffs kept out foreign goods. The state rationed key materials and centralized industry even more. The war after 1939 finally reduced the number of unemployed under a million.

Mussolini had come to see the West as ineffective and, except for Austria, Italy and Germany had no major conflicts. Once Mussolini diverted the Italian troops guarding Austria, Nazis came into the Austrian cabinet. On November 1, 1936, Mussolini met with Hitler and declared that Rome and Berlin formed an Axis around which the rest of the world must rotate. In November 1937, Mussolini joined the Anti-Comintern Pact that Germany and Japan had signed to fight Communism.

Italian fascism had never put race at center of ideology as Nazis had. Mussolini had a Jewish mistress, and some important leaders had close ties to the Jewish community in Italy. After 1936, Nazi influence on Italy increased. The first anti-Semitic laws in Italy in July 1938 revoked citizenship granted to foreign-born Jews since 1919. In 1938, Mussolini borrowed the goosestep as an "ancient Roman march." With the withdrawal of Italian protection, the Austrians tried to reach an accommodation with Hitler. The government wanted to hold an election to see if people would reject a union with Germany, but Hitler intervened and Nazi troops poured into Austria on March 11, 1938. Two days later came a formal union (***Anschluss***).

The Munich Conference

Now there was another reason for appeasement, the military advantage that Germany held. British and French stepped up their pace of rearmament. They had drawn up spending plans to build a modern air force in 1936, but none of these planes rolled off the assembly lines until the end of 1938. In the last twelve months before the war, they were outspending Germany vastly and when the U.S.S.R. was included, Germany was dwarfed. Most importantly, Britain was setting up its net of top secret RADAR stations that could detect aircraft, but it would not be ready until late 1939. Baldwin retired in 1937 and was succeeded by his fellow Conservative **Neville Chamberlain**. British military spending in 1938 was four times its 1935 level, with air force spending seven times higher. German military spending rose from 1 billion Reichsmarks in 1933 to 5 billion in 1935, 9.5 billion in 1937, and 30 billion in 1939. The German economy was starting to come apart and inflationary pressures were building. Hitler needed his war fast before he lost control.

After taking Austria, the Nazis laid claim to the German-dominated area of the **Sudetenland** in northern and western Czechoslovakia. This was also the area of the Czech fortifications. Without the Sudetenland, Czechoslovakia would be helpless. France had signed a defense treaty with Czechoslovakia, and the Soviets were willing to help if the Allies would let them march through Poland, which lay between the Soviet Union and Czechoslovakia.

Chamberlain was not willing to go to war for Czechoslovakia and did not believe that Britain was ready for war. He, French Foreign Minister Daladier, and Mussolini met Hitler at the **Munich Conference**. Hitler knew he had the military edge and wanted war in 1938. The agreement gave the Sudetenland to Hitler, who promised that he would leave the rest of the country alone. Chamberlain returned to London and cheering crowds. In March 1939, Hitler took over the rest of Czechoslovakia. Stalin was disgusted by the West's behavior, and Mussolini invaded tiny Albania to show his "equality" with Hitler. Britain increased its military spending by another 50 percent and reintroduced the military draft in April 1939.

Stalin Comes to Terms with Hitler

Stalin became increasingly disenchanted with the West and felt Britain and France would not mind if Hitler attacked him. He began to think about dealing with the Nazis. In April 1939, Stalin replaced the Jewish anti-Nazi Litvinov as foreign minister in favor of **Vyacheslav Molotov**. Britain and France made ironclad guarantees of security to Poland, but Stalin had ideas about carving it up. The West did not realize the danger until it was too late. Germany and Italy deepened their alliance in the **Pact of Steel**. On August 23, 1939, the governments announced the **Nazi-Soviet Pact** (also known as the Ribbentrop-Molotov Pact). Officially, the treaty was just one of non-aggression. But there were secret clauses that divided East-Central Europe into "spheres of influence": Finland and the Baltic States would go to the U.S.S.R., while the two powers divided Lithuania and Poland.

TIMELINE

1916	Easter Rebellion in Ireland
1922	Ireland gains dominion status
1931	Japan invades Manchuria
1933	Hitler becomes German Chancellor, establishes dictatorship
	Franklin D. Roosevelt becomes U.S. President
1935	Hitler denounces Treaty of Versailles
	Stresa Front
	Nuremberg Laws
	Italy invades Ethiopia
	India Act
1936	Hitler militarizes Rhineland
	Blum leads Popular Front government in France
	Military dictatorship in full control of Japan
1936–39	Spanish Civil War
1937	Republic of Ireland gains independence
	Japan expands war in China
1938	*Anschluss* between Germany and Austria
	Munich Conference: Hitler gains Sudetenland
	Kristallnacht
1939	Hitler takes the rest of Czechoslovakia
	Nazi-Soviet Pact

KEY TERMS

William Butler Yeats
Albert Einstein
Sigmund Freud
Easter Rebellion
Enabling Act
Nuremberg Laws
Franklin D. Roosevelt
Lytton Commission
The Stresa Front
Spanish Civil War
Munich Conference
Nazi-Soviet Pact

PRIMARY SOURCE DOCUMENTS

1916 Proclamation of the Irish Republic, http://www.fordham.edu/halsall/
  mod/1916proc.jpg
Nazi-Soviet Pact, http://www.fordham.edu/halsall/mod/1939pact.html

THE EARLY VICTORIES OF THE DICTATORS

The Attack on Poland

The German style of war during the Second World War came to be called *Blitzkrieg* (lightning war). This was not so much a long-planned strategy as a necessity. Germany had limited supplies of fuel, and its economy was not yet on a war footing. The Germans used war planes to destroy the enemy air force before it could get up in the air. They sent mass tank formations to punch a hole in the line and then their soldiers exploited the opening. Plunder would pay for some of the war because Germany's ability to tax and borrow was very limited. About 1.7 million German soldiers attacked Poland, which had an army of around 600,000.

Under the guarantee to Poland signed in May 1939, France would furnish military assistance by the sixteenth day after the German attack. By that date, however, Poland was on the verge of collapse. The French border raids on the Saar were useless. The British declined to launch air strikes on the Ruhr industrial area. To make matters worse, the Soviet Union invaded Poland from the east on September 17. Polish resistance ended by October 2. 60,000 Polish soldiers had died in the fighting. There was nothing left for the French to fight for, and they feared that Britain might make a separate peace. While Hitler waited for better weather, the French hoped Hitler was only bluffing an attack on the West.

The Winter War

Finland and the Baltic states were in danger from a Russian attack. They had been part of the Russian Empire before 1918. Finland had rebelled as elements of the army beat pro-Russian communists. After the war began, Latvia, Estonia, and Lithuania all signed treaties with the U.S.S.R. and gave it bases. Finland refused because it thought that after Stalin purged the army of commanders, Russia was too weak to launch a major attack.

Russia began to bomb the Finnish capital of Helsinki on November 30, 1939. Russia set up a puppet government and brought back 6,000 Finnish communists, but the communists inside Finland did not support Stalin. The Finnish parties came together to oppose the Russians. On the long northern frontier with few roads or railroads, Finnish soldiers on skis were able to hold back the much larger Russian forces. They hoped for foreign intervention, but none came. Only volunteer troops from Norway and Sweden aided their cause. 25,000 Finnish soldiers were killed and 45,000 wounded; that was one-third of the original Finnish army. In February 1940, the Finnish defenses broke, and the Russians poured in. A hard peace treaty took significant Finnish land and forced 12 percent of the people to move.

The Northern War

In June 1939, Hitler had offered non-aggression pacts to Sweden, Finland, and Norway, but each refused. Denmark accepted and noted that no Scandinavian country had aided it in 1864 when the Austrians and Prussians had attacked. Hitler planned a coordinated attack on both Denmark and Norway. 38,000 crossed the Danish border on April 9, 1940. Germany gave Denmark an ultimatum: surrender or see Copenhagen bombed into rubble. The Danish king and Prime Minister remained in their posts and the nation kept its independence by declining the German offer of a customs and currency union. Germany pressed Denmark to be the breadbasket of the Reich, and it grew 78 percent more crops than in the First World War.

Attack on Norway

In mid-December, Hitler met twice with the Norwegian fascist leader **Vidkun Quisling**, who urged Hitler to support a coup against the government. Hitler wanted to secure the iron ore base in Sweden and give his navy and air force a wider starting base against Britain. The German attack had to be intricate: an 11,000-man advance force went through British-controlled waters to seize long lines of ports. The British did not understand what was happening at first, and heavy seas prevented interception. A German heavy cruiser sank in the Oslofjord, so the Germans did not take the capital on the first day. The king, cabinet, and parliament escaped into the interior. Quisling proclaimed himself leader. French and British troops were unable to cope with the battle or northern conditions. There were few heavy weapons. The Germans had air superiority from Danish and southern Norwegian air bases and this hampered the British Navy.

In April, resistance in central Norway collapsed, and the Germans closed in on Narvik. The British, French and exiled Poles were able to demolish the iron ore route and put it out of action for a year. King Haakon, the Cabinet, and the military leadership escaped to Britain along with much of the merchant marine, which was the third-largest in the world behind that of Britain and the U.S.

The Attack on the West

Problems in France

France had severe internal political problems. There was a fascist movement with half a million followers. When the war broke out, Daladier outlawed the Communist Party which had swung to neutrality following the Nazi-Soviet Pact. The French commanders Pétain, Weygand, and Gamelin had resisted mechanization and air power ideas. Trench warfare haunted them, and they were unprepared for mobile war. General **Charles de Gaulle** (1890–1970) had pushed for the transformation of the French army into a long-term professional army that would be highly maneuverable. France had not begun to modernize its air force until 1938 and had only 500 first-line planes vs. Germany's 4,000 and Britain's 1,100 in September 1939. By May 1940, France had 1,300, Britain 1,350, and Germany 5,000.

On May 10, Hitler invaded the Netherlands and Belgium. The French had always expected that if attack came, they would be able to come into Belgium and establish the Meuse River as a defensive line, but neither Belgium nor the Dutch were able to slow down the German advance. The Dutch lost one-quarter of their army dead and wounded in just a week. The Germans broke through at Sedan, which military planners had thought could be protected by the thick forests and rugged lands of the Ardennes. The Germans cut off the entire British force along with 112,000 French and Belgian soldiers. They had to retreat from the port of **Dunkirk** and leave their heavy trucks and tanks behind. The deep divisions in French society proved fatal. The commanding general Maxime Weygand decided the fight was hopeless while de Gaulle urged a retreat to Brittany and the transfer of the government to North Africa. In five weeks of war, the French had lost 200,000 soldiers dead, 400,000 wounded, 75,000 civilians dead from bombing, and several hundred thousand soldiers taken prisoner. Although Prime Minister Reynaud wanted to fight on, the majority of the Cabinet voted to ask the Germans for a ceasefire on June 16.

Reynaud resigned and the ancient Marshal Philippe Pétain (1856–1951), a World War I hero, became the chief of state, assisted by the real power behind the throne, the right-winger **Pierre Laval** (1883–1945). Pétain surrendered to Germany, and the Republic dissolved in favor of a very authoritarian regime that the Germans allowed to operate under Pétain and Laval in southern France. This puppet state was called "**Vichy France**" after the small town that served as the capital.

Under the terms of the armistice, the Germans occupied three-fifths of France along the Atlantic coast and English Channel. Vichy would hold the rest but was responsible for keeping security. Germany annexed Alsace and Lorraine. There was a heavy indemnity, and the Germans kept French troops as prisoners of war and slave laborers until the end of the conflict. The Vichy regime arrested Léon Blum and sent him to a German concentration camp.

The French Parliament voted 468 to 80 to give Pétain the power to draft a new constitution. Pétain substituted *travail, famille, patrie* (work, family, homeland) for "*liberté, fraternité, egalité,*" the phrase of the 1789 revolution. Pétain blamed the defeat on society's selfishness after 1918. There was much talk about undoing the last hundred and fifty years of history and returning to a decentralized structure with a strengthened Catholic church, and old family structures. Vichy abolished free secondary education. On the other hand, a number of young technocrats emerged seeking to make France modern, efficient, and run as an authoritarian regime by a technical elite. They reorganized industry to favor the largest and most efficient. The government banned strikes.

In December 1940, Pétain dismissed Laval as Vice-Premier and replaced him with Admiral François Darlan because Laval was suspected of preparing a Nazi coup. Out of office, Laval preached more collaboration with Germany and returned in April 1942 as the real power. In November 1942, the British and Americans landed in North Africa. Darlan took the French forces there over to the Allied side, and Laval took dictatorial power. Vichy drafted 700,000 French laborers to work in Germany, established a fascist militia, and carried out a reign of terror against those who resisted. Germany occupied southern France.

French society on every level cooperated with Nazis. By one estimate, German soldiers had fathered 85,000 illegitimate children by 1943. Some writers and politicians criticized Vichy for being too conservative and wanted an all-out fascist regime. The Vichy government was also very cooperative in the extermination of French Jews. An October 3, 1940, Anti-Jewish Law had a stricter definition of Jewishness than the Nazis. Vichy barred Jews from most civil service positions and professions. In the German zone, roundups of Jews began in May 1941. By June 1942, all French Jews had to wear the yellow star. In July 1942, Laval turned over all foreign-born Jews to the Nazis in exchange for a promise to spare French Jews. Laval insisted that the Germans take Jewish children as well as adults and revoked all naturalizations of Jews since 1930. 75,000 French Jews went to death camps.

Britain Alone

When Germany invaded Poland, Chamberlain shuffled his Cabinet to make it a national coalition. In May 1940, Chamberlain resigned, and **Winston Churchill** became Prime Minister. Churchill was determined to fight Germany to the bitter end. Hitler thought that the British would be too demoralized to fight after the French debacle. Even though the French had destroyed one-third of the Luftwaffe, the Germans were so confident that they began their attacks with daylight bombing. Britain had a number of surprises: 1)RADAR (RAdio Detection and Ranging) had been invented to show the location of aircraft and its net was completed just before the end of 1939. RADAR could detect planes up to seventy-five miles from the coast. 2) The British had broken the German secret code. They only used this sparingly because they did not want the Germans catching on. 3) The British had better planes and pilots. The Germans gave up the idea of a direct attack by the end of 1940. By that summer, the British were producing twice as many fighter planes as the Germans. The Germans resorted to terror bombing of London and other population centers to break the British resistance. The Germans destroyed or damaged 20 percent of all British homes. This only made the British more determined to win.

The Attack on Yugoslavia, Greece, and Crete

In *Mein Kampf,* Hitler had emphasized attacks in the East and, although Britain was still fighting, Hitler turned in that direction. Churchill tried to warn Stalin and even sent reconnaissance photos, but Stalin refused to believe it.

In October 1940, Mussolini attacked Greece. The Greeks counterattacked and pushed well back into Albania. The British diverted 58,000 troops from North Africa to help Greece. Hitler wanted to secure the southern flank with Yugoslavia and forced that government to join the Axis in March 1941, but anti-German forces overthrew the Yugoslav government. The Germans launched a ten-day attack on April 6 with 650,000 men and bombed Belgrade to paralyze the high command. The Yugoslav army never fully mobilized; some fled to mountain hideouts. The Axis conquered Greece in three weeks; the British rescued their men but abandoned even more heavy equipment. The German tanks forced their way through "impassable" Greek mountains. In this fight, the Germans lost 4,500 men, the British had 11,840 casualties, and the Greeks 70,000. The British had to evacuate to Crete, where they felt secure, even though they lacked air cover and proper equipment. The Germans landed paratroopers and glider troops on Crete, seized the airfields, and drove the British out.

Operation Barbarossa

Germany allied with Hungary, Romania, and Finland for a massive attack on the Soviet Union that would use 3 million ground troops. On June 22, 1941, battle opened simultaneously along a 2,000-mile-long front. The greatest early success was the Center Group, which enfolded armies, took 400,000 prisoners, and the cities of Minsk and Smolensk. The Germans took Kiev on September 19 along with 665,000 prisoners. Then they moved south to take Crimea. Some people in the beginning, notably Poles and Ukrainians who had suffered under Stalin, greeted the Germans as liberators. When the Nazis stole their food, enslaved their workers, and treated them as "racial inferiors," some became anti-Nazi guerrillas.

By September, the Luftwaffe had destroyed 4,500 Soviet planes while losing but 2,000. In October, General Rundstedt had reached the Don River. The Germans had Leningrad under siege. But the Finns pressed no further than the 1939 boundaries, and the Murmansk rail line was only disrupted, not closed. British convoys to Murmansk began in August, and on November 6, 1941, U.S. Lend-Lease assistance began to flow to Russia.

Hitler made an all-out effort to take Moscow. The Germans captured another

650,000 Soviet troops. The German army was within forty miles of Moscow, but it reached the limits on both men and equipment, and drenching rains made passage hard. The Germans had lost 800,000 men, the Soviets had lost 1.5 million prisoners and an equal number killed or wounded. Stalin entrusted General **Georgi Zhukov** with the defense of Moscow. The temperatures fell to -40°F. Stalemate ensued. Stalin threw a hundred fresh Soviet divisions into battle and launched a counterattack while the Germans were completely unprepared for winter war. The Soviet Union was the only country in the War to use women as combatants, especially as snipers and bomber pilots. Hitler, infuriated, blamed his commanders and essentially destroyed the general staff by firing Generals Rundstedt, Bock and Leeb.

The Japanese Offensive

While Hitler carved out a European empire, Japan had expanded its operations from China to all of Eastern Asia. In September 1940, Japan moved into the French colonies of Southeast Asia. The U.S. placed an embargo on the export to Japan of all steel and scrap iron. Japan began to look at the oil-rich Dutch colonies. The U.S. gave increased assistance to Britain, and devoted most of its 1941 budget to the military. By the end of May, the U.S. was in a state of emergency. In June, the U.S. cut off oil exports to Japan, then froze all Japanese credits. Japan thought the United States could be driven back if it could destroy the American Pacific fleet anchored at **Pearl Harbor**, Hawaii. Japan attacked on December 7, 1941, and at the same time attacked American possessions such as the Philippines and Guam and the British colonies of Hong Kong and Malaya. The attack on Pearl Harbor appeared spectacular and killed over a thousand people, but the Americans raised and repaired all but two of their battleships from the shallow waters. The Japanese would have caused more real damage if they had destroyed the clearly-marked fuel tanks for the fleet. They had done only superficial damage and brought a huge enemy into the war. Germany and Italy also declared war on the U.S. Stupidity ruled the Axis. Roosevelt's main general, **George Marshall**, organized the enormous American war effort.

THE HOLOCAUST

Background

Germany was not the most likely candidate to carry out a mass extermination of Jews. Russia in 1900 was carrying out a mini-Holocaust by persecuting and killing Jews. Austria-Hungary was notoriously anti-Semitic. France was suffering through the Dreyfus Affair. Germany under William II seemed an island of tolerance by comparison, and yet it was Germany that organized the Holocaust.

The Nazis had established concentration camps such as Dachau, Buchenwald, and Bergen-Belsen as early as 1933. At first, the government only put communists, socialists, and other political prisoners into these camps along with common criminals. In the later 1930s, the government began to send some Jews to these camps. They were not extermination camps although tens of thousands died there from malnutrition and overwork. The Nazis installed gas chambers at Dachau but never used them.

When Hitler reached the height of his power in mid-1941, he decided to follow his Jewish policy to its logical conclusion. Conquests in Poland and the U.S.S.R. had brought millions of Jews under Nazi control: 3.3 million in Poland alone. During the *Anschluss, Einsatzgruppen* (Special Groups) of the SS formed a strike force for the political police and security intelligence services. Heydrich sent six *Einsatzgruppen* into Poland hinting at an "ultimate goal."

The Ghettos

Germany expelled all the Jews from the parts of Poland that it annexed and herded them eastward into the "Government General." Germany established ghettos in cities along rail junctions. By 1940, it had sealed these ghettos. They were very cramped: German officials estimated there were 15.1 persons per apartment and six or seven persons per room. Heydrich ordered the formation of a *Judenrat* (Jewish Council) of twenty-four rabbis and remaining influential personalities. It would register Jews and make sure the residents obeyed German orders. Fuel and food were scarce in the ghetto. The Warsaw ghetto had ninety-one deaths from hunger in 1940 and 11,000 in 1941. Typhus killed one-tenth of all the people in the Warsaw ghetto.

Final Solution

After the launch of Barbarossa in June 1941, the Nazis sent about 3,000 in *Einsatzgruppen* to kill Soviet Jews, who were identified as sources of communism. They may have killed a million Soviet Jews in 1941 and 1942. The *Einsatzgruppen* were too inefficient and slow. On July 31, 1941, Göring ordered a "final solution of the Jewish question" by which he meant massive extermination.

From 1933 to 1937, the government sterilized 200,000 with mental problems, hereditary diseases and even alcoholics in the name of racial purity. In 1939, Hitler instituted the euthanasia of 5,000 mentally deficient and physically deformed children. They also sterilized Roma and mixed-race children who had born to German women and French African troops occupying the Rhineland after the war. The government imprisoned and killed homosexuals. They went after the mentally ill, setting up euthanasia installations, gassing them in rooms disguised as shower chambers, and then burning the bodies. The government suspended this program in the fall of 1941 but used the model for the death camps.

At the **Wannsee Conference** (January 20, 1942), Heydrich outlined the details of the death camps and who is to be killed. He numbered 11 million Jews, including those in England, Ireland, and Switzerland. The government liquidated the ghettos and sent Jews to Poland. Officially, they were being resettled in the east. In March of 1942, the first group of Slovakian Jews arrived in Auschwitz. Railroad schedules and even military production had to make way for shipping Jews; the ghetto of Lodz was heavily involved in military production, and the army objected when it was liquidated.

Extermination camps were built outside of the greater Reich following the Wannsee Conference. Auschwitz had been a prisoner-of-war camp with good railroad connections and distance from populated areas. The Germans added a manufacturing concentration camp for slave labor and then a death camp. It was joined by Chelmno, Belzec, Majdanek, Sobibor, and Treblinka. These camps were used for the sole purpose of receiving, holding, gassing, and burning people considered "racially inferior" by the Nazis. About a million were murdered at Auschwitz alone.

In many areas, the Nazis' absolute control led to Jews being handed over. The murder toll included 75 percent of Dutch Jews, 80 percent of Czechoslovakian Jews, 60 percent of Yugoslavian Jews, and 80 percent of Greek Jews. Some countries cooperated eagerly, such as France. Others put up some resistance such as Belgium, which still saw half its Jews killed. Finland, Italy, and Denmark also resisted. About 20 percent of the Italian Jews were killed after the Germans fully occupied Italy. Bulgaria and Romania allowed foreign Jews to be killed but tried to protect their own Jews. About half of the Hungarian Jews were killed. The worst losses were in Poland, the Baltic countries, and Greater Germany, where 90 percent of the Jews were killed. About two-thirds of all European Jews were murdered in the Holocaust.

Hitler also imprisoned and killed the Roma and Sinti people (called Gypsies), who he put in the same low racial category as Jews. 40 percent of the one million Roma and Sinti in Europe were gassed. The Germans often treated the Slavic peoples as slave labor; perhaps 4 million Poles, Ukrainians and Belarussians died as slaves. Two to three million Soviet POWs were allowed to die. The Nazis shared with others on the Right a delusion that city workers really wanted to be farmers. They began to clear land of Slavic peoples with the idea of emptying German cities and establishing farms. The Nazis were out of touch with reality in many ways.

THE ECONOMICS OF WORLD WAR II

The economic balance was against the Axis, but superior generalship and combat qualities of armies had created a catastrophic situation for the Allies. The Germans had overrun the richest part of the Soviet Union, but remarkably the Soviets had not collapsed. They relocated over 500 factories to the east and began production in freezing weather even before roofs had been installed. By 1943, the U.S.S.R. was outproducing Germany in arms.

Starting in 1942, the economic fundamentals reasserted themselves. A war of attrition developed, with rising force numbers and rising losses. Superior GDP and population numbers outweighed superior military qualities. The Germans started rationing food in April 1942. As in World War I, the numbers of the colonial empires had not counted for much. In 1940, the Axis held the advantage by a GDP 40 percent larger than that of Britain and France combined, twice the population, 50 percent more territory. However, by 1942, with France out and the U.S. and U.S.S.R. in, the Allied lands had grown substantially richer since 1938 (the U.S. by more than 50 percent). The U.S. national debt grew by 400 percent, but the government kept inflation in check by freezing prices. The Axis had problems exploiting new lands in part because they had enslaved 8 million foreign laborers by 1944. By 1945, the Reichsmark had lost 99 percent of its value.

THE TIDE OF WAR TURNS

The North African Campaign

Mussolini had an even vaguer foreign policy than Hitler. He had always talked of the glory of the Roman Empire and had aimed at making the Mediterranean an Italian lake. This was a difficult proposition since British naval power dominated the Sea, but Mussolini had the advantages of land. If he could conquer the mainland of North Africa and southern Europe, it would weaken British naval power. Italy's immediate goal was to seize the Suez Canal by a pincer movement from North Africa and East Africa.

In August 1940, Italian troops from Ethiopia overran British and French Somaliland. Mussolini ordered troops from Italian Libya to drive against Egypt. They outnumbered the British by more than three-to-one but were inferior in tanks because Churchill had rushed the last British armored division to Egypt. The British got some reinforcements from the Commonwealth nations of India, Australia, and New Zealand. By February 1941, British had suffered 2,000 casualties while capturing 130,000 Italians. At the same time, the British sent a force to East Africa and forced the Italians out by April 1941.

Germany sent General **Erwin Rommel** to save Libya from becoming a British colony. The British force was weakened by its disastrous intervention in Greece. For a year, the front pushed back and forth between Egypt and Libya. In June 1942, **Bernard Montgomery** took command of the British forces and steadily built them up while the British Navy blocked Rommel's supplies. The British/Commonwealth forces outnumbered the German/Italian forces 150,000 to 96,000. Rommel also had to leave for medical treatment. Upon his return, Rommel, undersupplied and undermanned, unwisely launched an offensive. At **El Alamein** (October–November 1942) Montgomery won big; he lost one-tenth of his army, but Rommel lost two-thirds of his.

Operation Torch

The British and Americans decided that rather than try an immediate invasion of German-occupied France, they would attack what Churchill termed the "soft underbelly." Since the Germans and Italians were already depleted, and the Germans were mostly tied up in Russia, the Americans could land first in Northwest Africa, far from Rommel's forces, where only the Vichy French were providing defense. General Marshall appointed **Dwight Eisenhower** to command the American, British and Free French force that landed in November

1942. Then came a great stroke of luck. As the British and American forces reached Algiers, they unexpectedly found Admiral **Darlan**, who ordered Vichy forces to cease fire. Although Darlan was assassinated a month later, the sudden collapse of French resistance was a great blow to Italy and Germany. The Germans quickly reinforced Tunisia. Rommel won a couple of more victories but could not follow them up. Aided by codebreaking, the Allies sank the German supply ships. 275,000 Axis forces surrendered in Tunisia in May 1943.

The Fall of Mussolini

In response to Operation Torch, Mussolini dismissed eleven members of the cabinet. He said he would mobilize a million more men. Things grew worse as Italian communists launched paralyzing strikes in the winter of 1942/43. Mussolini urged Hitler to make peace with Stalin. As the American and British forces attacked Sicily on July 10, 1943, Mussolini feared letting the Germans in, lest he become a complete German puppet. Italian morale was low and surrenders were frequent. On July 24, Mussolini summoned the Grand Fascist Council. It had not met in a long time, but Mussolini thought this vaguely representative body might bolster his support. Instead it led to a ten-hour debate among the Fascist elite, and finally the council called upon the king to dismiss Mussolini.

On July 25, King Victor Emmanuel III compelled Mussolini to resign. The king appointed Marshal Badoglio as Prime Minister. The Fascist Party dissolved on July 28, and Badoglio opened negotiations. When Allied forces crossed the Straits of Messina on September 3, Italy surrendered. It agreed to join the war against Germany and hand over its navy, air force, and merchant marine. On September 12, German troops rescued Mussolini from prison; he announced formation of a new Republican Fascist Party, allied with the Germans. German forces fought the Allies and seized control of the leading cities. Forces loyal to Badoglio occupied Sardinia and the Free French took Corsica. The king and Badoglio fled south, and by the end of 1943, the Germans held most of Italy.

The Germans pulled back in Italy very slowly. The Apennine Mountains and many rivers made the advance of the Allies tortuous as the German commander had a strong line a hundred miles from Rome, anchored by Monte Cassino. This allowed the German to hold off forces that outnumbered them twenty divisions to seven. The Allies finally captured Rome on June 4, 1944.

RESISTANCE MOVEMENTS

The German Resistance

The German resistance was small, divided, and generally ineffective. The Nazis had put 200,000 political prisoners into camps before 1939. The Gestapo had also infiltrated many groups. The German resistance used little underground propaganda and no sabotage. It focused on organizing a sudden coup to kill Hitler and topple the Nazis. The main resistance focused among army officers and some Prussian nobles, notably General Beck and Count Helmuth James von Moltke, a relative of the generals of 1870 and 1914. The Nazis arrested Moltke and his aristocratic circle in early 1944. The military plotters pushed ahead. On July 20, 1944, Colonel Claus von Stauffenberg planted a bomb at Hitler's headquarters. By luck, Hitler escaped death. The conspirators were arrested and executed immediately. It should be noted that these officers had no intention of restoring liberal democracy. They wanted to set up a non-Nazi dictatorship and ask for peace while trying to keep German areas in Czechoslovakia, Poland, and Austria.

Resistance in Western Europe

After the Nazi conquest, collaborators outnumbered resisters vastly but as Hitler was forced back, the proportion reversed itself. The puppet rulers' fawning behavior towards Hitler and Nazi demands on men and matériel began to fan anger. Hitler's attack on the U.S.S.R. led the Communist Parties in each country to organize effective underground cells against the Nazis. Non-communist resisters tried to advance the values of democracy and liberalism in Christian Democratic movements, especially in the Catholic countries. They were deeply suspicious of communist motives because of the communists' ties to Moscow. From 1943 on, resistance groups became mass movements as the Nazi defeat seemed inevitable.

De Gaulle called for continued resistance and set up a Free French movement. The British gave him a daily radio program. De Gaulle had rocky relations with Churchill and nearly had an open break because he wanted to see a rapid liberation of France. American entrance into the war shook the confidence of the technocrats, and they looked for ways to straddle the fence. Some took to the hills of central and southern France and joined the resistance (*maquis*). Laval set up special courts and a French secret police, which relieved the German SS of having to deal with this problem. In the German north, there was broad resistance, but the southern resistance was mostly leftist. Only the Communist Front straddled both zones. 100,000 French were sent to concentration camps, and only 40,000 returned.

Resistance in Yugoslavia

Some of the most open and bitter fighting between resistance and Axis forces occurred here. Perhaps 2 million of the 14 million who lived in Yugoslavia died in the war. When Italy surrendered in 1943, Communist partisans under Josip Broz (revolutionary name **Tito**) filled the vacuum. In the summer and autumn of 1944, Yugoslavia was liberated not by Allied armies but largely by the Yugoslavs themselves. This gave Tito leverage after 1945 in keeping his independence from Stalin.

Resistance in Eastern Europe

In Poland, the uneasy truce between Communist and non-Communist resistors broke down in 1943, when the Germans found a mass grave in the **Katyn Forest** where Soviet soldiers had machine-gunned thousands of Polish officers in 1939. In Russia, the central military command loosely coordinated the guerrillas and partisans. Thousands of Soviet soldiers had escaped Hitler's initial blitzkrieg but were behind enemy lines and harassed the Germans.

Resistance in Scandinavia

The Germans required the Danish government to jail all known communists but enforcement was lax, and resistance sprang up by 1941 with underground newspapers and acts of sabotage following Hitler's attack on the Soviet Union. The mood in Denmark changed in mid-1943 as the Allies drove the Nazis out of Africa and invaded Italy. Suddenly the Germans no longer looked unbeatable. The Danish government helped smuggle 7,000 Jews across to neutral Sweden to keep them out of Nazis' hands. The British Navy constantly threatened to invade Norway and kept 300,000 Germans pinned down there as the Norwegian king in exile urged resistance over the radio. As the Nazi juggernaut faltered in Russia, Sweden started to move away. In June 1943, the Swedish government issued a pamphlet that in case of invasion, "Resistance shall be made under all circumstances." Sweden also allowed Norwegian exiles to train in "health camps," for the day of liberation. Sweden did not make a major cut in exports to Germany until after the Allied landings in Normandy.

THE GERMANS IN RETREAT

The Eastern Front

In the summer of 1942, the Germans opened a powerful drive aimed at taking **Stalingrad**. This city controlled traffic on the Volga River, especially the oil traffic from the Caspian Sea. The Germans wanted the oil for themselves and to deny the oil to the Soviet war effort. Stalin ordered the Soviets to stand and fight for Stalingrad block by block, building by building, and floor by floor. As the Germans were tied down in the city, the Soviets brought up more forces and surrounded the German army. Another bitter winter descended and on February 2, 1943, the German Sixth Army at Stalingrad surrendered 165,000 men and 1,000 tanks. The Germans had started with 300,000 soldiers. Only 5,000 eventually returned home twelve years later. The Germans staged strategic withdrawals while looking for opportunities to counterattack against extended Soviet lines. In July 1943, the Soviets and Germans fought a massive tank battle at Kursk. The Soviets came out on top and effectively destroyed the German Army Group Center.

American-made trucks, jeeps, and other motorized vehicles gave Russians much greater mobility so they could follow up victories. The U.S. provided the U.S.S.R. about $10 billion in arms and equipment. The Soviets lifted the siege of Leningrad in January 1944, and their first units entered southeast Poland. In March, they launched an offensive during the muddiest time in Ukraine. The Germans were completely surprised as the Soviet T-34 tanks and four-wheel drive trucks outmaneuvered Germans who were bogged down.

The Pacific War

For six months after Pearl Harbor, the Japanese ran through the western Pacific. They took the Philippines, the Dutch East Indies, Burma, and Singapore. In May 1942, the Japanese advance halted as Allied ships and planes stopped Japanese warships in the **Coral Sea** north of Australia. In June 1942, American and Japanese forces fought a bitter battle at **Midway**, with the Japanese losing all four of their aircraft carriers. This victory gave the U.S. naval superiority in the Pacific. With over a million Japanese troops bogged down in China, the rest of the Japanese army was scatted on various Pacific islands and the Allies, primarily the Americans, began to move an island at a time. A long offensive in southeast Asia ended in April 1945 with the Japanese defeated and losing 347,000 killed and wounded.

D-DAY TO THE END

Bombing Strategy

The Allies gained air superiority over Germany by February 1944. The loss of land was already beginning to starve German industry of labor. In 1943 and 1944, Germany produced 278 million tons of hard coal, 45 percent of which came from the Ruhr, 33 percent from Upper Silesia, and 8 percent from the Saar. As Alfred Mierzejewski has written, strategic bombing was generally ineffective until August 1944 when "transportation bombing" started. This concentrated on the rail centers in France, Belgium, and western Germany and secondarily on cut rail lines. In an extraordinary piece of luck, Allied bombers on October 26, 1944, hit a bridge in Köln and triggered the explosive charges. The entire bridge collapsed as one piece into the Rhine and could not be dislodged. Low water exposed the bridge and made traffic impossible, but high water meant barges could not get under the remaining bridges. There were coal shortages at the time when the Germans usually built up their winter reserves.

Operation Overlord

The **Tehran Conference** in November 1943 was the first face-to-face meeting among the three Allied leaders. Roosevelt and Stalin wanted a cross-Channel invasion to have top priority. Roosevelt appointed Eisenhower as Supreme Commander of the expeditionary force. Stalin had wanted a Channel invasion in 1943, but many said it was not possible until the Allies had driven most of the German submarines out of the Atlantic. The experiences of amphibious operations in North Africa, Sicily, and Italy had been very valuable.

The Allied forces landed in Normandy on June 6, 1944 (D-Day). By July 1, there were over 2 million Allied troops in France. Hitler would not order a retreat, and the Allies cut off large German forces. The Free French forces under de Gaulle captured Paris. By September 15, the Allies held so much ground that they had outrun their supply lines and had to stop and consolidate.

Hitler foolishly ordered a new offensive that came to be known as the **Battle of the Bulge**. The Germans diverted rail cars to bring supplies and soldiers to the Ardennes region. They told those factories short of coal to concentrate on finishing their arms products, so that once those were done, there would be long delays. The fighting and bombing trapped many trains in the Ardennes. They could get there but could not get back. Coal began to pile up in the Ruhr. In January 1945, the Russians burst into Upper Silesia, depriving Germany of that coal supply. Heavy bombing completely cut off the Saar. The Germans still had the trains but they were unable to run smoothly between the centers of industry. The other major iron ore source was Sweden, which cut off supplies to Germany on January 1, 1945. The Ardennes campaign destroyed the German infrastructure. By February, Ruhr coal production was down to 30 percent of normal as miners were pulled out to repair yards. The locomotives themselves lacked coal to get back to the Ruhr. Less than a third of railroad cars could operate. Arms piled up and rusted at factories, but there were no trains to deliver them to the front. The Ruhr was isolated by February 1945 and surrounded by April 1.

The Last Phase

The Russians rolled at great speed into Poland and East Prussia. They took Warsaw on January 17, Danzig on January 26, and Budapest on February 12. Russian forces gained the Oder River but were dangerously overextended. This delayed further action until the middle of March. The Germans blew up all the Rhine bridges except for the bridge at Remagen, which failed to detonate. The Allies poured thousands of troops across the bridge before it collapsed from the weight. Allied forces also advanced in Italy, pushing Germans across the Po River. Italian partisans caught Mussolini and his mistress, shot them, and then strung them up by their heels.

The U.S. moved south and east against Leipzig, Dresden, and Chemnitz. On April 16, the U.S.S.R. launched the final offensive against Berlin and surrounded the city ten days later. Desperate fighting followed, with Hitler hiding out in an underground bunker. On April 30 Hitler shot himself, and on May 7 came the formal German surrender.

By this time, Japan had been surrounded and was being bombed round the clock. A firebombing of Tokyo on the night of March 9, 1945, killed at least 80,000 people. The main Japanese army was still trapped in China.

The government ordered a draft of all men aged fifteen to sixty and women aged seventeen to forty. Even as their own diplomats urged them to surrender, the government pushed forward. It had up to 2 million soldiers of various quality available. On August 6, the U.S. dropped the first atomic bomb on the industrial center of Hiroshima, killing at least 50,000 people. The bomb was based on Einstein's principles of energy and mass that when the atom was split, it would release an enormous amount of energy. On August 8, following earlier agreements, the Soviet Union declared war on Japan. On August 9, the U.S. dropped a second atomic bomb on the port of Nagasaki, killing 40,000. By the end of 1945, another 50,000 had died in Japan of injuries and radiation poisoning from the bombs. An additional 60,000 died between 1946 and 1950 of the long-term effects. With half of the Cabinet wanting to fight on, Emperor Hirohito personally broke the deadlock and imposed surrender. The Second World War was over.

Aftermath

60 million had died, including about 25 million citizens of the Soviet Union, around 15 million Chinese, 6 million Poles, 4 million Germans, 2 million Japanese, and close to 2 million in Yugoslavia. The areas of Russia, Poland, Belarus, and Ukraine had seen two or three waves of brutal battle pass over them. The war had devastated coastal China. Extensive bombing had damaged many areas around the world. The United States had lost 300,000 dead, had largely undamaged territory, and emerged as the most powerful country in the world by far.

TIMELINE

1939	Hitler invades Poland, beginning of World War II in Europe
1940	Belgium, Netherlands, and France fall to Hitler
1941	Hitler invades Soviet Union
	Japan attacks United States
1942	American troops land in North Africa
	Stalingrad
1943	American troops land in Italy
1944	Allied invasion of Normandy in Operation Overlord
1945	Germany surrenders
	U.S. drops atomic bombs on Japan

KEY TERMS

Blitzkrieg
Operation Barbarossa
Pearl Harbor
George Marshall
Wannsee Conference
Stalingrad
Operation Overlord

PRIMARY SOURCE DOCUMENTS

Winston Churchill, http://www.fordham.edu/halsall/mod/1940churchill-finest.html

Vasili Grossman, http://www.sovlit.com/war/mainline.html

Chapter 15

THE WATCHFUL PEACE

During the War, the Allies had not wanted to show disunity. They had agreed that Germany should be rendered harmless, that there should be a United Nations, that the leading Nazis should be punished, and that Russia should receive security guarantees and have non-enemy countries on its border.

THE OUTBREAK OF THE COLD WAR

The Yalta Conference

Roosevelt, Stalin, and Churchill met at Yalta on the Crimea in February 1945. The U.S.S.R. was in a strong position since it held Bulgaria, Romania, Hungary, part of Yugoslavia, and much of Czechoslovakia. The U.S. had not crossed the Rhine and still had to contemplate an invasion of Japan. Many misinterpreted the Battle of the Bulge as indicating that the Germans still had plenty of fight left.

The Allies agreed to divide Germany and Austria into zones of occupation. Germany would pay heavy reparations to the U.S.S.R., Stalin agreed to declare war on Japan three months after the war with Germany ended. They also agreed that a United Nations Organization should replace the discredited League of Nations. There was long debate about the nations of East-Central Europe. Churchill particularly wanted Poland to have free elections since the Polish government-in-exile was centered in London. Stalin was angry that Romania,

Hungary, and Bulgaria had been allies of Nazi Germany and demanded governments that would not be hostile in the future. Yalta reached a rather vague agreement that the East European nations would hold free elections but would be pro-Soviet. How could one have free elections and not allow anti-Soviet parties to compete? Stalin had wanted a say in the government of occupied Italy, but Britain and the U.S. refused this.

The Potsdam Conference (July 1945)

Two months after Germany surrendered, the leaders met again, this time in the suburb of Potsdam outside of the ruined German capital of Berlin. This conference was supposed to start drawing up the official peace treaty to end the war. Franklin Roosevelt had died in April, and Harry Truman took his place. Churchill had hoped to capitalize on the victory by calling quick elections, but his Conservatives were crushed by the Labour Party and **Clement Attlee** became British Prime Minister. Churchill had wanted to preserve British naval dominance in the Mediterranean, but the U.S. disapproved. Truman hoped to impress Stalin with the revelation of the new atomic bomb, but Stalin made no concessions. Stalin refused all free elections, and Truman cut off aid that the wrecked Soviet Union desperately needed. The U.S. ended lend-lease and did not respond to a request for a $6 billion loan. Stalin did reaffirm his commitment to enter war against Japan and did so precisely three months after Victory in Europe (V-E) Day. The conference allowed the U.S.S.R. to take reparations out of the eastern zone of Germany but was vague about larger claims. An **Allied Control Council** of Britain, France, the U.S., and the U.S.S.R., would govern German affairs. The Conference recognized the Soviet annexation of land from Romania and Finland but not its takeover of the Baltic lands. Italy lost all of its overseas territories.

Change in American Opinion

By 1946, American opinion had shifted against the U.S.S.R. Conservatives had seen communism as a greater threat than fascism before World War II and now redoubled their efforts. Liberals, socialists, and ex-communists were suspicious, remembering communist behavior in Spain. Business interests were eager to roll back the New Deal and other measures taken in the Depression. Politicians fanned the fear that Stalin was planning some sort of world domination, just like Hitler had. This ignored the facts that the U.S.S.R. had just lost 25 million dead, its western part was wrecked, and its area of occupation had been chewed up in the war. The American government ended the demobilization of troops and extended the draft. The United States has never returned to a peacetime economy. In May 1946, former British Prime Minister Churchill described an "**Iron Curtain**" falling across Europe.

Communism in Western Europe

The Communist parties in France and Italy were strong and under Soviet domination. They came out of the war with strong credit because they had warned most loudly about fascism and had led much of the wartime resistance. In the elections of October 1945, the French Communists won the most seats, about one-third of the total. In elections of June 1946, the Italian Communists won 104 of 556 seats in Italian Parliament. To some, it appeared that Europe would go communist simply through elections. The U.S. began to pour secret funds to the other political parties to keep communists out of government.

Iran

Soviet troops had occupied northern Iran in 1941 when the British, Soviets, and Americans combined to oust the pro-Nazi Shah. With the end of the war, Iran asked the three nations to evacuate, but in November 1945, communists in northern Iran organized a separatist movement. Truman then threatened to drop atomic bombs on the Soviet Union, and the U.S.S.R. evacuated Iran in May 1946. From 1945 to 1948, the Soviets reduced their army from 12 million to 3 million.

Truman Doctrine

Communism was also rising in Greece and Turkey. The Soviet Union had denounced an earlier nonaggression pact with Turkey and demanded territorial adjustments in 1945. Meanwhile, a Greek civil war had re-opened in May of 1946 after the British installed a right-wing monarchy. By 1947, the British had exhausted themselves helping the Greeks against communist guerrillas, who were backed by Bulgaria, Yugoslavia, and Albania. Stalin was not particularly interested in the Greek communist cause.

In March 1947, Truman asked Congress for $400 million in military and foreign aid to help fighters against communism everywhere, beginning with military aid to Greece and Turkey. The Greek Communist rebellion ended in 1949. In July 1947, State Department aide **George Kennan** published an anonymous article repeating some of the main points he had made in a telegram to Washington. Kennan called for a long, patient **"containment"** policy to resist Communism in all quarters. Since the devastation and poverty caused by the War was helping Communist parties, Kennan also called for a program of massive economic assistance which would even be offered to the U.S.S.R.

REBUILDING WESTERN EUROPE

Conditions after the War

Europe east and west was flat on its back. Millions were starving, there was runaway inflation, and black markets flourished. Rationing would continue in France and Britain for years. More than 11 million Germans had fled or been driven out of the lands of the east and migrated to Germany. Many German cities were just heaps of rubble from Allied bombs. In February 1946, the daily German diet in the Ruhr consisted of two slices of bread, margarine, a spoonful of porridge, and two small potatoes. Even before the war ended, inflation had made the German currency worthless.

Western European cooperation was spurred by the Russian threat and American support. It was made possible by fact that four powers emerged as roughly equal: Britain, France, West Germany, and Italy. As long as no one power dominated, the others felt safe. Right after the war, Britain had been the biggest power, but it declined relative to the others and gave up its leadership to West Germany. The war had changed the political pattern. Much of the Old Right, from the conservatives to the radical right and fascists, had been discredited by collaboration with the Nazis. In occupied countries, communists and other resistance fighters had murdered tens of thousands of fascists and collaborators.

Voters who had supported the right-wing parties had little choice but to back the old centrist and democratic conservative parties. Out of this came a new philosophy in the Catholic countries, **Christian Democracy**. This combined Christian values, commitment to a generous social welfare state and a guarantee of human rights, with democracy and a greater adherence to property rights, along with a belief in strong government intervention backed by heavy taxes. It became the main conservative group in Italy, France, and West Germany. New leaders of this idea included **Alcide De Gasperi** (1881–1954) in Italy, **Robert Schuman** (1886–1963) in France, and **Konrad Adenauer** (1876–1967) in West Germany.

The social democrats began to revive with more distrust of communists than ever. Many had been killed or imprisoned during the Nazi Regime and realized that they must be more flexible and less committed to Marxist rhetoric. A new generation of pragmatic social democrats came to power.

Finally, there were the Communists, whose prestige had grown during the war. They were insignificant in West Germany and Britain, but very strong in France, Italy, and southern Europe through the 1970s.

The Marshall Plan

Truman and his Secretary of State George Marshall (the American World War II commander) announced a plan in June 1947 to provide a massive program of loans and gifts to Europe from April 1948 and to the end of 1951. In 2011 money, it might have been the equivalent of $650 billion. The goals were to promote production, bolster European currencies, and facilitate international trade. The **Organization for European Economic Cooperation** (O.E.E.C.) coordinated it. After the Marshall Plan ended, the O.E.E.C. continued as the **Organization for Economic Cooperation and Development** (O.E.C.D.). The Soviets were offered Marshall Plan aid, but Stalin would not accept outside controls over the eastern economy and rejected it. Western Europe responded with spectacular economic growth.

Conflict in Central Europe

A Spring 1947 Foreign Ministers' conference for a peace treaty fell apart over the issue of reparations. The Soviets said they were entitled to payments from the western zones of Germany under the Yalta agreement. The West said that the Soviets had not been providing the required food from the rural eastern zone. At the end of 1947, the Western zones began to coordinate an economic recovery program for western Germany. The Russians feared that the West was trying to revive Germany as a weapon against them. Tensions grew worse in 1948. In February 1948, the communists took over Czechoslovakia in a coup when the restored leader Eduard Benes resigned and Jan Masaryk, the son of the former president, was thrown out of a window. When cooperation broke down in Germany, the Soviets blockaded Berlin. Some urged Truman to use military action and attack the Soviet troops, but the American President responded with a non-offensive airlift to bring food and fuel. If the Soviet Union wanted to start a war by shooting down American aircraft, it could, but the U.S. would not fire the first shot. The **Berlin Airlift** was a famous success and the blockade ended in April 1949. The U.S., Canada, Britain, France, Belgium, Luxemburg, Netherlands, Italy, Portugal, Denmark, Iceland, and Norway formed the **North Atlantic Treaty Organization** (**NATO**) in April 1949 as part of the "containment" policy. In September 1949, the U.S.S.R. announced that it had exploded an atomic bomb. The next month, Communists under Mao Zedong took over China.

The New Security System

The security system of the 1940s and 1950s was not defined by grand world schemes and alliances. It was a **bipolar** system with only two great powers: the U.S. and U.S.S.R. The United States had a much larger and richer economy and a much more modern military, but after 1949 the U.S.S.R. was never too far behind in nuclear technology. The new order involved a careful understanding of where each country had interests: there would be no doubt what would happen if another country sent troops there. Neither great power could conquer the other and the fear of having their cities destroyed ensured cautious policies. The Soviet Union established a buffer zone of puppet governments in east-central Europe, while the United States acquired hundreds of military bases all around the world. They would fight "**proxy wars**" (such as Vietnam, Korea, and Afghanistan) through other countries but always avoided direct conflict. Unlike The Concert of Europe or Bismarck's European Order, this bipolar system did not end in war, so it is better called "The Watchful Peace" rather than the "Cold War." In the 1960s and 1970s, the bipolar system gave way to a multipolar system with five great powers as revived Japan, China, and Western Europe joined the U.S. and U.S.S.R. as great powers.

CONFRONTATION AND RECONSTRUCTION

Formation of the Soviet Bloc

East Central Europe after the War

Between 1945 and 1948, almost 100 million people came under the Soviet Union's sway. Finland managed to stay out of direct Soviet control by pursuing strict neutrality. Stalin had dissolved the Comintern in 1943 as a goodwill gesture. The **Comecon** became the main communist coordinating organization in Eastern Europe. In 1955, the Soviet Union, Poland, Romania, Hungary, East Germany, Bulgaria, and Czechoslovakia formed the **Warsaw Pact** as a military alliance.

The countries were restless under Russian domination. In 1953, East Germany felt secure enough to lift its curb on protests. Immediately, the workers of East Berlin engaged in mass strikes. Soviet tanks and troops put down the Berlin revolt on June 17, 1953. After this, the Communist East German government was very aggressive and constantly pushed for confrontation and war to drive the Americans, British, and French out of West Berlin. In the 1950s, it was very easy for East Berliners to cross to the west and then fly out. The Soviets tried to keep the East German government on a short leash.

The Challenge of Tito

Joseph Broz Tito (1892–1980) had led communist guerrillas against the Nazis in Yugoslavia and had occupied Belgrade before the Russians. This gave him leverage that no other country had. Tito quickly established a dictatorship and would not give the Soviets control of the army or police. Differences grew until March 1948, when the U.S.S.R. pulled out its military and technical advisers. Tito purged the pro-Stalin elements from the Yugoslavian Communist Party and in 1949 signed economic agreements with Western countries. Fixed elections backed Tito fully. The U.S. supplied military equipment, and Yugoslavia signed a mutual defense pact with Greece and Turkey.

The World Financial Situation

The policy-makers of the 1940s reacted against the lack of international cooperation that had made the Depression worse. In July 1944, the **Bretton Woods Conference** was held in the U.S. The guiding force was the British economist **John Maynard Keynes** (1883–1946). It set up the **International**

279

Monetary Fund (IMF) and the **International Bank for Reconstruction and Development** (later known as the **World Bank**). The gold standard was mostly abandoned since it had helped cause the Depression. Foreign countries could turn in their dollars for gold bullion. Since the U.S. held two-thirds of the world's gold, the dollar would be the standard for all other currencies. A 1958 agreement allowed currencies greater flexibility to move up and down where needed for adjustment. The Marshall Plan was in part a restoration of money which had flowed into the U.S. A devaluation of the major West European currencies solved other problems. As a condition for credits in 1947, Britain and France had to sign the **General Agreement on Tariffs and Trade** (GATT). A world of more free trade would be good for general development but also the world's biggest economy, the United States.

The Korean War

Korea had been occupied by the Japanese for many years. After Japan's defeat, Soviet troops entered Korea on August 9, 1945, American troops on September 8. In the north, the Soviet Union worked with the anti-Japanese guerrilla leader **Kim Il Sung** (1912–1994) to establish a communist dictatorship. The U.S. sought political stability without economic change. At first, it worked with the Japanese-installed government, then sought alternatives. The conservative landlord class led by **Syngman Rhee** (1875–1965) dominated southern politics. In August 1948, Rhee's group won elections, and the American occupation ended.

The North was the stronger state in 1950, with greater mineral and hydroelectric resources and was well-armed by the Soviets. It saw the South as a continuation of the Japanese occupation. On June 25, 1950, Kim launched an invasion of the South despite the cautions of Mao and Stalin. To many, this looked like a repeat of Japan's invasion of Manchuria. The security system could not fail as the League of Nations had failed in 1931. President Truman went to the United Nations. The U.S.S.R. was boycotting Security Council meetings because the U.S. and U.N. had refused to recognize Mao's victory, and instead the Chinese Nationalist representative sat in China's chair. With the U.S.S.R. absent, the Security Council voted to send an army to Korea led by the American general **Douglas MacArthur** (1880–1964). After some desperate fighting, the U.N. forces rallied and began to push north. The aim by October became the reunification of Korea by military force. China then entered the war sending hundreds of thousands of troops down into Korea and pushing the U.N. forces back with great loss of life. MacArthur talked of taking the war to

China with direct attacks to drive out Mao and was fired by Truman. Mao also sought to lure the U.S.S.R. into the war by talking of retreating and then having the Soviet Union drop atomic bombs on Chinese territory, killing Chinese and Americans alike. The Russians were appalled and believed Mao to be a little crazy. They were not going to turn this proxy war into a direct war against the U.S. The war bogged down by 1951. After two years of stalemate, they reached a ceasefire in July 1953, and the old division at the 38th parallel remained.

Mccarthyism in the United States

Truman had come into office with a very ambitious program known as the **Fair Deal**. Truman saw this as being parallel to social programs in Britain and other countries: raise the minimum wage, provide universal health care and public housing, expand social security benefits, and recognize the issues of civil rights. He saw this as the follow-up to the New Deal, which had stalled after 1936. In 1946, as part of the general post-war reaction, the Republicans returned in strength to control both the House and Senate. The Republicans threw most of the Fair Deal back at Truman and pushed through the **Taft-Hartley Act** (1947) over Truman's veto. This law limited labor union activity and changed the balance of power to favor the corporations.

In 1948, southern racists criticized Truman and walked out of the Democratic convention after it endorsed a liberal civil rights plank. The Republicans felt certain that they would win in this Democratic split. To their shock, Truman was reelected and the Democrats retook control of the Congress. The Republicans not only criticized Truman and the Fair Deal, but also began to hint that there were traitors in the Administration. Taft-Hartley remained in place, the determined opposition of the American Medical Association derailed health insurance, and a Senate filibuster killed the civil rights bill. The U.S. military budget soared from $13.5 billion to $50 billion. The Maoist victory in China, the shock of the Soviet atomic bomb, and the outbreak of an unpopular war in Korea combined with the very anti-Communist rhetoric which the Administration had used caused a hysteria to grow, which focused on the figure of U.S. Senator **Joseph McCarthy**. In February 1950, McCarthy falsely claimed that the U.S. State Department was riddled with communists and communist sympathizers. Under a McCarthyite law, communist organizations had to be registered, and the U.S. could exclude foreigners for any reason from visiting. In 1954, despite Republicans now holding the White House, McCarthy focused on the U.S. Army and accused the Secretary of the Army of covering up a communist spy ring. The Army's lawyer implied that McCarthy was overseeing a homosexual gang and discredited him. The Republican-controlled Senate censured McCarthy for his activities. The Democrats retook control in 1954 and sharply limited McCarthy's power. The McCarthy era was not confined to Washington. Hollywood cleaned out those who had once had communist ties and put them on a "blacklist." Universities denied tenure and fired professors believed to have dangerous views or those who would not sign loyalty oaths. Over 6 million Americans were investigated, imprisoned, or fired from their jobs. McCarthy even reached back 200 years to censor Tom Paine's *Common Sense*, a key document of the American Revolution.

The Republicans ran a campaign against Truman's "containment" policy and called for a "rollback" of communism, which of course would mean war with the Soviet Union and its allies. In 1952, Dwight Eisenhower won the presidency and appointed **John Foster Dulles**, who had prominently called for rollback, as Secretary of State. Instead Eisenhower brought an end to the Korean War, where 33,000 Americans had died. Instead of an invasion, Dulles promised American assistance to any people who rebelled against their communist government.

WESTERN EUROPE IN THE 1950S

The Federal Republic of Germany (West Germany)

Adenauer and the Constitution

As the occupation zones split between east and west, the western states held elections and sent representatives to a Parliamentary Council in order to draw up a constitution. In September 1948, the Council met in the small city of Bonn and elected **Konrad Adenauer** as President. Adenauer had been a prominent member of the Catholic Center Party before the war and the Mayor of Köln. The Council passed a **Basic Law** (not a Constitution). Drawing upon the lessons from Weimar, the Chancellor was given more power and made fully responsible to the Bundestag. The election system provided a modified two-party system rather than proportional representation. The Basic Law restored federalism as the states would choose members of the Federal Council (*Bundesrat*) that could delay, but normally not block, action from the *Bundestag*, the body elected by the people. Provisions in the Basic Law allowed the states in eastern Germany to apply for admission to the Federal Republic whenever they chose.

Three major parties emerged. Adenauer led the Christian Democrats (CDU), made up mostly of members of the Catholic Center. With the east gone, West Germany was more Catholic and the old Nationalists had lost their base. The CDU became the main conservative party. The Christian Socialist Union (CSU), the Bavarian branch of the CDU, was slightly more conservative. The Social Democrats (SPD) reemerged in much the same form and drew most of their support from the working class. Finally, the Free Democrats (FDP), a smaller party, combined the moderate parties of the Weimar Republic with some elements of the extreme Protestant right. The first popular national elections were held in August 1949 with the Christian Democrats and their allies the Free Democrats gaining a slight majority. Adenauer became the first Chancellor of the Federal Republic.

The Economic Miracle

By 1949, Germany was already well on the way to economic recovery following the currency reform. Despite all the damage, Germany still had a lot of well-educated and productive people. West Germany took a share of the Marshall Plan, and this spurred the economy further. West Germany was already close to its 1936 level of industrial production. In January 1950, the government lifted the last rationing restrictions. Industrialists agreed to the labor unions' demands for **Co-Determination**, which put union leaders on boards of directors, gave unions a big say in the governance of industry, allowed union leaders to look at the real accounting books, and gave workers a stake in the plants they worked in. Exports spurred tremendous growth in the 1950s. Middle-class Germans continued to flee the East and brought their training and education.

Adenauer's Final Years

After Adenauer's eightieth birthday in 1956, people kept expecting him to retire but he stayed on as Chancellor. By the early 1960s, Germans were becoming increasingly restless and looking for new leadership. At the same time, West Germany's weakness was shown with the construction of the **Berlin Wall** in 1961. The East Germans built a wall dividing their part of Berlin from the West to make it harder for easterners to flee. This was seen as necessary to stabilize the situation. Although it had joined NATO, the Federal Republic could do nothing without the approval of the United States. The Social Democrats' call for dialogue with the East seemed more attractive. Adenauer's problems came to a head in 1962 over the *Spiegel* Affair. A leading newsmagazine criticized the Defense Minister repeatedly and printed government documents in which the army admitted that it could not defend West Germany from a Soviet attack. Adenauer ordered a break-in into the magazine's offices and arrested the editor-in-chief. To many, this smacked of Gestapo tactics. Adenauer promised to resign.

The Fourth French Republic

Charles de Gaulle had returned with great prestige and wanted a new republic with a strong president, namely himself. However, the elections favored continuing proportional representation and a similar system to the Third Republic. De Gaulle resigned in protest and founded a party opposed to the system and in favor of a new constitution. The Fourth Republic had to make governments without the Gaullists or the Communists and this led to shaky and short-lived coalitions. The governments were capable economically. The economist **Jean Monnet** (1888–1990) drew up a comprehensive plan for economic reform. He worked to make industry more efficient, update farming methods, and guide the Marshall Plan aid to key industries. France led the way in national economic planning by a democracy. The plan emphasized heavy industry so that France became an industrial country for first time. By 1956, French industrial production was 50 percent above its pre-Depression high. The plan transformed agriculture as the holdings of the small farmers became more profitable. Population, which had been stable from 1840 to 1940, now climbed by 12 percent while national income rose 85 percent.

Clement Attlee in Britain

Attlee launched an ambitious plan after becoming Prime Minister in 1945. He had to cope with continued austerity because so much money had gone into the war effort even though Britain had not been occupied. Britain's economic decline had continued as its trade lost even more markets. In 1946, the government had to re-impose food rationing which lasted until 1954. Britain was overextended with its military and colonies. The Attlee government provided wider benefits for health, old age, and unemployment; it gave free medical care to all registered British subjects. It nationalized the coal industry, communications, and the Bank of England in the hope that this would make the British economy more efficient. Finally, despite sharp opposition, it nationalized the iron and steel industries. It gave compensation in all cases. The elections of 1950 gave Labour a very narrow advantage. Another election in 1951 returned the Conservatives under Churchill. He had run on a platform of rolling back Labour programs and resistance to decolonization. He carried out neither.

The End of Empire

Roosevelt and the U.S. had wanted the Europeans to give up their colonies. There had been some unrest in the colonies in the years between the wars, but the Europeans had kept control. The Japanese takeover of colonies during World War II had proved that Asians could beat Europeans. The Europeans easily rebuffed American demands but soon found that they could no longer afford colonies while trying to rebuild from war damage.

India

In 1942, Indian leaders rejected limited autonomy and called for immediate independence while Britain was at a disadvantage during the War. The British responded by jailing Indian leaders, including Gandhi. Three million people died during a terrible Bengal famine in 1943, souring relations with the British even more. After the war, Muslim-Hindu rivalry split India along the lines of geography and religion. Religious riots in 1946 left thousands of dead. The Muslim League refused to participate in the drawing up of a constitution. In 1947, Britain announced that it would pull out that year. Negotiations created an independent India, with 350 million people, and Pakistan with 75 million to the east and west sides of India. Some 12 million people had to be exchanged between borders and during exchanges, attacks would occur and about a million died. 60 million Muslims remained in India.

The Middle East

The European had let a number of areas go during the inter-war years. The Saud family had ousted the sharifs of Mecca, the British allies in Arabia, after World War I. Britain compensated its friends by putting them on the thrones of the new nations of Iraq and Jordan that had been in the Ottoman Empire. Egypt gained independence under British protection. France also gave independence to Syria and Lebanon. The remaining area was the mandate of Palestine, which the League of Nations had entrusted to the British. The British had promised in World War I to consider the creation of a Jewish homeland and decided to give the Jews a portion of the mandate. The territory of the West Bank was left undetermined but would probably become an independent Arab state. When Israel gained independence in 1948, there was immediate war. Jordan occupied the West Bank and annexed it.

The Suez Crisis

Europe still wanted to control key areas and the African colonies. In 1952 nationalist army officers led by **Gamal Abdel Nasser** ousted the pro-British king of Egypt. The British under Churchill and his successor **Anthony Eden** sought to preserve British control over the Suez Canal and the right to station troops in the canal zone. Egypt turned for help to the Soviet Union. The U.S. canceled aid for the Aswan High Dam on the Nile. Egypt retaliated by nationalizing the Suez Canal. Britain, France, and Israel worked out a secret plan. Israel invaded the Sinai Peninsula in October 1956. The British and French occupied the canal zone in the name of "peacekeeping." The U.S. and U.S.S.R. joined together to force them down and get Israel out of the Sinai. This marked the end of British and French influence over Middle East and hastened decolonization.

The French War in Vietnam

During World War II, the Japanese had occupied the French colony of Vietnam in Southeast Asia. Vichy French officials cooperated without any problem. **Ho Chi Minh** (d.1969) led a mainly communist guerrilla movement against the Japanese and wanted an independent Vietnam after the Japanese defeat. Negotiations broke down as France wanted to retake Vietnam. The French defended their colony with French soldiers and members of the foreign legions, which included a large number of former German prisoners from the Second World War. The communist takeover of China gave Ho a decisive advantage. The U.S. rushed arms and aid to the French. In 1953, the French built a huge fortified camp at **Dienbienphu** on the Laotian border and put in a garrison. The guerrillas cut it off with mortars and anti-aircraft guns obtained from China. President Eisenhower, although declaring that area was of crucial importance, would not send American air forces to relieve the siege. On May 9, 1954, the French surrendered. The Geneva Accords of 1954 called for a temporary division until elections for the whole country took place. The southern Prime Minister Ngo Dinh Diem (d.1963) refused all elections because he would lose to Ho Chi Minh. Vietnam became divided between a communist north and an American-backed south, but the north was still determined to unite the country.

War in Algeria

France was very sensitive about the decolonization process. Defeat in World War II had wounded its national pride, and decolonization seemed to add insult to injury. Unlike the British, French fought hard for some possessions, notably Vietnam and Algeria. Algeria had been part of France since 1830. 1.2 million French dominated the 9 million Muslims in Algeria. After

Dienbienphu, terrorism and guerrilla warfare grew in Algeria as the Muslims sought independence. French put down the revolt brutally and sent in draftees. This brought the war home to French families. Some soldiers had been fighting nonstop since 1939 and were weary. Up to 500,000 French troops were involved at the peak of fighting, and a million Algerians died. When rumors grew of the government opening peace talks in May 1958, the French army in Algeria revolted and occupied Corsica. The government had no way to put down the revolt and gave in to the army's demand that de Gaulle return as leader.

De Gaulle called for autonomy and self-determination once both sides reached a truce. A 1961 referendum among the French supported de Gaulle's initiative. Army leaders again rebelled, and a secret army of terrorists tried to kill de Gaulle. In 1962, Algeria gained independence and many Europeans left. The French reasoned that if they could not hold Algeria, they might as well let their other African possessions go.

GENESIS OF THE EUROPEAN COMMUNITY

International Cooperation after World War II

Out of the devastation of war, a feeling grew that Western Europe's only hope was a move toward unity. Economic cooperation was seen as especially important because of the effect of the Great Depression, which had led to economic isolationism, the rise of Hitler, and the Second World War. The largest postwar political parties, Christian Democrat, Socialist, and Communist, were all internationalist. The mass availability of road and air transportation made Europe a very small place. The mass ownership of televisions and radios made Europe more cosmopolitan. At night, one can pull in dozens of different languages over the AM band. Finally, the guest workers who came to Germany and France from Italy, Spain, Yugoslavia, and Turkey, although disliked by many, created a greater understanding of other cultures.

The Marshall Plan and the Organization for European Economic Cooperation set the pattern. The countries' representatives also met in a Congress of Europe to discuss a union. By 1949, there were already agreements for full economic union between France and Italy and among Belgium, the Netherlands, and Luxemburg (Benelux). By 1950, there were three united organizations: NATO in Brussels, OEEC in Paris, and the Council of Europe in Strasbourg. These set the foundations for subsequent developments.

France became convinced that a hard line against Germany was self-defeating. The Foreign Minister Robert Schuman and the architect of French economic recovery Jean Monnet drew up the **Schuman Plan** in 1950 for coal and steel cooperation. Monnet saw this as the first real step towards European economic integration. Under the plan, a single high authority would govern all French and German coal and steel production, and there would be an open market between the two countries in these products. It would encourage modernization and planning without nationalization. Britain foolishly refused to join. The **European Coal and Steel Community** began in April 1951 with France, West Germany, Italy, the Netherlands, Belgium, and Luxemburg as members. The Treaty of Rome in 1957 set up a **European Economic Community** (EEC or **Common Market**), starting with the six members of the coal and steel community. It aimed at abolishing customs barriers among members, permitting the free movement of labor and capital, and equalizing wages and social insurance programs. It would work in stages and had its headquarters in Brussels. In 1968, the EEC agreed to a common tariff with non-member states and free trade within the EEC. Britain finally applied for membership in 1963, but de Gaulle blocked it. He feared British economic power, disliked Britain personally, and opposed expansive social welfare programs. After de Gaulle's retirement, Britain was admitted to the Common Market, effective 1973.

THE MULTIPLE CRISIS OF 1956

Malenkov and Khrushchev

After the war, Stalin began a new crackdown. Stalin grew increasingly paranoid, and people feared that another purge was on the way. Stalin had his first heart attack in front of his lieutenants; it was followed rapidly by a second and Stalin died March 5, 1953. It was Stalin's will that **Georgi Malenkov** (1902–1988) succeed him in both positions of Prime Minister and General Secretary of the Communist Party. Malenkov had worked his way through the ranks of the party as one of Stalin's "new men" with little memory of the Revolution and had come into the Politburo in 1946. Malenkov's chief associates were Foreign Minister Molotov and Secret Police head Lavrenti Beria. Malenkov held both positions for only two weeks. The other Communist leaders apparently told Malenkov to choose one position, and he unwisely chose to remain as Prime Minister. **Nikita Khrushchev** took the position leading the Communist Party. Khrushchev was older than Malenkov and had started as an illiterate coal miner. The Communist Party had given him education and prestige, and he was devoted to his idea of communism.

There were immediate changes and a loosening of policy. The government allowed foreigners to travel more in the U.S.S.R. Beria was arrested on charges of treason in June 1953 either because he tried to stage a coup or because he was blamed for the Berlin uprising. In February 1955, Malenkov resigned as Prime Minister but remained in the Politburo. Nicolai Bulganin became Prime Minister, and war hero General Zhukov became Defense Minister.

Khrushchev and Bulganin

Reform and relaxation continued. Khrushchev reduced the size of the army, decentralized agriculture, pulled out of Austria, and recognized the Federal Republic of Germany. He also announced that he would aid the newly-independent nations of Asia and Africa and all who struggled against Western colonialism. In February 1956, the Twentieth Communist Party Congress opened. It was only the second meeting since 1936. Khrushchev electrified the Congress by publicly revealing and condemning Stalin's crimes. He claimed that Stalin was a semi-literate peasant who had wrongly murdered many party members. Stalin had bungled foreign policy and been unprepared for Hitler's attack. Khrushchev claimed that he was trying to return to true Leninism and break with Stalinism. Because Khrushchev had ordered the doors closed before he spoke, this became known as the **Secret Speech**. Stalin's body was removed from a place of honor next to Lenin and buried beneath twenty feet of concrete. The government released 4.5 million persons from prison camps in 1956. The reaction in the Soviet Union was fairly muted, but it set off a firestorm in the satellites because Stalin had installed most of their leaders. Riots broke out across Poland in June 1956. Soviet troops took up a position near Warsaw, ready for action. A number of reforms then put a more moderate Communist in charge of the Party and released the leader of the Polish Catholic Church from detention.

Hungary

U.S. Secretary of State Dulles had promised American aid to the peoples of Eastern Europe if they rose up against Communist dominance. As discontent rose in Hungary, the moderate former Prime Minister Imre Nagy was restored as leader of the Communist Party. Riots demanding sweeping reform stormed across Hungary in October 1956. On October 31, Nagy announced that Hungary would leave the Warsaw Pact and would have a multiparty system.

Soviet troops poured across the border. The Interior Minister, Janos Kadar, announced that he was taking control. The Hungarians, hoping for American aid, were cruelly disappointed. The United States was not going to break the Watchful Peace. Within a week, the Soviets had ruthlessly crushed the revolt. 200,000 Hungarians fled over the next year.

The Waning of International Communism

The crushing of the Hungarians led to mass disillusionment among leftists with the Soviet Union. Many who had been willing to back the Soviet Union or were wary of the U.S. now turned their back on the Russians. From this point on, the Soviets would only have popularity in the Third World or among those too young to have remembered communist outrages.

China

Khrushchev's secret speech embarrassed Mao because he was still praising Stalin. Khrushchev tried to soothe Mao by speaking of "many paths to socialism," and recognized Beijing as an independent center of doctrine. China felt Khrushchev's revisionism was a sellout, especially when the Soviet leader visited the U.S. in 1959. Khrushchev promised Soviet nuclear assistance even as he believed that Mao getting control of nuclear weapons was a very bad idea. The U.S.S.R. secretly told the Russian scientists to sabotage the Chinese nuclear program. When the Chinese realized this deception in 1960, they ordered the technicians out. China tested its first nuclear weapon in 1964.

Backlash in the Soviet Union

Bulganin, Malenkov, and Molotov led an attempt in the Politburo to dump Khrushchev. In June 1957, they won a seven to four vote, but Khrushchev asserted that only the Central Committee could oust him. He called an emergency meeting, and Zhukov brought army planes from around the nation to fly in the members. The Central Committee backed Khrushchev. Molotov, Malenkov, and Bulganin lost their positions. Unlike Stalin, however, Khrushchev did not murder his enemies. The bloodiness that had marked Stalin's time was draining out of Soviet politics.

CLIMAX OF THE COLD WAR

In the 1960s, the confrontation between the US and the Soviet Union came to the brink, and then both powers backed off, and relations between the two superpowers began to warm, despite the fact that Russian bullets were ending up in American bodies in Vietnam.

Confrontation in Latin America

The 1950s saw tension growing in Latin America. Since the Roosevelt Corollary, the United States had claimed the right to intervene and had done so repeatedly. When the reformist President Arbenz of Guatemala accepted political support from communists and seemed to threaten the United Fruit Company, the U.S. sponsored a military coup that overthrew Arbenz.

Communism in Cuba

In Cuba, a guerrilla movement led by **Fidel Castro** (b.1927) challenged a longtime dictator and ousted him in 1959 after Eisenhower declined to resupply the dictator with arms. No one quite knew what to make of Castro. He started as the commander-in-chief of a coalition government, but rapidly took control. Revolutionary courts executed 550 people. Castro's trip to Washington in April 1959 seemed to go well, but the next month he announced land reform and that no foreigners would be allowed to own farmland. He postponed promised elections and jailed other revolutionaries. Many, especially in the U.S., saw this as communism. Castro turned more anti-American. Cuban exiles flocked to Florida and plotted a counterrevolution. In 1960, Castro nationalized the economy, swung to the Soviet bloc, established an authoritarian regime, and launched an egalitarian socioeconomic policy. When Cuba nationalized American-owned oil refineries, the U.S. suspended its guaranteed purchases of Cuban sugar. Cuba then confiscated the rest of the American property, and the U.S. responded with a total embargo. Castro abolished an independent press and judiciary.

The American Central Intelligence Agency (CIA) was convinced that Castro was a Soviet puppet. It promoted clandestine plots such as exploding cigars. After becoming President, John F. Kennedy agreed to the **Bay of Pigs Invasion** (April 1961) by the exiles but would not provide American logistical support or air power. The invasion was a failure. In December 1961, Castro declared himself a Communist.

The Cuban Missile Crisis

In the fall of 1962, the U.S.S.R. began to build intermediate-range missile bases in Cuba. The U.S. discovered the activity with reconnaissance aircraft. It demanded that Khrushchev withdraw missiles from Cuba, and it put a naval quarantine on Soviet ships. War seemed imminent; what would happen if ships tried to force their way through? There seemed to be disarray in the Kremlin, as the ever-unpredictable Khrushchev sent two messages: one belligerent, threatening destruction; another conciliatory. Kennedy ignored the first message, replied to the second, and reached a deal: the U.S. would withdraw its short-range missiles in Turkey and would not invade Cuba; the U.S.S.R. could keep some forces in Cuba and would dismantle the missile bases there. Castro was now closely identified with the U.S.S.R.

After the crisis had brought the superpowers to the brink of nuclear war, both of them began to work for better relations. They installed a "Hot Line" between Washington and Moscow for instant communication. They signed the **Atmospheric Test Ban Treaty** in 1963, which banned all nuclear tests in the air, sea, or space. China denounced this. In 1964, Khrushchev announced a sweeping change in the Communist Party structure and its relation with the government. This was too much for Communist conservatives. They staged a coup in October 1964. Khrushchev learned of the coup while on a plane flying back from a vacation. He could have ordered massive resistance and bloodshed, but he had devoted his rule to ending Stalin's tradition of blood. He landed in Moscow and submitted to the coup leaders. **Leonid Brezhnev** took over.

The Vietnam War

As Diem lost popularity in South Vietnam, the United States sent increasing numbers of military advisers. A military dictatorship took over and murdered Diem around the time President Kennedy was assassinated. In August 1964, the U.S. government falsely claimed that North Vietnamese ships had attacked American destroyers in the **Gulf of Tonkin Incident**. The Congress authorized President **Lyndon B. Johnson** to take whatever action was necessary. Johnson cashed this blank check when he sent 75,000 troops to Vietnam in February 1965. When that did not stabilize the south, Johnson added increasing numbers of troops until they totaled half a million.

No headway could be made because the South Vietnamese government was very corrupt. Many American supplies and weapons ended up with the communist guerrillas. Despite torture and terror bombing and the death of 2 million Vietnamese, they were willing to fight on. A technological war in a land of jungle trails and self-sufficient villages did not have the same punch as when fewer bombs had been dropped on industrial Germany and Japan in World War II. Johnson did not want to bring China into the war by staging troop landings in the north.

The Tet Offensive in January 1968 was a massive attack throughout the south to demonstrate that the guerrillas had not been beaten. They even raided the American Embassy in Saigon, the capital of South Vietnam. The guerrillas were slaughtered and broken as an effective force. The fighting would be carried on by regular units of the northern army. Nevertheless the offensive shocked U.S. public opinion and Johnson. The American generals told Johnson they needed 250,000 men from the reserves to continue the war. College campuses erupted. Johnson announced that he would not run for reelection, that peace talks would begin, and that the bombing of the north would end.

Vietnam was caught up in American electoral politics. **Richard Nixon**, the Republican nominee, claimed to have a secret plan to end the war and encouraged the South Vietnamese dictator to drag his feet on peace talks. Nixon won a razor-thin victory and began a very slow withdrawal. In 1970, Nixon extended the war to neighboring Cambodia without any legal authorization. Nixon finally signed a peace in 1973. Within two years, North Vietnamese forces overwhelmed the south and united the country under a Communist dictatorship. Communists also took over in Cambodia and Laos.

NEW TRENDS OF THE 1960S

While the protests against the American involvement in Vietnam raged, a number of trends were growing and mixing with one another to show the way to a major change in society and culture. Most of these trends started before the Vietnam protests and have continued and developed up to the present day, exciting some people and disturbing others. Nevertheless, when people talk about "the Sixties," particularly in the U.S., this is what they mean.

The Economic Balance of Power

By the late 1960s, an important shift was clearly taking place in the economic balance of power. The world of the Cold War had been built on the fact that two great powers, the U.S. and U.S.S.R., stood victorious. Britain was badly damaged, Germany and Japan were flattened, France had been occupied. The colonial powers controlled much of the rest of the world. China was big but in the throes of a civil war. By 1970, this balance had changed considerably. The

U.S. and U.S.S.R. were still reckoned as the two leading powers of the world, although we may question the size of the Soviet economy. Germany and Japan had rebuilt themselves and had emerged as major economic powers. Britain and France remained considerable forces, and Italy was emerging as an economic power. The European Community had come together in Western Europe and was a growing power. The Communists had united China, even if its progress was uncertain. China and India were able to feed themselves and China had nuclear weapons. Other nations such as Canada, Australia, and Brazil were at least minor or regional powers. Most of Africa and Asia had been decolonized. Europe and Japan as well as the U.S. were conducting major research work.

By the 1960s, this diffusion of power made itself clearer. The U.S. had increasing difficulty maintaining the world's financial system and controlling the prices of gold (at $35 an ounce versus market rates of $150) and silver (at $1.25 an ounce). Because of the growing expense of silver, the U.S. stopped minting silver coins in 1964. De Gaulle of France took special delight in tweaking the U.S. He would exchange dollars for gold at the official rate of $35 an ounce and then sell it at the world market rate, draining gold from the U.S. De Gaulle pulled France out of NATO in 1966 with a great flourish, criticized the U.S. harshly over Vietnam, hinted that France and others might seek a third way between the U.S. and the U.S.S.R., and came to Canada to urge the liberation of Québec in 1967. Canada itself sold great amounts of wheat to the U.S.S.R. and China in the 1960s and reduced its contribution to NATO. The Iron Curtain was rusting away.

The Student Protests

Around the industrial western world, the baby boom after 1945 had created a large and self-confident pool of young people. Rich families in the Western world had moved steadily out of the cities and into the suburbs. Blue- collar workers making high wages in the steel or auto industries could send their children to college. There were more students than ever in the universities. In France, 14.5% of young people were attending universities as opposed to 4.5% in 1950. The West German rate also tripled.

As the number of college students had grown, so had student deferments. There were many ways of getting out of going to Vietnam: doctors' notes, the national guard, or civilian work in the Defense Department. Only a few defied the draft openly and fled to Canada or went into hiding. By 1966, massive protests filled the streets as students feared an end to deferments. Some parts of the movement became more radical. Some soldiers were glad that protesters were trying to end war and joined the anti-war movement when they came home. Soldiers began to refuse orders and murder officers they disliked; a giant anti-war banner was unfurled on an aircraft carrier. Other soldiers were bitter at those who avoided fighting and felt that protests prevented victory in Vietnam. Nixon would call them the "silent majority."

Environmentalism

Concern about destruction of the environment also became more urgent in the 1960s. Expansion of the suburbs in the 1940s and 1950s and the expansion of the road system to reach them worried many. Farmland and wilderness were disappearing. Neighborhoods in cities were being torn up to make way for highways. More and more cars spewed exhaust into air. Foul air and water were becoming commonplace. Bad smogs in London and Pittsburgh killed dozens. Dead fish washed up. Rivers caught fire. Oil and waste products fouled beaches. The world consumed enormous amounts of coal, oil, natural gas, and chemicals. In 1963, Rachel Carson published *Silent Spring* and warned of environmental consequences. In the late 1960s and 1970s, there was action: lead was taken out of gasoline, there was less coal burning or "scrubbers" cleaned the emissions, and governments funded nuclear power plants. The United States passed clean air and clean water acts and banned DDT and similar pesticides. The U.S. generally took the lead, and in the late 1970s, "Green" environmental movements emerged, notably in Germany, that pushed for limiting economic growth due to environmental concerns.

Feminism

A new women's rights movement began in the late 1950s. One can associate this latest movement with drives for economic and sexual freedom. Lower class women had always worked, often at lower wages than men at the same job. As the middle class and upper classes had grown in the West with prosperity, women were expected to stay home and run a household in stable nuclear families. During World War II, women had played prominent work roles while men were away at the front. The end of the war forced women out of the factory and other workplaces, restricted them to certain jobs of the lower-middle and lower class (nurses, waitresses, secretaries). By the 1950s, many middle-class women were feeling unfulfilled despite their comfortable lives and families. The percentage of married women in the salaried American workforce rose from 15 percent to 40 percent from 1952 to 1970. The French woman Simone de Beauvoir in her book *The Second Sex* (1949) put sexual relations in a Marxist context: men oppressed and exploited women and denied them positions of authority, leadership, and power. The American **Betty Friedan** in *The Feminine Mystique* (1963) also spoke of emptiness in life. Their cause was linked to civil rights movements, and laws against discrimination on the basis of sex became common in the 1960s and 1970s. By the early 1970s, about half of western women were having their last baby by age twenty-seven while their life expectancies were soaring past age seventy. Many sought new roles in society. Conservatives frustrated an attempt to pass an Equal Rights Amendment to the Constitution. The U.S. generally led in women's rights until about 1980. Most European countries expected women to remain family-raisers first and sacrifice their careers. This family concern led them to pass family leave laws for people with sick relatives and newborn children so they could take time off work without risking their jobs. The U.S. did not enact this until 1993. The Europeans also provided ample and affordable child care facilities for those women who did work.

Women also gained greater control over their bodies. Doctors developed the first oral contraceptives in 1960. These would be much easier and effective than other methods of birth control. "The Pill" decisively separated sex and reproduction. The western world legalized abortion in the late 1960s and 1970s. Family planning became much more possible, and women could put their career and family plans into perspective.

Even as women felt something was missing from life, a similar restlessness affected a number of men. Social pressures of men's responsibility for family weakened. Rates of illegitimacy have roughly tripled from the late 1950s. About half of all marriages ended in divorce as divorce laws were either approved or eased to make that more possible. At the end of the 1960s, a gay liberation movement began as homosexuals wanted the freedom to express their sexuality openly.

Terrorism

Reforms satisfied many of the 1960s protesters, but a few turned to violent action. Some areas felt that they should receive their own countries, such as Palestinians from Israel and Croatians from Yugoslavia. The idea of terrorism was to spread fear and paralyze society. This was demonstrated in 1972 when eight Arab terrorists seized the quarters of Israeli athletes during the Munich Olympics. In a bloody shootout, nine athletes, one policeman, and four terrorists died. Some of the countries allied with the Soviet Union helped supply training and materials to terrorists, worsening relations with the West. Terror against Israelis or Israeli institutions became common. German and Italian terrorists committed outrages that alienated many, and those governments used a measured and legal response to end the terrorist wave.

Northern Ireland also became the scene of violent terrorism. Discrimination against the Catholics persisted in the north even though the Catholic proportion continued to increase. In 1966, Protestant extremists staged a riot in Belfast to block concessions to Catholics. In April 1969, Britain sent troops to restore order. The Irish Republican Army began a terrorist campaign that extended through the 1980s, Protestant radicals countered with violence of their own, and over 2,500 died violently over the years. In the 1990s, settlements were finally reached with the help of U.S. President Clinton.

The New Technologies

The period after 1945 saw technology playing an ever greater role in the everyday life of people around the world, but especially among the middle and upper classes of the industrialized world. The technologies transformed both work and play. Not all technology was "new" in terms of being invented after 1945. Electrical generators had been devised before 1900, but electrification was a slow process, especially in rural areas. By 1950, most houses had electricity in the U.S., Canada, and Europe. Colonial areas had also had electrical lines built, but after independence many areas had problems keeping generators going. Blackouts were common. As households added more and more electrical devices, the need grew for more and more power, with oil generating most of that energy. After the oil crises of the 1970s, natural gas and nuclear power began to play more of a role. Air conditioning played a big role in the development of the U.S. It allowed a mass migration to hot southern states. It was much less important in underdeveloped countries and in Europe, which is generally cooler.

The airplane also existed before 1945, but air travel became increasingly common and cheaper. Railroads grew more decrepit and less used. After 1970, governments introduced faster, cleaner railroads to save energy and help the environment. Tourists, especially from the U.S., Japan, and Germany, were seen all over the globe. The world became closer.

The radio was another old piece of technology that flourished. The introduction of FM radio (invented 1933) gave a cleaner sound with less static. It became a natural home for music stations. It also provided for the spread of culture, especially American culture and music, to all parts of the world. The development of the transistor in 1948 led to miniaturization and smaller radios that could be carried around.

Television had been invented before the war, but was not introduced until afterward. TVs were first very small and very expensive. In the prosperity of the 1950s, more and more people owned televisions. Networks controlled by private corporations or by governments provided news and entertainment. People stayed in more and (probably) stayed up later. Movies felt stiff competition from TV and tried to do things to attract people back. The problem grew worse for the movies with the introduction of color televisions in the mid-1960s. By the late 1960s, censorship codes in the movies had given way to a rating system so that people would have some idea of the content of violence, nudity, and sex. In the 1980s, cable channels grew, and the domination of the networks in the U.S. fell. Bigger corporations bought all the U.S. networks. New press lords such as the Australian Rupert Murdoch rose to rival Hearst of the old days.

The use of rockets had taken a big step forward during World War II, especially ballistic missiles that went high into the atmosphere. The military continued to develop rockets. By the late 1950s, the U.S. and U.S.S.R. had Intercontinental Ballistic Missiles (ICBMs). In 1957, the Soviet Union fired a rocket into space carrying the satellite **Sputnik**. The U.S. feared an attack from above, and the "space race" was on. The Americans put their first satellite into space in 1958. Satellites would help communication. Better mapping of weather made for superior forecasting. In 1961, the U.S.S.R. again beat the U.S. in the race to put the first man into space. Kennedy announced his determination to put a man on the moon, and in 1969, astronauts planted the U.S. flag there. By that year, détente was on between the United States and Soviet Union, and the space race eased. Exploratory vehicles brought interesting discoveries, but many doubted that the costs were worth the trouble. Japan and Western Europe kept only modest space programs.

The discovery of the structure of DNA in 1954 was part of a flurry of medical advances. Scientists developed vaccines against polio. By 1975, the world had eradicated smallpox. Plastics made possible various devices for transplant, and organ transplants became common. Operations to prolong life caused life expectancy to grow in many countries, but the new medicine was very expensive.

The Xerox machine made possible multiple copies of any document. It eliminated the laborious retyping and use of carbon copies. It also made secrecy more difficult and publishing easier as people no longer needed a printing press to express themselves, just a typewriter and Xerox machine. Improvements in transistors and semiconductors allowed computers to become more common. Cumbersome computer tape and punchcards were replaced by disks, then by internal platters, then flash memory. Communication among computers improved, culminating in the Internet. By 1980, computers became cheap enough for families to buy them.

TIMELINE

1945	Yalta Conference
	Potsdam Conference
1946	Soviets evacuate Iran
1947	Truman Doctrine
	Marshall Plan
1948	Communist coup in Czechoslovakia
	U.S. Democrats favor civil rights for blacks
1948–49	Berlin blockade and airlift
1949	Soviets detonate atomic bomb
	NATO formed
	Communists take China
1950–53	Korean War
1951	European Coal and Steel Community
1952–3	U.S. and Soviets develop hydrogen bomb
1953	Stalin dies; Khrushchev begins rise
1954	French defeated in Vietnam
1955	Soviets evacuate Austria
	Warsaw Pact formed
1956	The Multiple Crisis in the Communist world
	Suez Crisis
1957	Treaty of Rome establishes European Economic Community
	U.S.S.R. launches Sputnik
1959	Castro takes over Cuba
1960	Birth control pill
1962	French leave Algeria
	Cuban Missile Crisis
1963	Friedan, *The Feminine Mystique*
	Carson, *Silent Spring*
	Assassination of U.S. President Kennedy
1964	Brezhnev replaces Khrushchev
1964–73	Intense phase of U.S.-Vietnam War
1969	U.S. moon landing

KEY TERMS

Yalta Conference
Potsdam Conference
Truman Doctrine
Marshall Plan
Berlin Airlift
Suez Crisis
European Economic Community

PRIMARY SOURCE DOCUMENTS

Truman Doctrine, http://www.fordham.edu/halsall/mod/1947TRUMAN.html
Nikita Khrushchev, http://www.fordham.edu/halsall/mod/krushchev-secret.html
Brezhnev Doctrine, http://www.fordham.edu/halsall/mod/1968brezhnev.html
George Marshall, http://www.fordham.edu/halsall/mod/1947marshallplan1.html

Chapter 16

THE HUMAN RIGHTS REVOLUTION

The Nuremberg Trials, 1945–1946

The horrors of World War II shocked the world, but especially public opinion in the United States. The victors could not just let the defeated Axis leaders slink into retirement and disgrace. Britain and the Soviet Union had favored "political disposition," meaning summary execution or imprisonment without trial. The Truman administration favored open trials as "morally superior." The scope would be sweeping to purge all who had done evil. In Germany, there would be an extensive investigation to find perpetrators and "denazify" German society. The German war crimes trials began at palace of justice in Nuremberg on November 20, 1945. The Allies held trials for the "main war criminals." The International Military Tribunal had representatives from the U.S., U.S.S.R., Britain and France. The Tribunal tried twenty-two prisoners for **conspiracy against peace, crimes against peace, violations of the laws of war, and crimes against humanity**. The defendants pointed out that the Allies were also guilty of crimes. Had not the United States carried out a holocaust against American Indians, and did it not treat African-American citizens poorly? What about Stalin's crimes? What about the treatment of the British and French colonies? The Allies admitted their shortcomings, but vowed that Nuremberg marked a new beginning for human rights and that they would never commit such crimes in the future.

Individual military governments held trials in their occupation zones. After the occupation, German courts held trials, and countries that had been occupied held trials for crimes committed on their soil. The Allies distributed millions of questionnaires with 131 questions asking how closely the person had worked with the Nazis. There was much trouble establishing the truth. With the coming of the Cold War, the Americans ended denazification in 1948 with 30,000 cases outstanding and were willing to look the other way as ex-Nazis came into the government and army. Adenauer's cabinet secretary had been the bureaucrat in the Hitler years who had drafted the Nuremberg laws. The American CIA smuggled many Nazi war criminals out of the country to escape justice.

The UN Charter and the General Situation

The 1945 Charter of the United Nations contained a Human Rights Declaration that called on all the nations of the world to respect the traditional human rights of people. Yet in 1945, the overwhelming majority lived in some kind of dictatorship or colonial rule and even in democratic countries such as the United States and France, voting rights were denied to some citizens. As long as western countries denied human rights in areas they controlled, it was quite difficult for them to dictate to others, and the West had been muted in its criticism of the dictators in Germany, Italy, and the Soviet Union.

The American Civil Rights Movement

The American prosperity of its Industrial Revolution finally trickled down to a number of blacks, and after 1910 there was a mass exodus out of the South into northern cities, where blacks could vote and have some additional rights. The joining of the blacks to the Democratic coalition in the 1930s and the participation of many black soldiers in World War II moved civil rights to the forefront. During the war, black civil rights leaders had campaigned for the "Double V": victory over the Axis followed by victory for equal rights. World War II accelerated the migration with a million African-Americans moving to northern cities for factory jobs. In 1948, President Truman announced desegregation of the army, and the Democratic Party adopted a strong civil rights plank in its platform. In 1954, the Supreme Court reversed its 1896 decision in **Brown vs. Board of Education** and began the desegregation of the school systems. Starting with a 1955 bus boycott in Montgomery, Alabama, **Martin Luther King, Jr.** spearheaded drives to treat blacks equally on buses and in restaurants and to abolish "whites only" bathrooms, hotels, and drinking fountains. After years of delay and filibuster, the Congress passed the **Civil**

Rights Act of 1964 and **The Voting Rights Act of 1965**. Economic inequality still remained a problem but at last a challenge had brought down the legal barriers of Jim Crow.

TURNING POINT

A New Diplomatic System

By 1969, the shift in the economic balance of power was having an effect on diplomatic relations. It was predictable that as Europe and Asia recovered from World War II, the relative position of the United States would fall. But the United States, on its own, had growing problems. First, the overcommitment to an American empire and an outsize military budget far beyond the defense needs of the U.S. eroded the economy year by year. By 1970, the economic decline had affected the ability of the American military itself as seen in Vietnam. Secondly, U.S. oil production peaked in the early 1970s. Until 1948, the U.S. had been the largest oil exporter in the world. Its ability to provide energy had been critical in World War II. Despite massive attempts at exploration and drilling and the arrival of the supergiant Alaska fields on line in the early 1980s, American oil production has never exceeded its 1970 peak and never will.

Nixon and his chief foreign policy adviser **Henry Kissinger** shifted away from the old Cold War situation. The "**Nixon Doctrine**" moved the security burden onto regional powers such as the Shah of Iran. Kissinger was an expert on Metternich's Concert of Europe, where all European powers had worked to maintain the peace. Now Kissinger saw a similar situation, a "Concert of the World" with the U.S., U.S.S.R., Western Europe, Japan, and China all equal partners cooperating to keep the peace. Others objected and believed the U.S. should keep special ties to Western Europe and Japan. Nixon and Kissinger accelerated a trend towards cooperation with communists that had been building since the Cuban Missile Crisis.

Ostpolitik in West Germany

The Western European nations also began to develop a foreign policy independent from the United States. France left NATO in 1966. West Germany had begun to explore its own policy with the eastern nations (*Ostpolitik* in German). In 1969, **Willy Brandt** became the first socialist Chancellor of Germany since

1930. He opened negotiations with the Soviet bloc nations and began new four-power talks on the status of Berlin. In 1970, West Germany signed a deal to build a Soviet natural gas pipeline and agreed to finance its construction. In the 1970s, many western banks provided loans to the communist countries.

Ostpolitik consisted of groups of treaties:

A) **Treaties of diplomatic recognition**: before Brandt, West Germany only had full diplomatic relations with one communist nation: the Soviet Union. Now, it recognized Poland, Czechoslovakia, Hungary, and Bulgaria. When he was in Warsaw to sign the Polish treaty, there was a dramatic moment as Brandt fell to his knees at the memorial to the Jews who died in the Warsaw ghetto.

B) **Treaties on Berlin**: A series of treaties normalized the situation in divided Berlin and allowed West Berliners to travel freely to East Berlin. The "city in crisis" atmosphere abated.

C) **Treaties between the Two Germanies**. These allowed both German states to join the U.N. and other international organizations. Bonn recognized East Berlin as the capital of East Germany.

Willy Brandt received the 1972 Nobel Peace Prize for these accomplishments.

Détente with the Soviet Union and China

Leonid Brezhnev (General Secretary 1964–1982) had been trained as an engineer and gained the ceremonial position of President under Khrushchev in 1960. In 1964, the conservatives in the Politburo, alarmed by Khrushchev's reforms, deposed Khrushchev and put in Brezhnev as General Secretary. Brezhnev began to reverse Khrushchev's reforms. Censorship grew, and the government declared dissidents mentally ill and packed them off to asylums. The Brezhnev years were ones of great decline in almost all sectors. Brezhnev's family was notoriously corrupt and millions of rubles disappeared into secret bank accounts. A small Communist elite of 17.5 million sucked the resources from the people. The Soviets also diverted more and more money into the military budget, although much Soviet military technology remained primitive. At a time when miniaturization and solid-state circuitry were becoming standard in Western equipment, the Soviet Union was still using vacuum tubes. The collapse of agriculture accelerated as the U.S.S.R. became dependent upon U.S. imports for grain. The leadership grew older and older.

Brezhnev and Nixon worked to each other's political benefit in a policy that became known as *détente*. They signed the SALT (Strategic Arms Limitation Treaty) to try to limit the growth of nuclear missiles. They also signed an **Anti-Ballistic Missile (ABM) Treaty** that sharply limited antimissile defenses.

The United States also joined the Conference on Security and Cooperation in Europe that was still trying to work out border changes left over from 1945.

Dubcek and the Czech Dissent

The decline of the U.S.S.R. led the countries of the bloc to begin to turn to the West for economic assistance and to try to stimulate consumer goods. In 1968, **Alexander Dubcek** (1921–1993) became leader of the Czechoslovak Communist Party. He called for "Communism with a Human Face," to allow for some human rights and some capitalist innovations. He introduced democratic changes in the structure of the Czechoslovakian Communist Party. He lifted restraints on free speech, and criticism of the Soviet system blossomed. These measures were known as the **Prague Spring**. Dubcek tried to assure the Russians that Czechoslovakia was not getting ready to rebel as Hungary had. On August 21, 1968, Soviet troops rolled into Czechoslovakia to oust Dubcek. Brezhnev proclaimed that once a country became Communist, it would not be allowed to leave. The Soviets installed a reactionary Communist government and ended the reforms.

Poland

Strikes racked Poland in 1970, and a more reformist Communist became leader. As part of establishing better relations with the Germans, Poland received billions of dollars from the West. The Polish debt was $2.5 billion in 1973 and $17 billion in 1980. This money was intended for industrial development and modernization but in fact it subsidized Polish consumers in the cities and Polish farmers by paying the farmers above market price and keeping prices artificially low. This meant ten years of uneasy peace but in 1980, strikes broke out again, centered in Gdansk where the Lenin shipyard had laid off many workers. The fired electrician **Lech Walesa** (b.1943) became leader of these strikes and established the **Solidarity Trade Union**. Solidarity signed up 8 million members in a country of 35 million. It was larger than the disintegrating Polish Communist Party. People feared another Soviet military intervention. However, intervention would certainly lead to a default on the loans and an end to further loans. The only Communist-dominated institution remaining, the army, staged a coup against the government as General **Wojciech Jaruzelsky** (b. 1923) took power, outlawed Solidarity, and arrested its leaders.

The China Card

It took years for American policymakers to accept that the decline in Chinese-Soviet relations was not some trick. In the 1969, the two nations nearly had a border war. Nixon and Kissinger were determined to "play the China card" and put Communist China into the West's camp, at least in official policy. This was a startling change since Nixon had once been an ardent McCarthyite. In 1971, the U.S. allowed the Communist government to represent China at the United Nations and hold its permanent seat on the Security Council. In February 1972 Nixon visited China and normalized relations. American companies such as Coca-Cola began to invest in China. By the late 1970s, the U.S. and China had exchanged ambassadors.

The End of the Bretton Woods Monetary System

As the old diplomatic system transformed, the U.S. acknowledged the relative weakening of its economic position. Pressure had built up on the U.S. gold supply, maintained at $35 per ounce, while the market price continued to climb to around $150. Inflation was also seen as a growing problem in the U.S. as Johnson and Nixon declined to raise taxes to pay for the Vietnam War. In 1971, Western European steel production surpassed that of the U.S. European and Japanese car imports began to take a major share of the U.S. market. By 1970, the U.S. gold reserves were officially valued at $11 billion. Western Europe held $50 billion in dollar reserves. On August 15, 1971, with no prior warning, Nixon suspended convertibility in gold and allowed the dollar to "float" to its true level. From this point on, gold would only be sold at the market level. The market would revalue currencies each day as they floated. The Japanese Yen, Deutsche Mark, and Swiss Franc became major currencies along with the dollar. The E.E.C. countries established a Monetary System to keep their values roughly in line with periodic adjustments. Over the years, dollar value in other currencies has fluctuated wildly. When Nixon cut the last ties to gold, he removed a drag on the economy but encouraged inflation since only the U.S. Federal Reserve Bank and consumers' decisions determined the money supply.

Democracy in Southern Europe

Spain under Franco

Franco's dictatorship in Spain survived despite the defeat of his patrons Hitler and Mussolini. Franco had been careful never to declare war on anyone. The Cold War led the U.S. to bury previous differences. In 1960, it provided $63 million in Marshall Plan aid for Spain, even though it had not been a battlefield in the war. Spain allowed the U.S. to establish air and naval bases in 1953 and the U.N. admitted Spain in 1955. In 1969, Franco named **Juan Carlos** (b.1938) of the royal Bourbon dynasty as his successor to quiet the monarchists. Franco died in 1975 after a long illness, and Juan Carlos was crowned king. He appointed Adolfo Suarez (b.1932) as Prime Minister to restore democracy. Many Socialists and Communists returned from exile, and there was fear that the Civil War could resume or that Spain might become dominated by the Communists, as another outpost of independent "Eurocommunism." A general attempted on two occasions to stage a coup against the government, but the strong support of Juan Carlos for democracy foiled the coups. Spain legalized divorce and began to reduce the power of the Church in private lives.

Portugal

There had long been a series of dictators. Antonio de Oliveira Salazar was dictator from 1932 to 1968. He had helped Franco gain power and remained a close ally. After he suffered a stroke and retired, Portugal grew discontented. The country was bankrupting itself fighting independence forces in its African colonies. On April 25, 1974, a group of left-wing army officers overthrew the government in a nearly bloodless revolution and invited the exiled liberals to return. Portugal released its colonies.

Greece

Greece also began a rocky experience with democracy in the 1970s. The civil war against the communists had ended in 1949. The military and the king were the main forces as a series of weak parliamentary governments ruled. In 1967, a military junta took full control. When the king tried to resist, the junta forced him into exile. In 1974, the junta overstepped its power by trying to stage a military coup to take control of Cyprus. This coup triggered an invasion from Turkey, which defeated the Greeks and took the northern part of the island. Massive protests filled the streets. The junta invited the exiles back, and 69 percent of the voters approved a republic.

The Helsinki Accords

Since the United States had improved its civil rights record, a number of Democratic senators took the issue of human rights into the international arena. They called on the Soviet bloc to loosen its tight emigration law and allow dissidents to leave. This group was suspicious of Kissinger's détente policy. Nixon had to resign after trying to overthrow the U.S. Constitution and put himself above the law in the "Watergate scandal." His successor Gerald Ford signed the accords with the Soviets in 1975. These agreements officially put an end to World War II and recognized the changes in the Soviet and Polish borders that the Soviet Union had drawn. In return for this, the Soviet bloc nations agreed to respect human rights. The Accords established "Helsinki Watch" committees in every country, although none ever formed in East Germany. Although human rights were not generally respected and Helsinki Watch committee members were often jailed, the Committees served as the first nucleus of opposition to the regimes.

The Energy Crisis

As the economies grew in Western Europe, the U.S., and Japan, they became increasingly dependent on oil supplies. Western Europe and Japan were very dependent; by 1973, US imported 15 percent of its oil supply from Middle East. The **Organization of Petroleum Exporting Countries** (OPEC) had been formed in 1960, but had little effect until after 1969. Between 1950 and 1973, demand for oil increased fivefold, while reserves grew eightfold. However discoveries of new oil fields peaked in 1965. Between 1969 and 1979, the oil price increased from $1.20 per barrel to $41. A series of blunders by Nixon's administration delayed the Alaska Pipeline a full five years. Nixon also did not act in 1969 when a small band under Muammar Qadaffi took over oil-rich Libya. Nixon actually wanted oil prices to rise, so that the Shah of Iran could afford to buy weapons to fulfill his role under the Nixon Doctrine. When the oil companies tried to prevent Qadaffi from raising prices, Nixon threatened antitrust action against them.

This came to a head in 1973. Demand for oil grew rapidly with the Clean Air Act, which pushed companies away from coal. Nixon had imposed wage and price controls in 1971 in order to postpone inflation until after the 1972 election. The decision to allow the dollar to float forced the oil price in dollars higher. By 1973, after the controls were lifted, oil was up to $5 a barrel. When the U.S. supported Israel in the Yom Kippur War of 1973, the Arab oil exporters declared an embargo. The total available oil only dropped by 7 percent, but panic and poor distribution made for shortages. On the open market, oil reached $17.40 per barrel.

Carter and Human Rights

Jimmy Carter beat Ford in 1976 and made human rights a much greater foreign policy goal. Carter not only criticized the Soviet bloc countries but also traditional U.S. allies and dictators in the Philippines, Iran, and Nicaragua. In 1979 came a second oil shock. A revolution overthrew the Shah of Iran in February 1979, and the "spot" price of oil rose to $23 a barrel. Largely due to the actions of oil companies, there were regional oil shortages and the price began to rise again by the summer of 1979. The market peaked at $41 a barrel, and then settled in the mid-30s. Republicans blamed this on Carter's criticism of the Shah. The oil shock touched off another round of inflation, which had partly subsided in the mid-1970s during a recession. Carter used drastic measures to end the inflation. These caused an economic recession, and Carter lost his reelection bid in 1980. Carter's conservation projects meant that the oil consumption level of 1979 was not exceeded until 1996. This kept the price low and brought prosperity without inflation.

THE DRIVE FOR EUROPEAN UNITY

In 1979, with great fanfare, the members of the E.E.C. held the first elections for a **European Parliament**. Christian Democrats and Social Democrats across the continent faced off and won most of the seats with various centrist parties and the British conservatives cooperating on certain occasions. Despite great hopes, the European Parliament did not make much of an impact.

With political integration foiled, Europe turned back to economics. Most nations of West Europe belonged to the E.E.C. by the 1980s. The newest members, mostly not industrialized and rural, retained some customs and special provisions. In the 1980s, some feared that Western Europe was falling behind the U.S. and Japan as innovators. Leaders agreed to the **Single European Act** (1987), to take effect January 1, 1993. It would abolish frontiers, national rules and subsidies, and there was hope for a common social policy to aid the poorer nations, a central bank, and even a common currency. The E.E.C. became the **European Union**. As the implementation faltered, European leaders met at **Maastricht** at the end of 1991. They agreed to form a united European currency, the Euro, which replaced eleven national currencies in 2002. Other countries have joined "Euroland" since then.

"PEOPLE POWER" IN THE PHILIPPINES AND HAITI

In 1986, there was rapid change in what had seemed two firm dictatorships. The Philippines had achieved independence after World War II but was ruled by the dictator Ferdinand Marcos since 1965. As an anti-Communist, he had enjoyed strong U.S. support except for the Carter years. In 1983, his leading political opponent was murdered at Manilla Airport. The opponent's wife, **Corazon Aquino**, began a campaign to oust Marcos. Marcos announced elections that he planned to fix, but international observers arrived to monitor the elections. When it was clear that Aquino had defeated him, Marcos called out the army. Under pressure from the U.S. Congress, Marcos fled the country and Aquino took over, inspiring many.

Just a few weeks later, one of the most brutal dictatorships in the world, Haiti, also saw an eruption of "people power" as Haitians defied enforcers, took to the streets, and the dictator fled. Haiti eventually held elections and chose the priest **Jean-Bertrand Aristide** (b.1953). A military coup overthrew Aristide, but Aristide was restored in 1994 after pressure from U.S. President Clinton. After Clinton left office, Aristide was again forced into exile.

RUSSIA UNDER GORBACHEV

Hard Choices

By the time of Brezhnev's death in 1982, the Soviet bloc was in bad shape. It was deeply in debt to the West, corruption was rampant, and its economies were in decline. The high price of gold and oil had sustained much of the economy, but those materials lost more than two-thirds of their value in the 1980s. Communist membership was falling, and in Poland the party had crumbled and left the army in charge. For Brezhnev's successors, it seemed that the only choices were widespread economic reform, democratization, or the imposition of a military dictatorship like Poland's. When the first policy was tried and failed, the choice was the military or democracy.

The Interregnum

In 1979, the Soviet Union felt its hold on a puppet regime in Afghanistan slipping. Brezhnev committed massive forces and got bogged down in guerrilla war. Jimmy Carter's adviser later said there was a deliberate strategy to bleed the U.S.S.R. in a proxy war. The Reagan Administration that succeeded gave massive assistance to Muslim fundamentalists who flooded into Afghanistan. With its economy staggering under the military burden, the Afghan war was the straw that broke the Soviet Union's back, and its economy went into free fall.

After Brezhnev's death in 1982, the Soviet Union had two weak and short-lived leaders. In 1985, the Politburo chose its youngest member **Mikhail Gorbachev** (b.1931) as the first post-Stalinist leader. Gorbachev cautiously endorsed reform and began to speak about *glasnost* (openness) and *perestroika* (restructuring), but it was unclear what he meant precisely. He had to share power with more conservative men. When the **Chernobyl** nuclear plant melted down and killed hundreds in 1986, the Soviet government said nothing until Swedish scientists detected radioactive clouds. He asked to see Dubcek on a trip to Czechoslovakia and was denied by the Czech leaders. Real change remained scanty. Gorbachev seemed caught between the old conservative members of the Politburo and newer, impatient members who wanted to see faster action. The most vocal reformer in the Politburo was the Moscow Party Chief **Boris Yeltsin** (1931–2007). Yeltsin was dismissed from the Politburo in 1988 after challenging Gorbachev in a speech. Meanwhile, the Soviet economy continued to crumble.

The Scrapping of the Stalin Constitution

In October 1988, Gorbachev decided that only sweeping political changes could transform the U.S.S.R. He convened the rubber-stamp Supreme Soviet and won its agreement for a series of changes. The President, not the Prime Minister, would name the Cabinet, and would preside over a new elected body, the Congress of People's Deputies. On closer inspection, it was clear that many seats in this Congress would be reserved for Communists, but some seats actually would be contested. Gorbachev apparently hoped to tap into democratic strength and support without the Communist Party surrendering its leading role.

The end of the Stalin system sparked nationalism in the Baltic countries and then in Russia. Latvia, Lithuania, and Estonia all agitated for fuller rights and then for independence. In Russia, some called for a revival of Stalinism, others for a return to the Czarist era. In the spring of 1989, the Congress met and featured some notable dissidents including Yeltsin, Andrei Sakharov (d.1990), the famous physicist and dissident, and other new figures. Some prominent Communists, running unopposed, had been confirmed by less than 50 percent of the voters and lost their posts. In the spring of 1989, the last Soviet troops pulled out of Afghanistan. After Yeltsin and others declined to stand for Soviet president, the Congress elected Gorbachev. The new constitution allowed voters to choose the Presidents of the Republics of the Soviet Union.

THE REVOLUTIONS OF 1989

Poland

Unlike other bloc leaders, General Jaruzelsky welcomed Gorbachev and his reforms. Jaruzelsky's military coup had worked temporarily, but the economy continued to decline. Any attempt at economic reform would have to be done on a broad-based political basis or there would be rioting. Poland's 1988 economy was 13 percent smaller than it had been in 1978. The foreign debt loomed large. In November 1987, Jaruzelsky allowed the people to vote on economic reforms to restructure the Polish economy. The voters rejected all the measures, including price increases, by a large margin. The government tried to impose price increases in 1988, and riots swept the nation. With the Polish Communist Party not functioning and no other options, Jaruzelsky had to turn to Walesa.

The general hoped to win Solidarity's support for unpopular economic measures and harness its political energy without surrendering power. Jaruzelsky and Walesa agreed to a new Polish parliament in which the Communists and their traditional allied parties were guaranteed 65 percent of the seats in the lower house. In the June 1989 elections, Solidarity swept all of the remaining 35 percent of the seats and took ninety-nine of 100 Senate seats. The long-dormant allied parties suddenly rose against the Communists, and Solidarity aide **Tadeusz Mazowiecki** became Prime Minister. Jaruzelsky became President but found more and more power slipping from his hands. In 1991, Jaruzelsky gave up and Walesa took over as President.

Hungary

The Revolution passed most peacefully in Hungary. In May 1988 younger Communists forced out Janos Kadar, who had ruled since the 1956 revolution. Kadar's economic program had been called "Communism with a human facelift" in a reference to Dubcek. The new group wanted supported Gorbachev-type reforms but change swung out of control. As late as May 1989, the Hungarian Communists said they would not risk their position for six to eight years. They did not take the **Democratic Forum** forces seriously. But they did open the fortified border with Austria, took down the barbed wire fence, and put in some reforms. By October 1989, the Communists had renamed themselves Socialists and jettisoned Leninist dogma. This angered the hard-liners while not appeasing the reformers. The Parliament instituted a multiparty system and legalized opposition parties. 100,000 gathered on October 23 to cheer the new constitution and urge a break with the U.S.S.R. The Hungarian Communist Party collapsed from 720,000 to 30,000 members overnight. On November 26, Hungary held its first free elections. On March 25, 1990, Hungary's voters ended communist rule.

Germany

The D.D.R. (East Germany) seemed to be one of the most stable Soviet bloc states after the Berlin uprising of 1953. While legal emigration continued, the Secret Police (**Stasi**) kept tight reins on dissent. The Helsinki Final Act had authorized native "monitoring groups" to ensure that countries respected human rights but, unlike Poland, Czechoslovakia, or even the U.S.S.R., the D.D.R. had no Helsinki watch group. By the summer of 1989, dissent seemed small and unorganized. The leader, Erich Honecker, had fallen gravely ill with a gall bladder ailment, and there seemed to be a lack of will at the top. In September 1989, 7,000 citizens of the D.D.R. who had been vacationing in Hungary refused to go back and demanded passage to the West. After long agonizing, Hungary let them go, much to Honecker's displeasure. Within two weeks, thousands were fleeing via Hungary and an opposition party had formed. 200,000 left from September through November. Honecker did not want to seal the border with Hungary (another Communist state) and was preparing to celebrate the D.D.R.'s fortieth anniversary. At that celebration, on October 4, Gorbachev apparently told Honecker that he had to resign, but the German would not listen. On October 7, frenzied crowds in East Berlin cheered Gorbachev and denounced Honecker. Police waded into the crowds and beat up people. Two days later, a huge demonstration was planned in Leipzig. Honecker signed orders for troops to fire into the crowd. Honecker quickly lost support even from the Old Guard, and was forced to resign on October 18 in favor of Egon Krenz, the head of the Stasi.

Krenz, the youngest member of the D.D.R. Politburo, tried to promote a Gorbachev-like plan of reform and renewed the ability of Germans to travel to Hungary and Czechoslovakia. On November 4, 500,000 East Germans protested and demanded full democracy. Even thousands of Communist Party members demanded a clean sweep. The Politburo dismissed Krenz and installed Hans Modrow, who was seen as even more reformist. The government then tried to announce liberalized travel restrictions, but the crowds took this as a signal for unlimited travel and stormed the Berlin Wall, destroying it.

Events were now completely out of anyone's control. The New Forum, which had organized many of the protests, wanted a reformed D.D.R., but the flood of voices calling for unification overwhelmed it. Modrow agreed to free elections for March 18, 1990. The campaign was now dominated by Western politicians campaigning in the East. The CDU won a comfortable victory by promising a rapid unification with the West. The Four Powers sat down and reached a final German settlement, which mainly involved West Germany writing a large check to the Soviet Union. With only a few bumps in the road, the two Germanies became one again on October 2, 1990.

Czechoslovakia

Hard-liners had ruled Czechoslovakia since 1968. They had no respect for Gorbachev and insulted him. On November 17, 1989, students demonstrated against the government. When the regime tried to disperse them, the police injured over a hundred. Rumors spread that one student had been killed. 50,000, and then 500,000 protested and demanded the return of Alexander Dubcek. Millions went out on strike and paralyzed the country. Only massive violence could put it down. The Czech Communists declined to do that and resigned. An opposition group, the **Civic Forum**, was cobbled together at the Magic Lantern Theater by **Vaclav Havel**, a playwright and dissident. On December 9, the Communist President left. Havel became Czechoslovak President, and Dubcek became Speaker of the Parliament.

Romania

Romania resorted to all-out violence as China had and Honecker had wanted. The dictator **Nicolai Ceaucescu** had been a favorite of the West in the 1970s because he had supported Dubcek and taken a slightly different foreign policy stand than the Soviets. Ceaucescu's harsh repression led to the estrangement of the people. Corruption and destruction of property were commonplace. As the other communist countries fell, Ceaucescu tried to spur Romanian nationalism against the Hungarians living in Romania. His attempt to crush an uprising led only to bloodshed as security forces shot randomly into the crowd of protesters in December 1989. On December 21, Ceaucescu tried to hold an official rally in the capital of Bucharest to show how beloved he was, but as he stood on the balcony, protests swept through the crowd. Ceaucescu gave orders to the security forces to kill as many as needed and fled by helicopter. The infuriated crowd overwhelmed the forces and stormed the palace. Rebels caught Ceaucescu and his wife, gave them a summary trial, and executed them. The security forces fought street-to-street battles but finally were beaten. A number of communists broke away from the dictator at the last minute and were able to hold power.

THE END OF THE SOVIET UNION

The Soviet economy continued to collapse as Gorbachev declined to make radical changes. The crumbling of the Soviet bloc in the Revolutions of 1989 intensified demands. Gorbachev tried to meet the demands of the right and then the left in succession. Internationally, he was a triumph, but the people at home generally despised him. In May 1990, the elected Parliament of the Russian Federation chose Yeltsin as Russian President; Gorbachev remained Soviet President. The 1990 Communist Party Congress was a parody of previous triumphs. It was marked by sharp divisions, attacks on Gorbachev, and the resignation of several prominent members from the Party, including Yeltsin.

1991 was the year of decision. It began with action against the Baltics as troops were used to suppress the movements while American attention was distracted in Iraq. Gorbachev now seemed to be with the hard-liners. The demands of Russia and the other republics, many of which were controlled by reformers, became louder and louder. They demanded a federal system with less central power. Gorbachev again shifted left to sign a sweeping treaty to give the republics more power. On the day before Gorbachev was to sign this treaty, elements of the military and secret police staged a coup to seize power. They did not work through the old Stalinist system, using the Party, Politburo, or Central Committee. The coup was bungled badly. Many army units stood on the sidelines. The hard-liners had no solutions for change. Yeltsin rallied the support of people in Moscow. The plotters lost courage and pleaded for mercy.

The U.S.S.R. was left in turmoil. The Congress dissolved itself and gave all power to Gorbachev, Yeltsin, and a special council they set up. The council granted the three Baltic states full independence, declared the Communist Party illegal, and confiscated its property. Leningrad's name was changed back to St. Petersburg. In December 1991, Yeltsin and the other republic presidents (except Georgia) signed an agreement abolishing the Soviet Union and setting up the Confederation of Independent States. Not only had communism ended, but the Russian Empire of 300 years had come crashing down in pieces.

TIMELINE

1945–46	Nuremberg War Crimes Trials
1954	*Brown vs. Board of Education* decision in U.S.
1964	U.S. Civil Rights Act
1965	U.S. Voting Rights Act
1968	Dubcek and Prague Spring
1969	Willy Brandt becomes West German Chancellor
1969–74	First Energy Crisis
1971	Nixon cuts last ties of dollar to gold
1975	Helsinki Accords
	Franco dies; end of Spanish dictatorship
1979–89	Soviet-Afghan War
1980	Solidarity union founded in Poland
1981	Jaruzelsky seizes power in Poland
1985	Mikhail Gorbachev becomes head of Soviet Union
1986	Chernobyl disaster
	Dictators overthrown in Philippines and Haiti
1989	Revolution sweeps East Germany, Poland, Czechoslovakia, Romania, Bulgaria, and Hungary
1991	Soviet Union ends
	Maastricht Treaty

KEY TERMS

Ostpolitik
Alexander Dubcek
Lech Walesa
Helsinki Accords
Maastricht Treaty
Mikhail Gorbachev

PRIMARY SOURCE DOCUMENTS

Franklin Roosevelt, http://usinfo.org/facts/speech/fdr.html
Robert Jackson, http://avalon.law.yale.edu/imt/imt_jack01.asp
United Nations General Assembly, http://www.fordham.edu/halsall/ mod/1948HUMRIGHT.html
Martin Luther King, Jr., http://history.hanover.edu/courses/excerpts/111mlk.html
Corazon Aquino, http://halohalonghalo.blogspot.com/2008/09/inagural-speech-of-president-coeazon.html

ABOUT THE AUTHOR

Edmund Clingan was born and raised in New York City and received his B.A. in History from Queens College and his M.A. and Ph.D. from the University of Wisconsin-Madison. In 1988/89, he studied at the University of Bonn, Germany, as a Fulbright Scholar. His books include *Finance from Kaiser to Führer: Budget Politics in Germany, 1912–1934* and *The Lives of Hans Luther, 1879–1962*. He is currently Associate Professor of History at Queensborough Community College of the City University of New York.